P9-DUB-190

Ongoing Revision:
Studies in Moral Theology

Other Books by Charles E. Curran

Christian Morality Today
A New Look at Christian Morality
Contemporary Problems in Moral Theology
Catholic Moral Theology in Dialogue
The Crisis in Priestly Ministry
*Politics, Medicine and Christian Ethics: A Dialogue with Paul
   Ramsey*
New Perspectives in Moral Theology
Dissent in and for the Church (Charles E. Curran, Robert E.
   Hunt, et. al.)
*The Responsibility of Dissent: The Church and Academic
   Freedom* (John F. Hunt and Terrence R. Connelly with
   Charles E. Curran, et. al.)
Absolutes in Moral Theology? (editor)
Contraception: Authority and Dissent (editor)

Ongoing Revision:
Studies in Moral Theology

CHARLES E. CURRAN

Fides Publishers, Inc.

Notre Dame, Indiana

Copyright: 1975, Fides Publishers, Inc.
Notre Dame, Indiana 46556

Library of Congress Cataloging in Publication Data

Curran, Charles E
  Ongoing revision : studies in moral theology.

  Includes bibliographical references.
  1. Christian ethics—Catholic authors—Addresses,
essays, lectures. I. Title.
BX1758.2.C83   241   75-28450
ISBN 0-8190-0612-2

To

Lucille and Jack

Kay

Jan and Ernest

Contents

Introduction

The changes that have occurred in Roman Catholic thought and life in the last decade have been felt in a particularly acute way in the area of moral theology. Part of the reason stems from the practical aspect of moral theology which intimately affects people's lives. Systematic and dogmatic theology have experienced the same changes, but the more theoretical aspects of these disciplines do not affect the daily lives of people. Many proposals about Jesus Christ or original sin are quite different from what they were in the past, but their impact is almost negligible on everyday life.

Roman Catholicism in the United States has often found its own self-identity in terms of its moral theology. Roman Catholics are different from others because of their agreement on certain specific moral questions—contraception, abortion, divorce. In the light of this self-understanding many Roman Catholics react very negatively to any possible change in these teachings. One of the primary emphases in this book is that Roman Catholic self-identity should not be found in terms of such specific moral questions. Such a change in self-identity will not come about easily. One can understand the resistance to such change, and at times the vehemence which accompanies these debates. On the other hand, there are some Roman Catholics who have become so disenchanted with some of the particular teachings of the Catholic Church that they claim to find no value or meaning in the tradition of moral theology.

In this context, ongoing revision well characterizes the work of moral theology today. Synthetic and comprehensive studies of moral theology will probably not be done for some time. Moral theology can never jettison its own past, but at the same time it must always be revised in the light of the changing realities of the present and the eschatological pull of the future. The essays brought together in this book illustrate this process of the ongoing revision of moral theology. Newer understandings of moral theology are proposed and explained in the light of their differences but also their continuity with the past. Perhaps the most important general characteristic is the insistence on the effects of pluralism. Moral theology today exists in an ecumenical age which requires dialogue not only with other Christians but with other religious ethics and with humanistic and philosophical ethics. In addition, these essays consider some of the specific points in which different solutions are being proposed— divorce, civil law and morality, the fifth commandment, the principle of the double effect and cooperation in a pluralistic society. Here too an attempt is usually made to show how the concepts have developed and why different approaches are required today. The final chapter reflects on the personal and theological influences that have influenced my understanding of the ongoing revision of moral theology.

I want to thank publicly all those who have assisted and encouraged my research in moral theology. Friends, colleagues and staff at the Catholic University of America have continued to be most helpful and supporting—especially James A. Coriden, Chairperson of the Department of Theology for the past two years and Carolyn T. Lee together with her associates Shirley Potasky and David Gilson in the theology library.

I am also grateful to the following publishers and periodicals for allowing me to publish in this volume studies which originally appeared in their publications: *The Proceedings of the Catholic Theological Society of America* for "Catholic Ethics, Christian Ethics and Human Ethics"; *Chicago Studies* for "Pluralism in Moral Theology" and "The Fifth Commandment: Thou Shalt Not Kill"; *The Jurist* and *The Proceedings of the Canon Law Society of America* for "Divorce in the Light of a Revised Moral Theology"; *Conversations* for "Civil Law and Morality: Abortion and the Churches"; International Congress Commemorating the Seventh Centenary of the Death of Thomas Aquinas for "The Principle of the Double Effect"; *The Linacre Quarterly* for "Cooperation in a Pluralistic Society"; The American Academy of Religion and Scholars Press for "Paul Ramsey and Traditional Catholic Moral Theology," which originally appeared in *Love and Society: Essays in the Ethics of Paul Ramsey,* ed. James Johnson and David Smith; Paulist Press for "Ongoing Revision: Personal and Theological Reflections," which originally appeared in *Journeys,* ed. Gregory Baum.

1

Catholic Ethics, Christian Ethics,

and Human Ethics

In one sense the title of this chapter has been a perennial question. Catholic and/or Christian ethics have constantly needed to reflect on their own identity *vis-à-vis* other types of ethics whether they are religious ethics or philosophical ethics. However, this questioning has become even more acute in the last few years. Our own age in many ways can be characterized as a time of crisis and radical questioning on the most ultimate of issues, namely, the God issue. It should not surprise us that the same type of questions arise about the identity of Christian and/or Catholic ethics in relationship to other ethics.

THE CONTEXTS

To situate the discussion it will be helpful to indicate the major contexts within which the questioning about the identity of Christian and/or Catholic ethics has arisen in the last few years. The first context is the dialogue between Christians and non-Christians in the modern world. All men of good will—to use a phrase employed by Pope John XXIII in addressing his encyclical letter *Pacem in Terris* to these people as well as to the bishops and members of the Roman

1

Catholic Church[1] —seem to share many of the same ethical values as Christians. In actual experience, Christians have worked side by side with non-Christians for the same social causes and ethical concerns. Many Catholics and Christians have personally experienced with nonbelievers the common ethical concerns which unite them, and they frequently feel more in harmony with the ethical concerns of non-Catholics and non-Christians.

Such a practical experience has been mirrored in the more theoretical realm through dialogue with atheists and with Marxists. These two types of dialogue and discussion characterized much of Roman Catholic theology in the 1960's. The Pastoral Constitution on the Church in the Modern World devotes a large section to the phenomenon of atheism and, generally speaking, recognizes positive values in this phenomenon.[2] "While rejecting atheism, root and branch, the Church sincerely professes that all men, believers and unbelievers alike, are to work for the rightful betterment of this world in which we alike live. Such an ideal cannot be realized, however, apart from sincere and prudent dialogue" (n. 21).

In a parallel way with Marxism, while the Roman Catholic Church rejects the materialism and atheism of Marxism, there

---

1. Pope John XXIII, *Pacem in Terris, Acta Apostolicae Sedis* LV (1963) 257. For a readily available English translation: *Pacem in Terris*, ed. William J. Gibbons (New York: Paulist Press, 1963).

2. Pastoral Constitution on the Church in the Modern World, nn. 19—21. The most available and reliable English translation of the documents of Vatican Council II is *The Documents of Vatican II*, ed. Walter M. Abbott (New York: Guild Press, 1966).

3. For theoretical aspects of this dialogue, see Roger Garaudy and Quentin Lauer, *A Christian-Communist Dialogue* (Garden City, N.Y.: Doubleday, 1968). For practical aspects of this dialogue, see Peruvian Bishops' Commission for Social Action, *Between Honesty and Hope: Documents From and About the Church in Latin America* (Maryknoll, N.Y.: Maryknoll Publications, 1970).

4. Coenraad van Ouwerkerk, "Secularism and Christian Ethics," *Concilium* XXV (1967), 97—139.

has been a growing recognition of the agreement on many issues confronting society and also in some countries a growing practical alliance between Marxists and some Christians and Roman Catholics.[3] In this same connection, the phenomenon of a theology of the secular and of secularization has also had its impact on the identity of Christian ethics.[4] Thus the contemporary experience has brought to Christian consciousness, probably more so than in preceding times, the recognition that there are great similarities between Christian ethics and non-Christian ethics.

The second context in which the question of the identity of Christian ethics occurs is on the level of theological theory, especially involving a rethinking of three important sets of concepts—nature-supernature; creation-redemption; Church-world. An older Catholic theology seemed to hold a dualistic approach, reserving some things for the area of nature and others for the area of supernature. Contemporary Roman Catholic thought has been trying to overcome that dichotomy. In a speculative context, Karl Rahner has employed the concepts of the supernatural existential and the anonymous Christian to overcome the dichotomies between nature and supernature and between creation and redemption.[5]

On the level of action and moral theology, Gustavo Gutierrez emphasizes the concept of one history to overcome both the dichotomy of nature and supernature and the dualism of creation and redemption and thereby shows a proper relationship between the Church and the world. There are not two histories, one profane and one sacred, juxtaposed or closely linked. There is only one human history and human destiny, irrevocably assumed by Christ, the Lord of history.

5. For an exposition of Rahner's thought, see William C. Shepherd, *Man's Condition: God and the World Process* (New York: Herder and Herder, 1969).

Gutierrez himself recognizes that such an acceptance of only one history, a Christ finalized history, raises the suspicion of not sufficiently safe-guarding divine gratuitousness or the unique dimension of Christianity.[6]

Gutierrez then develops the reasons for his position. The Bible itself establishes a close link between creation and salvation. In this light the understanding of the relationship of Church and world must be changed. In an older approach it was thought that the salvific work of God was present primarily in the Church and not in the world, but such an approach can no longer be accepted. The building of the temporal city is not simply a stage of humanization or preevangelization as was held in theology until a few years ago; rather it is a part of a saving process which embraces the whole of man and all human history.[7] "The perspective we have indicated presupposes an uncentering of the Church, for the Church must cease considering itself as the exclusive place of salvation and orient itself toward a new and radical service of people."[8] The Church is the universal sacrament of salvation, but the work of salvation is a reality which occurs in the one history of the world.

While agreeing with the general thrust of such an approach, I personally have some problems and difficulties which might better be called amendments or modifications. Contemporary theology must overcome the dichotomies between nature and grace and between creation and redemption which were present in an older Catholic thought. But in overcoming the dichotomies there is the great danger of seeing everything in terms of the supernatural and of redemption. Roman Catho-

6. Gustavo Gutierrez, *A Theology of Liberation: History, Politics and Salvation* (Maryknoll, N.Y.: Orbis Books, 1973), p. 153.
7. *Ibid.,* pp. 153–160.
8. *Ibid.,* p. 256.

lic theology, as well as Christian theology and human thought in general, in the late 1960's suffered from a naively optimistic approach that too often forgot about human limitations and sinfulness and mistakenly gave the impression that the fullness of the eschatological future was readily within our grasp. The stark realities of war, violence, hatred, and the inability of nations and individuals to live in peace and harmony have shattered such an illusion. My modifications to the approach taken by Guttierrez would insist that liberation is a long, hard, difficult process that will never be fully accomplished, but the Christian must be committed to strive to make liberation more present in our society. In my judgment, much of the disillusion which characterizes life today, both in the world and in the Church, comes from the crushing of a naive optimism which forgot about the realities of limitation, sin and the eschaton as the absolute future. In addition, I have difficulty in accepting any one concept as being all-controlling in ethical theory, even if that concept is liberation. In the past, for example, an overemphasis on freedom resulted in the doctrine of laissez-faire capitalism.

A third context in which the question of the identity of Christian and/or Catholic ethics arises refers to the methodological change which has occurred in Roman Catholic moral theology and which to some extent was influenced by the broader theological realities mentioned in the second context. To illustrate this changing methodology, compare the 1963 encyclical *Pacem in Terris* of Pope John XXIII with the Pastoral Constitution on the Church in the Modern World.

Pacem in Terris stands in the tradition of the papal social encyclicals beginning with *Rerum Novarum* of Leo XIII, who decreed the teaching of thomistic philosophy and theology in Catholic universities and seminaries and employed the natural law concept to questions of the social and economic order. The sources of the papal teaching were often referred to as

reason and revelation, but the heavy emphasis rested on
reason and natural law.[9]

Pacem in Terris was addressed not only to Catholics but to
all men of good will. The methodology employed by the
encyclical was in keeping with such an address, since the
basic appeal was not to the scripture and revelation but to
human reason. At the very beginning of the encyclical Pope
John insisted that peace on earth can be firmly established
only if men dutifully observe the order laid down by God the
Creator. The Creator has imprinted an order in the universe
in which we live and in the hearts of men. In the nature of
man and of the universe, conscience can find the order and
the norms by which men are guided to live together in peace
and harmony. Appeal is thus made only to creation, human
nature, and human reason which all men share in common
whether they are Christians or not.[10]

The revival of Catholic moral theology, which first appeared in the 1950's and can be illustrated in the pioneering
work of Bernard Häring,[11] insisted that moral theology must
be rooted in the scriptures and in grace and not just in reason
and in human nature. This newer emphasis was encouraged
by the dialogue with other Christians which was beginning to
occur at that time in a more regular and visible way. Protestant ethics had consistently emphasized the primary place of
revelation and the need to see Christian ethics in this context.
The Decree on Priestly Formation of Vatican II declared
"special attention needs to be given to the development of

9. For explanations and commentaries on the papal social encyclicals see J.Y.
Calvez and J. Perrin, *The Church and Social Justice* (Chicago: Henry Regnery Co.,
1961); John F. Cronin, *Social Principles and Economic Life* (Milwaukee: Bruce
Publishing Co., 1959); John F. Cronin, *The Social Teaching of Pope John XXIII*
(Milwaukee: Bruce Publishing Co., 1963).

10. *Pacem in Terris,* nn. 1–7.

11. Bernard Häring, *The Law of Christ,* tr. Edwin G. Kaiser, 3 vols. (Westminster, Md.: Newman Press, 1961, 1963, 1966).

moral theology. Its scientific exposition should be more thoroughly nourished by scriptural teaching. It should show the nobility of the Christian vocation of the faithful and their obligations to bring forth fruit in charity for the life of the world" (n. 16).

The Pastoral Constitution on the Church in the Modern World tries to propose such a new framework and methodology for its consideration of the political, social and economic problems of our day. No longer is the methodology based on creation alone or human nature alone, but the document addresses these questions in the light of the gospel and of human experience (n. 46). The methodological approach of the Pastoral Constitution on the Church in the Modern World can most adequately be described as a history of salvation approach which sees man's life in the world in the light of the whole history of salvation—creation, sin and redemption, and not merely on the basis of creation alone. Thus the tone and methodology of this document differ greatly from *Pacem in Terris*.

At first sight the very obvious methodological differences between the older papal encyclicals and the Pastoral Constitution on the Church in the Modern World seem to indicate there is a heavy insistence on the distinctively Christian aspect in social ethics which was lacking in the approach of the hierarchical magisterium before that time. However, a deeper investigation of the question raises some contrary indications. The factors mentioned in the second context above—the overcoming of the dichotomy between nature and supernature and between creation and redemption—are also very much present in this document. There are also some startling individual statements about the identity of the fully human and the Christian. These questions will be discussed later in greater detail.

A fourth and final context refers to the specifically Catholic aspect of the question. Post *Humanae Vitae* Catholic theology acknowledges the possibility and right of dissent to the authoritative or authentic, noninfallible teaching of the hierarchical magisterium. The possibility of dissent extends much more broadly than just to the specific question of the condemnation of artificial contraception which was proposed in *Humanae Vitae*. Theoretically, within Roman Catholicism today there are proposals going contrary to the official teaching of the Church on such questions as sexuality, abortion, euthanasia, and divorce.[12] In practice it also seems that many Catholics do not accept and follow the official teaching of the Catholic Church on specific moral questions.[13]

At the same time in the last few years many Catholics have expressed their belief that the Roman Catholic Church can and should speak out on any number of ethical questions facing our society. The war in Southeast Asia was the occasion on which many Catholics deplored the fact that the Catholic bishops of the United States did not give clear teaching to their people, although individual bishops made statements condemning American involvement in the war and finally the American bishops as a whole did issue a statement calling for the American withdrawal from Vietnam.[14] There have also been calls for explicit Church teaching on questions such as prison reform, condemnation of the death penalty, backing particular groups of workers in their labor struggles, etc.

These two signs of the times, which in some ways appear as conflicting, contribute to the milieu in which theologians

12. For a survey of recent developments in moral theology consult the "Notes on Moral Theology" which usually appear twice a year in *Theological Studies*.

13. For references to European questionnaires showing such divergences from the official teaching of the hierarchical magisterium, see Franz Böckle, "La Morale Fondamentale," *Recherches de Science Religieuse* LIX (1971), 331, 332.

14. "Resolution on Southeast Asia," a statement issued by the Roman Catholic Bishops of the United States in November 1971, is available from the Division of Justice and Peace, USCC, 1312 Massachusetts Ave., N.W., Washington, D.C. 20005.

raise the question about a distinctive and specific Roman Catholic ethics.

A DISTINCTIVELY CHRISTIAN ETHIC?

This essay will consider first the question of a distinctively Christian ethic and then only later the question of a distinctively Roman Catholic ethic. Any solution depends on a comparison between Christian ethics and other religious and human ethics. In the past few years, particularly within Roman Catholicism, this question has been raised about the material content of Christian ethics. Does the material content of Christian ethics add anything distinctive to human ethics; and, if so, what?

One must be careful not to prejudice the argument. The question cannot be settled merely by comparing the ethical conduct proposed in the scriptures with the ethical conduct exemplified in the lives of nonbelievers. In one sense scripture proposes the objective and somewhat ideal teaching which all would have to admit is not always verified, even in the lives of Christian believers. A comparison can be made by studying the content of the ethical teaching proposed in scripture with the content of morality as expressed in the writings of another religion or of a philosopher. It is possible, for example, to compare the teaching of the Old Testament with the ethical content proposed by those who lived in the same historical circumstances. Some comparative studies have been made, but they are quite limited.[15] Comparative historical studies will always constitute an important aspect of the debate, but at the present time no one can claim to have

---

15. Francesco Compagnoni, *La specificità della morale cristiana* (Bologna: Edizioni Dehoniane, 1972), pp. 27–61; Carroll Stulhmueller, "The Natural Law Question the Bible Never Asked," *Cross Currents* XIX (1969), 55–67.

made an exhaustive comparative study of the ethical teaching of the Old and New Testament with the teaching proposed by nonbelievers living in somewhat the same historical and cultural milieus.

In these discussions there can also be valuable data derived from experience and history. Does our own experience indicate that there is a specifically different Christian ethical content? Obviously our own personal experience is necessarily limited so that no conclusive answer can be drawn from experience alone, although it can contribute insights to a final solution of the question. Can history itself indicate that the moral content of Christian ethics has differed from the moral content of non-Christian ethics? Here again it is very difficult, if not impossible, to do an exhaustive historical study to determine if there is a difference between the content of Christian ethics and of non-Christian ethics, but again some helpful insights can be obtained through history. In my judgment, the limited data we have from both experience and history give no clear evidence of indicating a distinctive content to Christian ethics. Even some who would admit to the existence of a different content recognize that history cannot prove the existence of a specifically Christian ethic as far as content is concerned.[16]

While all the above approaches to the question are helpful, they cannot at the present time give a definite and certain answer to the question of the existence of a specifically different content in Christian ethics. Such approaches unfortunately are necessarily incomplete. This essay will now concentrate on the more theological and theoretical approaches to the question of a specifically different material content in Christian ethics.

16. James M. Gustafson, *Christ and the Moral Life* (New York: Harper and Row, 1968), p. 238; Donald Evans, "A Reasonable Scream of Protest," in *Peace, Power and Protest,* ed. Donald Evans (Toronto: The Ryerson Press, 1967), p. 5.

Some preliminary points deserve attention so that the question can be properly stated and pursued. Sometimes discussion about the specific contents of Christian ethics *vis-à-vis* others is only in terms of norms or precepts.[17] In my judgment such a description of the material content of ethics in general and of Christian ethics is much too narrow. The material content of ethics also includes other elements besides norms—attitudes, dispositions or virtues; goals and ideals; moral judgments. One cannot reduce the material content of ethics just to the question of rules and norms.

Secondly, it should be noted that the question about a distinctively Christian content to ethics and especially the denial of such a distinctive content in comparison with human ethics has arisen primarily in the context of Roman Catholic theology. There has been some discussion of the question among Protestants but comparatively little in the form of this specific question.[18]

This fact is not surprising but rather coheres with the basic theological thrust of Catholic and Protestant ethics, although one must be careful in speaking about either Protestant ethics or Catholic ethics as if either was a monolithic system. Classical Protestant ethics has generally down-played the human and the role of the human in Christian ethics. Roman Catholic ethics on the contrary has insisted on the goodness of the human, and its natural law tradition claimed that human reason on the basis of its understanding of humanity can arrive at true ethical wisdom and knowl-

17. Compagnoni, pp. 17, 18.
18. For one Protestant author who denies the existence of a distinctively Christian content in ethics, see John Macquarrie, *Three Issues in Ethics* (New York: Harper and Row, 1970), pp. 87–91. Macquarrie, as an Anglican theologian with a strong emphasis on philosophy, is very much in the mainstream of the Roman Catholic tradition on this question. For a Protestant critique of his position, see Hideo Ohki, "A New Approach to Christian Ethics," *Lexington Theological Quarterly* VII (1973), 11–26.

edge. Catholic ethics traditionally has given a very important place to the human, whereas classical Protestant ethics has seen Christian ethics as starting from God and his action and not from man.[19]

The Pastoral Constitution on the Church in the Modern World of Vatican II, despite its newer methodological approach, still remains in basic continuity with the Catholic emphasis on the human. The acceptance of the goodness and importance of the human can be illustrated by a number of statements in the document itself. "Above all the Church knows that her message is in harmony with the most secret desires of the human heart when she champions the dignity of the human vocation restoring hope to those who have already despaired of anything higher than their present lives. Far from diminishing man, her message brings to his development light, life and freedom. Apart from this message nothing will avail to fill up the heart of man. 'Thou hast made us for Thyself, O Lord, and our hearts are restless till they rest in Thee' " (n. 21). A little further on, the document describes the ultimate vocation of man as in fact one, and divine (n. 22). Jesus who entered world history as a perfect man revealed to us that God is love. "At the same time He taught us that the new command of love was the basic law of human perfection and hence of the world's transformation. To those therefore who believe in divine love He gives assurance that the way of love lies open to all men and that the effort to establish a universal brotherhood is not a hopeless one" (n. 38).

The encyclical letter *Populorum Progressio* of Pope Paul VI follows the same general method of the Pastoral Constitution on the Church in the Modern World and also illustrates that the Catholic tradition has at the very least a high regard for

---

19. Paul Lehmann, *Ethics in a Christian Context* (New York and Evanston: Harper and Row, 1963), especially pp. 165–367.

the human. *Populorum Progressio* builds its teaching around the concept of development. Since human beings, like all of creation, are ordered to their Creator, they should orientate their lives to God, the first truth and supreme good. By reason of union with Christ man attains to a new fulfillment of himself, to a transcendent humanism which gives man his greatest possible perfection.[20] Later, the pope comments that modern man is searching for a new humanism embracing the higher values of love and friendship, of prayer and contemplation, which will permit the fullness of authentic development (n. 20).

The discussion about a specific content of Christian ethics takes place, at least in Roman Catholicism, in the light of this basic acceptance of the goodness and importance of the human as well as its continuity with grace. This essay does not intend to summarize all of the writing which has appeared on this question in the last few years. Rather, the different positions will be illustrated and criticized. Interestingly, many Catholic authors writing on this subject in the last few years have denied the existence of a specifically different material content in Christian ethics, although there have been two distinct and different approaches in arriving at this conclusion. On the other hand, there are also some authors who affirm a Christian ethic which does not contradict human ethics but does add a distinctively Christian content beyond the human. It is only in the last few years that the question has been raised in the exact terms in which it has been raised now. For that reason, it would be an almost impossible task to determine how other thinkers in the past would have responded to this question because the question was not really posed exactly the same way as it is now.

20. Pope Paul VI, *Populorum Progressio, Acta Apostolicae Sedis* LIX (1967), 265, n. 16. For an available English translation see *On the Development of Peoples,* commentary by Barbara Ward (New York: Paulist Press, 1967).

The position affirming a distinctively Christian content.[21]
One of the characteristics of Roman Catholic moral theology
has been its heavy emphasis on anthropology as the starting
point of Christian ethics, and the opinion affirming a specific
material content to Christian ethics can readily find a basis in
anthropology. The comparison, however, is not between the
sinful nature of man and the redeemed nature of man. There
is no doubt about the great contrast existing here as illustrated, for example, in Paul's description of those who walk
according to the flesh and those who walk according to the
spirit. Likewise, the call to conversion as it is frequently
proposed in the scriptures is not a call to man as such but
rather to sinful human beings.

The "human" which is under discussion in the comparison
of the human and the Christian must be that which pertains
to the nature of man as such and not to the historical state of
man after the fall. Since Catholic ethics has often accepted
the axiom *agere sequitur esse,* then the starting point should
be an anthropological understanding of the Christian as such.
Christianity definitely adds a specific element in the area of
anthropology. Faith and grace are the decisive elements in a
Christian anthropology.

What do faith and grace add to ethics? A new way of being
(life in grace) must result in a new way of acting. The
teachings of Jesus indicate how he does extend the ambit of
the human for those who are his followers. He calls for love

21. The following section, while bringing in other aspects, will basically follow
the position proposed in an unsigned article "Esiste una morale 'cristiana'?" *La
Civiltà Cattolica* CXXIII (1972) III, 449–455. As illustrations of the wide attention given to this problem in different countries and of the position affirming a
distinctive content in Christian ethics, see René Coste, "Loi naturelle et loi
évangélique," *Nouvelle Revue Théologique* XCII (1970), 76–89; J. Gründel,
"Ethik ohne Normen? Zur Begründung und Struktur christlicher Ethik," in *Ethik
ohne Normen?* ed. Gründel-Van Oyen (Freiburg: Herder, 1970), 11–88; Dionigi
Tettamanzi, "Esiste un'etica cristiana?" *La Scuola Cattolica* XCIX (1971), 163–
193.

of enemies, humility, renunciation, nonviolence, virginity for the kingdom. The radical demands of gospel morality, including the cross and love of enemies, are not mere counsels but constitute ethical demands that go beyond the human and flow from the new life of those who are in Jesus Christ. The scriptural ethical teaching indicates that the gift of new life in Christ Jesus calls the Christian to act in a different way so that there is a specifically different material content in Christian ethics. However, the existence of an irreducibly specific Christian morality does not mean that such a morality stands in opposition to human morality. Christian morality goes beyond the human, but it is in the last analysis a fulfillment of the human and not in any way a contradiction of the human.

The above argumentation definitely shows the Catholic matrix out of which it comes. The Protestant approach would tend to see greater discontinuity between the human and the Christian; for example, human ethics is based on man giving his neighbor his due in accord with the rights of the neighbor, whereas Christian morality responds not to the rights of the neighbor but to the needs of the neighbor.[22]

Many theologians within the Protestant tradition do give some importance and value to the human. This more positive relationship between the Christian and the human can best be described in the model of the Christian transforming the human. This concept of transformation implies not only continuity between the human and the Christian but also some discontinuity, so that occasionally the Christian ethical demands will go against the purely human demands.[23] How-

22. Paul Ramsey, *Basic Christian Ethics* (New York: Charles Scribner's Sons, 1950), pp. 1–152.

23. For an explanation of this model in contrast to other possible models, see H. Richard Niebuhr, *Christ and Culture* (New York: Harper Torchbook, 1956). Paul Ramsey has explicitly adopted such a model of transformism in his later writings especially *Nine Modern Moralists* (Englewood Cliffs, N.J.: Prentice-Hall, 1962).

ever, it is important to point out that in Catholic thought the
human, or the natural, is a metaphysical and ahistorical
concept referring to the meaning of man as such apart from
either the fall or grace, whereas the Protestant concept of the
human is more historical, referring to the actual human condition.[24] This difference of perspective is very significant but
still does not completely explain away the divergences between Catholic and classical Protestant thought on the relationship between the human and the Christian. On the other
hand, liberal Protestantism is often more willing to see a great
continuity between the human and the Christian and at times
even an identity.[25]

Denial of a distinctively Christian content. A comparatively
large number of Catholic authors in the last few years denied
the existence of a specifically different material content in
Christian morality.[26] There are two possible ways of attempting to justify this assertion. The first approach, which
begins from an abstract ahistorical notion of the human and

24. Josef Fuchs, *Natural Law: A Theological Perspective* (New York: Sheed
and Ward, 1965), pp. 85–122.
25. Lloyd J. Averill, *American Theology in the Liberal Tradition* (Philadelphia:
Westminster Press, 1967).
26. The following list is illustrative and does not intend to be a complete
bibliography on the subject. The authors cited do refer to other references to the
question. Jean-Marie Aubert, "La spécificité de la morale chrétienne selon Saint
Thomas," *Le Supplément* XXIII (1970), 55–73; Franz Böckle, "Was ist das
Proprium einer christlichen Ethik," *Zeitschrift für Evangelische Ethik* XI (1967),
148–158; James F. Bresnahan, "Rahner's Christian Ethics," *America* CXXIII
(1970), 351–354; Josef Fuchs, *Human Values and Christian Morality* (Dublin:
Gill and Macmillan, 1970), especially 112–147; Fuchs, "Gibt es eine spezifisch
christliche Moral?" *Stimmen der Zeit* XCV (1970), 99–112. The same article
appears in Fuchs, *Esiste una morale cristiana?* (Rome: Herder, 1970), 13–44;
Fuchs, "Esiste una morale non-cristiana?" *Rassegna di teologia* XIV (1973),
361–373. Richard A. McCormick, "Notes on Moral Theology," *Theological
Studies* XXXII (1971), 71–78; Bruno Schüller, "Typen ethischer Argumentation
in der katholischen Moraltheologie," *Theologie und Philosophie* XLV (1970),
526–550; René Simon, "Spécificité de l'ethique chrétienne," *Le Supplément*
XXIII (1970), 74–104. For a more complete bibliography, see Compagnoni, pp.
172–182.

from a theological perspective based on creation, asserts that the material content of Christian morality adds nothing to the material content of human morality understood in a metaphysical way. The second approach, which begins from the historical order of the human and from a theological perspective based on an understanding of redemption and grace, asserts that the human as we know it today is already influenced by grace so that Christians cannot claim a distinctive content to their ethics which cannot be found in the ethics of non-Christians or others existing in this world.

The approach based on creation has been followed by most of the authors. Interestingly, some theologians (e.g., Aubert, Compagnoni, Fuchs) claim that Thomas Aquinas supported such a position even though he did not formulate the question as it has been proposed in the last few years.[27] Aubert arrives at this conclusion on the basis of Aquinas' teaching on the virtues and on the new law. In his treatise on the virtues Thomas integrated the human virtues into the Christian perspective. Charity is the form of the virtues so that charity thus becomes the efficient and the final cause ordering the human virtues to their ultimate end. But charity is expressed in and through the moral virtues which thus constitute the material cause of Christian ethics. From the viewpoint of material causality the human and the Christian are the same. Aubert also points out that Aquinas acknowledges that the law of Christ introduces man into a radical newness, but the Angelic Doctor explicitly states that the law of Christ does not of itself add any new moral prescriptions to the human.[28]

The proponents of this position do not deny a specifically distinct Christian ethics as such, but they do deny that there

27. Aubert, *Le Supplément* XXIII (1970), 55–73; Compagnoni, pp. 63–96; Fuchs, *Rassegna di teologia* XIV (1973), 306.
28. Aubert, *Le Supplément* XXIII (1970), 64–70.

is a distinctive material content to Christian ethics. Thus, such a position makes a distinction between the material and the formal element in Christian ethics or between the transcendent and the categorical aspects.

In explaining this position, following paragraphs will develop the exposition of Joseph Fuchs who has written more articles on this subject than any other Catholic author—although other positions will also be mentioned. According to Fuchs there is a twofold aspect in morality. There are the particular, categorical moral values such as justice, fidelity, or goodness which are present in the moral act itself. In addition, and even more importantly, in the realization of particular moral values in individual actions the person attains and realizes himself as a person before the Absolute, who is God. The realization of the self occurs in every specific act but we are often conscious of it only in a nonthematic and nonreflexive way, whereas the realization of a particular moral value in an action usually occurs with a thematic and reflexive consciousness. The self-realization of the person which occurs usually in a nonthematic and nonreflexive way in every moral act is the more important and determining element of the individual moral act.[29]

The believer, however, can thematize and understand this relationship as a person before the Absolute in terms of a relationship in the Spirit through Jesus Christ to the Father. Although the Christian is not always reflexively conscious of this in every act, nevertheless this relationship is present as the most profound aspect in the moral life. Fuchs refers to this as Christian intentionality, understood as the decision for Christ and the Father, which is present and orientating the life of the believer as the most important aspect of Christian morality.[30]

29. Fuchs, *Esiste una morale cristiana?* pp. 17, 18.
30. *Ibid.,* pp. 18, 19.

The categorical content of Christian morality, as distinguished from Christian intentionality or the transcendental aspect, is fundamentally and substantially human, or a morality of humanity. The Christian teaching on creation establishes the existence of man among men in this world, with the Creator God requiring that men should live and act in accord with their multiple relationships.[31] Human morality, which Fuchs prefers to describe as *recta ratio* and not as natural law because of certain connotations connected with the concept of natural law, is the medium in which the Christian transcendentality realizes itself. Authentic human morality demands that the individual person live in accord with his relationships with God and with his interpersonal relationships with others working and striving with them for the formation of the world and of humanity. Fuchs goes on to indicate that the teachings of scripture, as well as theologians such as Thomas Aquinas, Suarez, and even manualists such as Vermeersch and Zalba, maintain that Christian ethics does not add anything to the material content of human ethics.[32]

Fuchs and other defenders of this position realize that they must respond to the strongest arguments proposed in favor of a specifically distinct Christian ethical content—the anthropological argument and the argument derived from the moral teachings of scripture. Fuchs believes that those who argue for a new Christian action based on the new Christian being wrongly see Christ as a teacher of morality rather than as a redeemer of fallen man and correlatively see in the Church the duty to teach morality rather than to enunciate and communicate salvation. The newness that Jesus brings is not a new moral teaching but rather a new man, born in the spirit rather than a man of the flesh, in Pauline terms. To the new

31. *Ibid.*, pp. 22, 23.
32. Fuchs, *Rassegna di teologia* XIV (1973), 364–367.

Christian *esse,* there does correspond a Christian *agere.* This new Christian being calls the Christian person in faith, charity and the following of Christ to manifest his new existence by living in a Christian manner the true human morality. The material content remains the demands of human morality as such.[33]

What about the biblical teaching on love of God and man, especially the love of enemies, self-denial even unto death, the role of the cross in the life of the Christian, care for those people who are in need and who contribute nothing to society? Francesco Compagnoni devotes one chapter of his book, which was originally a doctoral dissertation, to show that the scriptures do not add any moral content to human morality.[34]

In what sense is the command of charity in the New Testament a new commandment? Aubert responds to this question by citing Pope Leo XIII who, in the encyclical *Sapientiae Christianae,* maintains that Jesus called his commandment new not because mutual love was not prescribed by the law of nature itself but because the manner of loving was completely new and unheard of. The newness in the New Testament commandment of love arises from its relationship to the fallen nature of man—the flesh in the Pauline sense. If one understands humanity in the metaphysical sense and not in the sense of fallen man, then there is no fundamental difference in the command to love. The natural law itself entails the precept of love of God and of other men as the expression of the specifically human tendency, for as a spiritual being man has as his end to tend toward God and love him and to love his images who are other persons.[35]

Fuchs raises the question about a distinctive Christian con-

33. *Ibid.,* p. 369.
34. Compagnoni, pp. 27–61.
35. Aubert, *Le Supplément* XXIII (1970), 67.

tent in the teaching of the Sermon on the Mount and in the law of the cross. But he points out that the antitheses in the Sermon on the Mount are between the new man and sinful man and not between the new man and humanity as such. Human nature or *recta ratio* does call for man to love God and love neighbor. For fallen man this exigency of humanity requires renunciation, sacrifice and the cross so that such a man can free himself from the egoism which is not a part of humanity as such. The law of the cross for fallen man does not add a new material content beyond the human but rather shows how the essential demand of humanity is to be achieved by fallen man.[36]

Interpretation and critique. Although these two positions come to a different conclusion about the material content of Christian ethics, they are in no sense diametrically opposed. Obviously, within the Catholic tradition those who have proposed a specifically different content to Christian morality also recognize that much of the content is the same as that of human morality. Most of Catholic ethics in the past has been based on the natural law. Contemporary official Church documents speak of Christian morality as being the truly, or fully, or perfectly human, so that even what is different from the human must not be opposed to the human but rather be in continuity with it and ultimately the fulfillment of the human.

On the other hand those who deny any specific Christian content in morality do admit that grace and the supernatural are necessary for man (fallen man in this historical situation) to live in accord with human morality.[37] In addition, Aubert recognizes that the demands of charity lead to the importance and place of some human virtues such as humility whose importance purely rational reflection is not able to

36. Fuchs, *Esiste una morale cristiana?* pp. 25–27.
37. Fuchs, *La Rassegna di teologia* XIV (1973), 373.

perceive. He goes on to point out that man has need of these virtues even in his natural state and not only because he is marked by sin and in need of salvation.[38]

Compagnoni affirms that the precepts of the new law add nothing to the material content of human morality, but they do bring about a radicalization of the precepts of human morality. Although the content of the moral precepts remain the same, they become more clearly manifest and their implications are seen more readily. Above all, since grace now permits their realization, they are able to develop everything that is contained in them even virtually, as is evident in the Christian understanding of the virtue of humility.[39]

Fuchs himself is willing to admit that there are human moral truths which are *per se* accessible to human intelligence but in fact are not known by some men. He draws the comparison with what Vatican Council I said about man's natural knowledge of God. Reason is able to achieve this knowledge, but man because of his fallen state often does not acquire such knowledge.[40] These authors thus acknowledge some limitations in reason's ability to arrive at the full understanding of human morality.

Although I deny there is a specifically different content to Christian ethics that is not available to all other human beings and other ethics, I prefer to propose the reasoning in a different manner. There are, in my judgment, difficulties with the argument based on creation and the metaphysical concept of humanity implied in such reasoning. Such a metaphysical concept of humanity is truly an abstraction which does not correspond to any given historical state of human existence. As a matter of fact, human beings are existing in the one order of creation and redemption in which all are

38. Aubert, *Le Supplément* XXIII (1970), 64.
39. Compagnoni, p. 95.
40. Fuchs, *Rassegna di teologia* XIV (1973), 373.

called to a saving and loving union with God. It will always be difficult, if not impossible, to say what belongs to the metaphysical state of man as such, because one can never abstract that perfectly from the influence of grace and sin, which are always a part of human existence as we know it.

The proponents of the first mode of reasoning admit that historical man cannot live according to such moral precepts without the help of grace. In fact, existing human beings cannot even know these moral teachings expeditiously, with certitude and without any mixture of error, without grace, if we are to fully apply the analogy Fuchs drew between reason's ability to know God as the beginning and end of all things and the ability to know human morality. One is thus employing reason to propose the content of human morality and at the same time admitting that human beings in this world will experience great difficulty in arriving at a knowledge of human morality. Likewise, one could bring an argument against the position proposed by Fuchs analogous to the argument brought against a natural knowledge of the existence of God.

The way in which these theorists have dealt with the questions of Christian love, the Sermon on the Mount, and the law of the cross indicates a weakness in the approach itself. They assert the abstract content of human morality itself as calling for love of God and of neighbor and working together for the good of society. This nucleus then becomes present in different historical situations. The historical situations referred to here are not just the changing cultural and historical relativities of human history but also involve the changes in the so-called history of salvation.[41]

The condition of fallen man will somewhat change the materiality of human ethics. Love of neighbor for fallen man will now involve renunciation, sacrifice, and the cross. Be-

41. Fuchs, *Esiste una morale cristiana?* p. 26.

cause of egoism, sin, and selfishness, love of neighbor will be experienced as the cross and a self-emptying. Fuchs asserts that the non-Christian or the atheist experiencing his own egoism is able to recognize that in this situation renunciation, sacrifice, and the cross are able to be part of the realization of humanity.[42] It seems difficult to assert that human reason, considered in the abstract, even though it is present in human beings in the midst of a sinful world, can understand that in this situation humanity calls for sacrifice, renunciation, and the cross.

There is another very possible alternative. Human beings might come to the conclusion that such a world is not rational and does not seem to make any sense on these grounds alone. At least, many human beings historically have come to that conclusion and not the one proposed by Fuchs and others. I have grave doubts that suffering, sacrifice, and the cross are historically verifiable as rational. Such an approach does not seem to give enough importance to the reality of sin and what effect it has on man and reality. There is such a thing as the mystery of evil or the mystery of iniquity which is so strong that in the midst of it rationality does not shine through. In the midst of suffering and unrequited love one could very easily conclude to the irrationality of the whole human enterprise. I do not want to say that sin totally does away with some aspects of the rational, but I do think sin has more effect than the proponents of this position are willing to admit. This approach to the question seems too abstract, ahistorical, and overly rational to be fully satisfying.

One further point can be made. Aubert maintains that the material cause of Christian morality is the same as human morality, but the final and formal causes are different. Fuchs writes of a specific Christian intentionality and Christian motivation, but this is expressed in the medium of human

42. *Ibid.,* pp. 26, 27.

morality. In the light of the thomistic reasoning explicitly employed by Aubert, one can ask if the formal element should not have some affect on the material element. Is there not a reciprocal causality between them so that the form in some way does effect the matter? The thrust of my critical remarks is that the mode of reasoning does not seem able to conclusively prove the thesis that human morality understood in the metaphysical sense has the same content as Christian morality.

Another approach. My own approach to this question begins with the actual historical order in which we live and not with an abstract concept of the metaphysical notion of the human. The Christian knows only one historical order—man created, fallen, and redeemed. The human beings that we know are under all these influences. Roman Catholic theology has consistently acknowledged the universal salvific will of God by which a loving father calls all men to salvation. Redemption and saving grace are offered to all men and exist outside the pale of the Catholic and the Christian.[43] Theologians have developed various theories to explain precisely how the reality of God's saving gift occurs, but it is not necessary for us to mention these at the present time. One theory, for example, maintains that in moral choice man is ultimately confronted with the absolute and in this way the saving gift of God can come to him.[44]

By understanding the human in this historical sense of man existing as created, fallen, and redeemed, the specifically Christian aspect of morality is going to be even less than that proposed by the other approaches to the question. The human can also share in the intentionality and motivation

43. Pastoral Constitution on the Church in the Modern World, n. 22.
44. Compagnoni (pp. 121, 122) criticizes Fuchs, with whom he is in fundamental agreement, for basing his argument on theological hypotheses when it is not necessary.

corresponding to the redeeming gift of God's love even though these are not present in a thematic way or in an explicitly Christian manner. The specific aspect of Christian morality is the explicitly Christian way in which this is known and manifested. But what the Christian knows with an explicit Christian dimension is and can be known by all others. The difference lies in the fact that for the Christian ethics is thematically and explicitly Christian. Earlier I stated my conclusion in this way: "Obviously a personal acknowledgement of Jesus as Lord affects at least the consciousness of the individual and his thematic reflection on his consciousness, but the Christian and the explicitly non-Christian can and do arrive at the same ethical conclusions and can and do share the same general ethical attitudes, dispositions and goals. Thus, explicit Christians do not have a monopoly on such proximate ethical attitudes, goals and dispositions as self-sacrificing love, freedom, hope, concern for the neighbor in need or even the realization that one finds his life only in losing it."[45]

Again, it should be pointed out that this position is not in total opposition with, and in some ways might even be reconciled with, the other two approaches to this question. For example, Dionigi Tettamanzi admits that if human ethics refers to the metaphysical concept of man as such, then Christian ethics does have a distinctive content; but if human ethics refers to man historically existing in the one given order, then the human and the Christian coincide.[46]

Joseph Fuchs has also insisted upon the fact that grace and salvation are offered to all men even those outside the pale of explicit Christianity. Fuchs' latest article on the question is entitled: "Is There a Non-Christian Morality?" Just as in the

---

45. *Catholic Moral Theology in Dialogue* (Notre Dame: Fides Publishers, 1972), p. 20.
46. Tettamanzi, *La Scuola Cattolica* XCIX (1971), 193.

case of the question about Christian morality, his answer is both yes and no. Fuchs maintains that in the last analysis there is only one historical moral order and the ultimate meaning of the human is Christian.[47]

Norbert Rigali has pointed out that the above approach is true of "essential" ethics but not of existential ethics. Existential, personal, or individual ethics has to be taken into account. The Christian as an individual belongs to the Christian community (the Church) and recognizes moral obligations existing within this particular framework. Such an example illustrates that individuals precisely because of their individuality will experience different moral calls and obligations.[48] Certainly one must accept the existence of such a personal and individual aspect of morality. I merely want to recall that the non-Christian too can perceive personal obligations of self-sacrificing love and service which are to be carried out in accord with his own individuality and circumstances.

Although this study has outlined three different approaches to the question of the specific content of Christian morality, it must always be recalled that there is general agreement within the Roman Catholic tradition that the human plays a large role in Christian morality. The practical differences between the second and third approach are not that great, and they result primarily from a different concept of the human. In the second opinion the human is understood in a metaphysical way as referring to humanity as such, apart from the realities of the history of salvation, whereas in the third opinion the human is understood as that which is historically existing here and now in terms of human beings

47. Fuchs, *Rassegna di teologia* XIV (1973), 361–373.
48. Norbert J. Rigali, "On Christian Ethics," *Chicago Studies* X (1971), 227–247. For a similar emphasis see Richard Roach, "Christian and Human," *The Way* XIII (1973), 112–125.

created, fallen, and redeemed. When speaking of the content of Christian ethics being the same as human ethics, I have frequently used the terminology fully, truly, or authentically human so that the sinful element does not enter in.

The moral theology of the manuals of theology also gave very great importance to the role of the human in Christian ethics. Even those who assert that there is a specifically different Christian content to ethics will also recognize and accept the fact that there is much content which the Christian shares with the human. As pointed out before, the teaching of the hierarchical magisterium on social matters was explained almost exclusively in terms of the natural law which is common to all mankind. In addition, those teachings which can be looked upon as most distinctively Catholic, such as the condemnation of contraception, sterilization, abortion, euthanasia, as well as the principle of the double effect, have all been based on natural law which is available to all mankind. Even the Catholic teaching on divorce has been proposed in the name of the natural law. Thus, within the Roman Catholic tradition all would have to admit that a very large place in Christian morality has been granted to a human morality. Translated into other terms this means that Christian morality must always be open to and learn from the true insights of a human morality. Christian morality in no way can ignore the meaning of the human but must work together with all other sciences and human experiences in trying to discern what precisely is the human.

The reasoning as developed in this section has talked in theory about the fact that truly human ethics and Christian ethics can have the same material content. The material content is only one aspect of any ethics as a thematic discipline. Christian ethics will always differ greatly from other ethics because it must reflect upon and thematize the ethical reality in terms of the explicitly Christian. This discussion has been limited to the rather narrow question of the material content of ethics as understood in terms of concrete ethical judgments, norms and proximate dispositions, attitudes and goals even including self-sacrificing love. Christian ethics as a theological and ethical discipline must reflect upon the Christian life in an explicitly and thematically Christian way so that by definition it does differ from all other religious or philosophical ethics.

A DISTINCTIVELY CATHOLIC ETHIC?

Is Catholic ethics different from Christian and human ethics, and, if so, what are the specifically different characteristics? An adequate response to this question must again distinguish between Catholic ethics in practice as lived and proclaimed by the Church and reflective ethics which as a theological discipline takes place in the Catholic tradition.

On the practical level of the ethics taught by the Catholic Church one can point to certain specific teachings proposed by the hierarchical teaching office in the Church and at times denied by many other people in contemporary society. In discussing the question of a specifically Catholic ethics, G. B. Guzzetti proposes some of these ethical teachings as what specifies and distinguishes Catholic ethics from all others—the indissolubility of every true marriage, the purity of marriage against all onanism, the inviolability of any human life from direct attack, especially the condemnation of abortion and euthanasia.[49] One could add to this list other specific moral teachings that have been proposed by the hierarchical teaching office in the Catholic Church, but Guzzetti does mention those which are well known and in the popular mind represent what is specific and distinctive about Catholic ethics.

A further investigation of these distinctive moral teachings

---

49. G. B. Guzzetti, "C'é una moral cristiana?" *Seminarium* XI (1971), 549.

in the Roman Catholic Church reveals two other distinctive aspects of Catholic ethics. These teachings are proposed by the authoritative, hierarchical teaching office in the Church. They have their force, therefore, not only on the basis of ethical arguments but also because they are proposed authoritatively by the Church. In addition, the hierarchical magisterium proposed all these specific teachings as being based on the natural law. It is true that in the case of divorce references are also made to the scriptural teaching,[50] but the specific and distinctive teachings proposed in Catholic ethics are based on the natural law.

At the present time, however, these three aspects—the specific teachings themselves, the natural law basis and the authoritative teaching role of the Church are being questioned within Roman Catholicism. In terms of the specific teachings mentioned by Guzzetti and popularly understood as what specifies Catholic moral teachings, many Catholic theologians are expressing their disagreement with the official teaching of the Church. Responsible Roman Catholic theologians have called for changes in the teaching of the Church on artificial contraception, sterilization, divorce, abortion, euthanasia, the principle of the double effect with its prohibition of direct killing, and even in other matters of sexuality. In addition, samplings of public opinion indicate that many individual Catholics disagree with the official teaching of the Church on these positions.[51] These specific teachings can no longer be regarded as what is distinctive about Catholic ethics.

The natural law invoked by the hierarchical teaching office in arriving at these conclusions has in theory always occa-

---

50. For documentation of the comparatively late (nineteenth and twentieth centuries) emphasis on natural law as the basis for the prohibition of divorce, see John T. Noonan, Jr., "Indissolubility of Marriage and Natural Law," *The American Journal of Jurisprudence* XIV (1969), 79–88.

51. See footnote 13.

sioned some question and uneasiness on the part of Catholics. On the one hand, the natural law is said to be available to all men because all share human nature and human reason, but, on the other hand, on the basis of such a natural law the hierarchical teaching office in the Church has arrived at ethical conclusions which many people in our society do not accept.

The key to the understanding of this apparent dilemma lies in the ambiguous concept of natural law. Natural law in the broad sense of the term refers to the humanity and reason which all men share in common. Natural law in the more restricted sense of the term refers to a particular understanding of humanity based on nature as a principle of operation in every living thing including human beings. Man's nature thus determines how he should act. The official teaching office used the more restricted concept of natural law to arrive at its ethical conclusions. Such an understanding of natural law resulted in a moral methodology which was primarily deductive, somewhat ahistorical and tending toward the possibility of absolute certitude in moral matters. The problem was intensified by the fact that such a restricted notion of natural law was authoritatively imposed as the methodology to be followed in Catholic moral theology and thus did constitute a distinctive characteristic of Catholic ethics.[52]

Today Catholic theologians are rejecting this very restricted notion of natural law so that it no longer is the characteristic and distinctive aspect of Catholic ethics. In the place of a monolithic ethical theory there now exists a plurality of ethical methodologies within Roman Catholicism with a greater emphasis on induction, *a posteriori* argumentation,

52. For a somewhat typical overview of the question of natural law with a bibliography, see Jean-Marie Aubert, "Pour une herméneutique du droit natural," *Recherches de Science Religieuse* LIX (1971), 449–492.

experience and a recognition of the lack of absolute certitude on specific moral issues. Thus what at one time, especially from the end of the nineteenth century, was distinctive about Roman Catholic ethical teaching no longer holds today.

The third distinctive aspect which characterized Catholic moral teaching in the recent past was the authoritative teaching of the hierarchical teaching office on these matters. The post *Humanae Vitae* Church now realizes that the possibility of dissent from specific moral teachings was present even in the manualistic understanding of the role of the hierarchical teaching office, although it was not popularly known by the vast majority of Roman Catholics.[53] It is important to understand the ultimate reason for the possibility of dissent so that the ramifications of such dissent on the future developments of ethics in the Catholic Church can be properly judged. The ultimate theological reason for the possibility of dissent on specific moral teachings comes from the impossibility of achieving absolute certitude in the light of the complex elements involved in any specific moral judgment or teaching. The older and restricted natural law approach characteristic of past Roman Catholic theology added weight to the argument that absolute certitude could be achieved on such issues.

It is no coincidence that the three elements which were distinctive characteristics of Catholic ethical teaching in the past are breaking down today and no longer true. Newer ethical methodologies only underline the reasons supporting the possibilities of dissent from authoritative Church teaching and at the same time argue against the specific teachings that have often been proposed by the hierarchical magisterium in the name of a restricted concept of natural law in the past.

---

53. For a summary of much of the literature which appeared on the occasion of *Humanae Vitae*, see Richard A. McCormick, "Notes on Moral Theology," *Theological Studies* XXX (1969), 645–668.

Even at the present time one can no longer say that any or all of these three characteristics are distinctive of Roman Catholic ethics.[54] In the future it will be even more evident that these three characteristics do not distinguish Roman Catholic ethics from other Christian ethics.

Such an understanding with its heavy ecclesiological overtones calls for a marked change in the way in which the Catholic Church understands and carries out its teaching function in the area of morality. The hierarchical Church still appears to cling to the older understanding. The American mentality and the experience of the Catholic Church in this country have tended to emphasize Catholic identity primarily in terms of the observance of the moral teachings which have been proposed by the Church and thought to be the distinctive sign of being Catholic. If one insists on seeing the unity of the Catholic Church in terms of specific moral teachings, that unity will quickly be shattered. This is not the place to find either the unity of the Catholic Church or the distinctive aspect of Roman Catholicism. This same warning applies to those who want the Church to give absolutely certain answers on specific social and political questions facing society. In all these matters I think that the Church at times should teach on specific moral questions but in so doing cannot exclude the possibility that other members of the Church might come to different conclusions. From an ecclesiological perspective it is necessary to recognize that the hierarchical magisterium is only one part of the total teaching function of the Church and in some way all members of the Church do participate in that teaching function. Unfortunate consequences have arisen from associating the teaching function with the juridical aspect of the Church and from restricting the teaching office

---

54. A more detailed development on these three points is found in my article, "Moral Theology: The Present State of the Discipline," *Theological Studies* XXXIV (1973), 446–467.

to giving authoritative answers to particular problems. In this connection it is necessary to recognize the need for the personal responsibility of the individual but also the limitations and sinfulness that can affect every individual. Within the community of the Church the individual can find help and guidance in conscience formation. This is not the place to develop in detail how the Church should carry out its teaching function in the area of morality, but what has been said here and elsewhere sketches some possible approaches.[55]

There is no doubt that many would dispute the understanding of Catholic moral theology which has just been presented. The consequences of such an understanding are only beginning to be felt in the practical life of the Church; and one can see, without claiming any great insight into the future, that many tensions and problems will accompany the growing awareness of this understanding. In many ways the remaining studies in this book develop and defend such an understanding of moral theology. The next chapter responds in detail to a lengthy criticism of the concept of pluralism in Catholic moral theology which I have been proposing. Subsequent essays show how the approach to many specific teachings is being revised even though there remains opposition to these revisions.

From the perspective of moral theology or Christian ethics as a thematic and reflexive discipline, I believe there are some characteristics which have consistently been a part of the Roman Catholic theological tradition. The most distinctive

---

55. Daniel C. Maguire, "Moral Absolutes and the Magisterium," in *Absolutes in Moral Theology?* ed. Charles E. Curran (Washington: Corpus Books, 1968), 57–107; Maguire, "Moral Inquiry and Religious Assent," in *Contraception: Authority and Dissent,* ed. Charles E. Curran (New York: Herder, 1969), pp. 127–148; Maguire, "Teaching, Authority and Authenticity," *Living Light* VI (1969), 6–18. For helpful insights on the same question from a Protestant perspective, see James M. Gustafson, *The Church as Moral Decision Maker* (Philadelphia: Pilgrim Press, 1970).

characteristic can best be described as an acceptance of mediation. Christian ethics, like any theological or religious ethics, ultimately sees man's ethical behavior in terms of his relation to God, and more specifically at times, to the will of God. Catholic ethics has generally seen God's will as mediated through other things; for example, the older concept of natural law as the participation of the eternal law in the rational creature is an excellent illustration of such mediation. The anthropological basis which has been a traditional starting point for Roman Catholic ethics likewise exemplifies the reality of mediation. The generic emphasis on the human in Catholic moral theology illustrates the practical consequences of mediation.

In an analogous manner the role of the Church in moral matters again exemplifies mediation. The Church mediates the presence of the risen Lord to all mankind. The same basic concept of mediation can be found in the traditional Catholic emphasis on scripture *and* tradition. Such a concept of mediation is opposed to a direct and immediate approach to God and the will of God. Even in the transcendental approaches in which there is no reflexively conscious knowledge of an object as such, the presence of God is still mediated through the consciousness of the subject. One can legitimately affirm that in general the Roman Catholic theological tradition in the area of morality has been characterized by its insistence on mediation.[56]

In conclusion, this essay has maintained that there is a Christian ethic insofar as Christians are called to act and Christian ethicists reflect on action in the light of their explicitly Christian understanding of moral data, but Chris-

56. As an illustration of this point, see Eric D'Arcy, " 'Worthy of Worship': A Catholic Contribution," in *Religion and Morality: A Collection of Essays,* ed. Gene Outka and John P. Reeder, Jr. (Garden City, N.Y.: Anchor Press/ Doubleday, 1973), pp. 173–203.

tians and non-Christians can and do share the same general goals and intentions, attitudes and dispositions, as well as norms and concrete actions. The difference is in terms of the explicitly Christian aspect as such which manifests itself especially on the thematic level. Likewise there is a Catholic ethic insofar as Catholics act and Catholic theology reflects on action in the light of a Catholic self-understanding, but this results in no different moral data although more importance might be given to certain aspects such as the ecclesial element. From the theoretical viewpoint of moral theology as a theological discipline, an emphasis on mediation has characterized the Roman Catholic approach and differentiates it from other Christian ethics.

2

Pluralism in Catholic Moral Theology

In a recent assessment of contemporary Catholic moral theology, and in the previous chapter, I pointed out that pluralism now characterizes Catholic moral teaching both in methodologies employed and in the solutions to particular moral questions involving such issues as medical ethics, abortion, conflict situations which had previously been solved in terms of the principle of double effect, some questions of sexuality and divorce. Pluralism on these specific moral questions was justified from the viewpoints of ecclesiology and of moral methodology.[1]

In reacting to this assessment Thomas Dubay has acknowledged the accuracy of the description of pluralism on specific moral questions in the writings of Roman Catholic theologians, but he disagrees with the evaluation given to this fact.[2] Dubay closes his article with several unanswered questions that moral theologians should explore (pp. 501–506). In the interest of pursuing the present discussion and hope-

1. Charles E. Curran, "Moral Theology: The Present State of the Discipline," *Theological Studies*, XXXIV (1973), 446–467. A slightly expanded version of this article may be found in my *New Perspectives in Moral Theology* (Notre Dame, Indiana: Fides Publishers, 1974), pp. 1–46.
2. Thomas Dubay, "The State of Moral Theology: A Critical Appraisal," *Theological Studies*, XXXV (1974), 482–506.

fully of clarifying some of the reasons proposed, I will respond to the more important questions he raised.

THE FIRST QUESTION

Dubay proposes his first question: "Is habitual and frequent dissent from authentic, noninfallible teaching in the Church biblically or theologically justified?" (p. 501). Dissent in the past was a rare phenomenon considered permissible only within narrow limits and confined to the pages of scholarly publications. It is academically unacceptable that an exception should now be blown up into a rule (pp. 501–2).

Yes, the possibility of frequent dissent from existing teachings of the authentic, hierarchical magisterium on specific moral matters is theologically justified today. Dubay and all Catholic theologians admit in theory the possibility of dissent from such authentic, noninfallible teaching of the hierarchical magisterium. The disagreement centers on whether or not such dissent can be frequent.

What is the ultimate theological reason for the possibility of dissent—be it rare or frequent? In my judgment the ultimate reason is epistemological. On specific moral questions one cannot have a certitude which excludes the possibility of error. Such an epistemological approach distinguishes the degree of certitude which can be had depending on the degree of generality or specificity with which one is dealing. As one goes from the general to the more specific, the possibility of a certitude which excludes error is less. One can be quite certain, for example, that murder is always wrong, but the problem is to determine in practice what is murder.

One can assert with great certitude that a Christian should be a loving, self-sacrificing person of hope and a sign of the fruits of the Spirit to the world, but one cannot know with

great certitude how to solve conflict situations involving
human lives. Roman Catholic theology in the past has solved
the question of conflict situations which might involve killing
or abortion on the basis of the understanding of the principle
of double effect. Such a solution rests on a philosophical
understanding of human actions in which the meaning of
direct effect is defined in terms of the physical structure of
the act itself. Such a solution is based on one philosophical
understanding of the human act, but many people, including
Roman Catholic theologians today, point out the inadequacy
of that particular philosophical understanding as a solution to
conflict situations.[3] Chapter 6 considers the principle of
double effect in greater detail.

Catholic teaching should, in season and out of season, with
great certitude, proclaim that the Christian must respect life.
One, however, cannot have such certitude in determining
precisely when death occurs. Catholic moral theology has
been willing to recognize the difficulties in determining precisely when death does occur.[4] In a somewhat similar way it
seems that one cannot have absolute certitude about when
human life begins. The solution to the question of abortion
ultimately rests on determining the beginning of human life.
The judgment about the beginning of human life cannot
claim to be so certain that it excludes the possibility of
error.[5] One cannot exclude from the Church of Jesus Christ a

3. Cornelius J. van der Poel, "The Principle of Double Effect," in *Absolutes in
Moral Theology?* ed. C.E. Curran (Washington: Corpus Books, 1968), pp. 186–
210; Leandro Rossi, "Diretto e indiretto in teologia morale," *Rivista di Teologia
Morale,* III (1971), 37–65.

4. Edwin F. Healy, S.J., *Medical Ethics* (Chicago: Loyola University Press,
1956), pp. 380–383.

5. For indications of some diversity already existing among contemporary
Roman Catholic authors on the question of the beginning of human life, see
Abtreibung—Pro und Contra, ed. J. Gründel (Würzburg: Echter, 1971); *Avorte-
ment et respect de la vie humaine,* Colloque du Centre Catholique des Médecins
Français (Paris: Editions du Seuil, 1972); D. Mongillo, F. D'Agostine, F. Com-

person who holds that the test for the existence of individual human life is the same at the beginning of life as at the end of life—that is, the presence of brain waves. Even though I personally would not hold such an opinion, I cannot exclude anyone who does from the Church of Jesus Christ.

Why is the possibility of such dissent now recognized to be much more frequent than in the past? There are three factors contributing to this changed understanding. First, the emphasis on historical consciousness in moral theology has affected theological methodology and the understanding of certitude in the area of theological ethics. A more historically conscious methodology, as illustrated in the Pastoral Constitution on the Church in the Modern World which begins its consideration of substantive questions by discerning the signs of the times, employs a more inductive methodology. The old methodology in Catholic moral theology tended to be more deductive so that the conclusion that one reached was just as certain as the premises from which one started, provided the logic was correct. A historically conscious methodology gives greater appreciation to the reality of continuing historical change and the need to begin, not with an abstract, universal, essentialist statement, but rather with the concrete, historical realities with which we live. Such a changing methodology with its emphasis on a more inductive approach will never be able to achieve the type of certitude which a more deductive methodology claimed to achieve.[6]

Second, contemporary moral theology recognizes the impossibility of an absolute identification between the physical aspect of the act and the moral description of the act. In fairness it should be pointed out that for the most part

pagnoni, "L'Aborto," *Rivista di Teologia Morale,* IV (1972), pp. 355–392; Richard A. McCormick, S.J., "Notes on Moral Theology: The Abortion Dossier," *Theological Studies,* XXXV (1974), pp. 312–359.

6. Bernard J.F. Lonergan, *Method in Theology* (New York: Herder and Herder, 1972), pp. 153–234.

Catholic moral theology has avoided the problem of identifying the physical structure of the act with the moral aspect. Thus, for example, our theology never claimed that all killing is wrong but only that all murder is wrong. One can have great certitude in claiming that all murder is wrong, but there might be more difficulty in determining in particular cases whether a specific act is murder or not.

In a similar way Catholic moral theology taught that lying is always wrong, but in the last few decades many theologians do not define a lie as the lack of correspondence between what I say and what is in my mind. The malice of lying consists in the violation of my neighbor's right to truth. Not every falsehood (defined in a somewhat physical way as the correspondence between what is uttered and what is in my mind) is a lie (defined in a moral sense).[7] However, the physical is a very important aspect of the human or the moral, and at times the moral is the same as the physical. In this world, my humanity cannot be separated from my physical, corporeal existence. There is a definite danger in some contemporary ethical discussions of not giving enough importance to the physical aspect, but one cannot merely assert that the physical is always the same as the moral.

In my judgment the areas of questioning today in Catholic moral theology are especially those areas in which the human moral act has been identified with the physical structure of the act itself. The areas under discussion today can generally be reduced to five—medical ethics, the solution of conflict situations which traditionally were solved by the application of the principle of double effect, abortion, sexuality, and divorce. There is not an opportunity here to develop fully an approach to these different questions, but rather the aim of this particular section is merely to seek intelligibility. Why is there questioning today about these particular issues?

7. J.A. Dorszynski, *Catholic Teaching about the Morality of Falsehood* (Washington: Catholic University of America Press, 1949).

Why is it that it will be very difficult to achieve on these questions the certitude which we thought we had in the past? The answer is that in all of these questions one cannot automatically make the identification of the human moral act with the physical structure of the act itself. In medical ethics involving questions such as contraception and sterilization, the older Catholic approach defines the morally wrong act in terms of its physical structure. The principle of the double effect understands the direct effect as the *finis operis* of the external act itself. In the question of sexuality, some ask why the physical act of sexual intercourse alone is permitted only between husband and wife even though many other acts such as revealing most intimate secrets can be done with one who is not a spouse? Some people today argue that human life does not begin at conception because according to them the human is more than just the biological, the physical and the genetic. I do not agree with all these new approaches. At times the human act is the same as the physical structure of the act, but such an identity cannot be accepted with a certitude that excludes the possibility of error.

Here again, there are a number of different epistemological approaches being taken by contemporary moral theologians on the basis of which they deny the position that the moral aspect is always identifiable with the physical aspect of the act itself. Moral theologians such as Milhaven, McCormick, and Schüller have insisted on the need to judge the morality of actions in terms of the consequences and seek justification for good acts in terms of proportionate reasons.[8] A more

8. Richard A. McCormick, S.J., *Ambiguity in Moral Choice,* The 1973 Pere Marquette Theology Lecture (Milwaukee: Marquette University, 1973); John Giles Milhaven, "Objective Moral Evaluation of Consequences," *Theological Studies* XXXII (1971), pp. 407–430; Bruno Schüller, S.J., "Zur Problematik allgemein verbindlicher ethischer Grundsätze," *Theologie und Philosophie,* XLV (1970), pp. 1–23; Schüller, "Typen ethischer Argumentation in der katholischen Moral Theologie," *Theologie und Philosophie,* XLV (1970), pp. 526–550.

relational or phenomenological approach judges the morality of actions not in terms of the physical structure of the act but rather in terms of the manifold relationships with God, neighbor, the world, and self.[9] Other Catholic theologians such as Capone, Fuchs, Janssens and Knauer agree in distinguishing between moral evil and ontic evil although they might not all employ the same terminology. Such authors often appeal to the thomistic distinction between the interior act and the exterior act. The decisive factor in determining the moral act is the internal act, especially the intention, and not just the external act itself.[10]

All of these approaches to the evaluation of the moral act differ from the approach of the past which often spoke of intrinsically evil actions in terms of the physical structure of the act itself. These contemporary approaches differ among themselves, but they agree in proposing an evaluation of the human moral act which includes so many other considerations that one cannot identify the human moral act and the physical structure of the act with such certitude that the possibility of error is excluded.

In a sense the debate about contraception in the Roman Catholic Church in the 1960's necessarily involved more than just the question of contraception. Some "conservative" Catholics, perhaps in an exaggerated way, pointed out that a change in the teaching on contraception would involve a change in other teachings of the Catholic Church. In one sense they were correct. The methodological approach em-

9. William H. Van der Marck, *Toward a Christian Ethic* (Westminster, Md.: Newman Press, 1967), pp. 41–79.

10. Domenico Capone, "Il pluralismo in teologia morale," *Rivista di Teologia Morale,* VI (1974), 289–302; Joseph Fuchs, "The Absoluteness of Moral Terms," *Gregorianum,* LII (1971), 415–458; Louis Janssens, "Ontic Evil and Moral Evil," *Louvain Studies,* IV (1972), 115–156; Peter Knauer, S.J., "La détermination du bien et du mal moral par le principe du double effet," *Nouvelle Revue Théologique,* LXXXVII (1965), 356–376; Knauer, "The Hermeneutic Function of the Principle of the Double Effect," *Natural Law Forum* XII (1967), 132–162.

ployed in justifying the condemnation of artifical contraception was the same general approach used to justify some other Catholic teachings. Logically, the call for a change in the teaching on contraception will also have reverberations in other matters where the same methodological difficulties occur. Even if one does not advocate different conclusions on the specific questions mentioned above, at least the newer methodological approaches realize that one's conclusions on these questions cannot have the same type of certitude as that proposed in the older methodology.

Third, contemporary Catholic theology acknowledges the overly authoritarian understanding of the Church which prevailed in the Catholic ethos until the last few decades. This authoritarian overemphasis also had its ramifications in the area of moral theology. Free theological discussion on many questions, such as the possibility of parvity of matter in sexual sins or the solution of conflict situations in the question of abortion, was not allowed. In the earlier article I tried to show at great length how an overemphasis on an authoritarian imposition of moral methodology and of solutions to particular moral problems arose and intensified from the time of the nineteenth century. Decisions of the Holy Office were sufficient to prevent any discussion of the particular questions mentioned above and other questions such as direct sterilization. Since older Catholic teachings on specific moral questions were often based on a monolithic methodology which is no longer accepted and were imposed in an extrinsic and authoritarian way, one must now expect there will be greater disagreement with such teachings.

THE SECOND QUESTION

The second question proposed by Dubay is: "Does not a 'right' to frequent dissent and public teaching of it postulate two magisteria in the Church?" (p. 502). Dubay correctly notes my intentional references to the "hierarchical magisterium" and concludes that my position does postulate two magisteria in practice.

Again one must recall that Dubay acknowledges the possibility of dissent from authentic, authoritative, noninfallible Church teaching. Anyone who admits such a possibility must deal with the same question. In theory one can at times go against the hierarchical magisterium and thus appeal to other criteria or sources of teaching. The question thus stands not only for one who would admit more frequent dissent but for anyone who in conformity with the Roman Catholic self-understanding admits the possibility of dissent from authentic, noninfallible Church teaching.

The key to the solution of such a question again involves a consideration of the reasons justifying the possibility of dissent. The theological reason for dissent rests on the epistemological recognition that on specific moral questions one cannot have that degree of certitude which excludes the possibility of error. The ultimate ecclesiological reason justifying dissent is that the hierarchical magisterium is not the only way in which the Church teaches and learns. A loyal Roman Catholic must acknowledge the hierarchical teaching office and the special assistance given by the Holy Spirit to such an office. However, since the hierarchical teaching office is not the only way in which the Church teaches and learns, the loyal Catholic can, and at times should, test this teaching in the light of a broader perspective.

The teachings of the Second Vatican Council show that the hierarchical magisterium is not the only way in which the Church teaches and learns. The Declaration on Religious Freedom begins by recognizing in the conscience of contemporary human beings the demand for a responsible freedom with regard to free exercise of religion in society. "This Vatican Synod takes careful note of these desires in the minds of men. It proposes to declare them to be greatly in accord with truth and justice" (n. 1). In the light of this assertion, one can ask when the teaching on religious liberty became true. The moment a document was signed in Rome? No, the teaching had to be true before that time. The hierarchical magisterium changed because it learned from the experience of people of good will.

Many of the documents of the Second Vatican Council insist on the importance of dialogue, not only with other Christians, but with nonbelievers, professionals, scientists, and others. Dialogue implies that one can and does learn from others. History illustrates the truth of the assertion, for the Roman Catholic Church has been taught by others, even nonbelievers. One should not wonder at this because a basic Catholic premise in moral theology is that our moral teaching is often based on our humanity and human reason which we share with all persons.

The Constitution on the Church proclaims that the holy people of God shares in the prophetic office of Christ (n. 12). Theology has traditionally spoken about the threefold office of Jesus as priest, prophet, and king. Through baptism the individual Christian shares in these threefold functions of Jesus. The liturgical movement found a deep theological basis in the fact that through baptism all Christians share in the priestly office of Jesus. The existence of the priesthood of all believers does not deny the need for a special hierarchical priesthood, but the complete priestly ministry in the Church cannot be identified solely with the hierarchical office of priesthood. So too, the fact that all Christians share in the prophetic teaching office of Jesus does not take away from the need for a hierarchical teaching office, but such a hierarchical teaching office cannot be identified with the totality of the teaching office and function in the Church.

The ultimate theological reason why all Christians share in

the teaching function of Jesus comes from the fact that the primary teacher in the Church is the Holy Spirit, but the Spirit dwells in the hearts of all the baptized and in some way in all persons of good will. The possibility of dissent from authoritative, authentic, noninfallible Church teaching rests on the theological reality that all the baptized share in the gift of the Spirit, and the hierarchical, noninfallible teaching office in the Church has never claimed to have a total monopoly on the Spirit.

The Constitution on the Church acknowledges that all people in the Church are given different gifts (n. 12). We are reminded of St. Paul's recognition of the different charisms and gifts which are given in the Church—some are called as apostles, prophets, teachers, workers of miracles, healers, helpers, administrators, speakers in various kinds of tongues (1 Corinthians 12:27ff). The role of the prophet exists in the Church and is not always identified with the hierarchical teaching function. The prophets both in the past and in the present have continually taught the whole Church. There arises the difficult question of the discernment of the Spirit and the discernment of the true prophet. But at least one has to admit that the acceptance of the authoritative, noninfallible teaching of the hierarchical magisterium cannot always be an ultimate test of the true prophet, although the prophet, like all others, must give due weight to this consideration.

The ecclesiology proposed in the Second Vatican Council clearly indicates that the hierarchical teaching office is not the only way in which the Church teaches and learns. This is the theological foundation for the teaching also accepted in the Constitution on the Church that dissent from authoritative, authentic, noninfallible Church teaching is a possibility for the Roman Catholic. The frequency of such dissent will depend on the other factors mentioned in response to the first question. In this connection, Dubay also raises the question of public dissent but elsewhere at great length I have justified public dissent in the Church.[11]

THE THIRD QUESTION

Dubay proposes a third question: "Is a contradictory moral pluralism a weak effort to make a virtue of necessity?" (p. 503). Earlier, Dubay has recognized the need to distinguish between complementary pluralism which is a healthy part of the life of the Church and contradictory pluralism which destroys the unity of the Church. Such a contradictory pluralism also diminishes the support of a secular observer who will not pay attention to a group who cannot speak out authoritatively and with one voice on important matters (pp. 91–92).

As an introductory note, it is important to point out that here and in other matters Dubay's differences are not only with my interpretation but with the approaches taken by many well recognized Roman Catholic moral theologians writing today. Dubay expressly admits, "For the most part, I have no problem with Curran's factual description of the pluralism situation" (p. 484). My explanation of this situation attempts to give meaning and intelligibility to the fact of pluralism which we both admit. Dubay does not want to admit the legitimacy of such contradictory pluralism which he recognized does exist in the writings of many Roman Catholic moral theologians today.

The consequences of Dubay's position are staggering—the many Catholic moral theologians today who are questioning various teachings of the Church and proposing alternate solu-

---

11. Charles E. Curran, Robert E. Hunt, et al., *Dissent In and For the Church: Theologians and Humanae Vitae* (New York: Sheed and Ward, 1969), 133–153.

tions are not truly within the pale of true Catholicity. In the light of such an interpretation, the Roman Catholic Church would be in the awkward position of acknowledging that probably the majority of Roman Catholic moral theologians who actually contribute to theological journals are not truly Catholic. But his question still remains—am I and many others merely making a virtue out of necessity?

While recognizing the rightful need and place for complementary pluralism, Dubay denies the possibility of contradictory pluralism on important moral questions. I contend that the Roman Catholic Church has now and always has had a contradictory pluralism even on important moral issues. The Catholic Church has been catholic enough to embrace both a William Buckley and a Dorothy Day, or in a wider context a Generalissimo Franco and President Julius Nyerere. There are Catholics who are for capital punishment and Catholics who are against it. The majority of Roman Catholics (rightly, in my judgment) were against the open shop, but some Catholics approved it. There are Roman Catholics who were in favor of the American involvement in Vietnam and Roman Catholics who were opposed to it. Some Roman Catholics are pacifists; others accept various forms of just war theory. Some Catholics favor busing as a means of overcoming racial imbalance in schools; others are opposed. Some Catholics believe that smoking is morally wrong because it is harmful to health, while other Catholics are willing to justify cigarette smoking.

There can be no doubt that a contradictory pluralism already does exist within the Roman Catholic Church on important moral matters. Many of the issues mentioned above pertain to the area of social ethics, but they constitute very important issues facing Catholics and the total society. It is strange that so often one tends to think of moral theology only in terms of personal morality and forgets the very important aspect of social morality. However, some of the examples above belong to the realm of personal morality, so it is not sufficient to say that contradictory pluralism can exist on the level of social morality but not in the sphere of personal morality.

The reason explaining the possibility of such pluralism in both cases is the same—the epistemological reason because of which on specific moral questions it is impossible to have the type of certitude that excludes all possibility of error. The unity of the Church has coexisted in the past and even now in the present with contradictory pluralism on very important moral issues. All references to the need for unity in the Church as proposed in scripture and mentioned by Dubay must take account of this fact—contradictory pluralism on important moral questions does not destroy the basic unity of the Church.

How can one attempt a more positive explanation and reconciliation of the unity of the Church and the possibility of pluralism on specific questions. A good starting point for such an explanation would be the well accepted axiom—*in necessariis, unitas; in dubiis, libertas; in omnibus, caritas.* There can and should be unity in terms of the general values, goals, attitudes, and dispositions that the gospel and human experience call for. Here attention centers on such things as the beatitudes of Matthew, the fruits of the Spirit proposed by Paul, or those basic Christian attitudes such as care, love, hope, forgiveness and compassion which should characterize the life of the Christian. However, as one descends to specifics and to more particular acts, then it is impossible to have the type of certitude that exists on the level of greater generality. The question of unity and pluralism finds its solution in terms of the epistemological question. Unity is present at the level of greater generality, but as one descends to particulars the possibility of pluralism arises because in the midst of such complexity one cannot exclude the possibility of error.

Once one recognizes that even contradictory pluralism has existed in the Roman Catholic Church in the past on important moral matters, both social and personal, it is now helpful to try to indicate the scope of the new areas in which pluralism is emerging. A survey of the literature seems to limit these questions to the following areas—medical ethics, direct and indirect voluntary as a solution to conflict situations, sexuality, abortion, and divorce. These questions cover only a comparatively small part of the Christian life and should not be identified in any way with the totality of the Christian life or with the totality of the concerns of Christian ethics.

Too often in the past few years moral theology has so riveted attention on the situation ethics debate that occasionally moral theologians have forgotten the many other aspects of Christian ethics such as attitudes, virtues, goals, dispositions, and values in the Christian life which can never be simplistically reduced to the one question of whether or not there is a norm. Likewise, as Dubay also points out, there are many more important topics and concerns in the Christian life such as the paschal mystery, the imitation of Jesus, and the Christian's call to perfection.

Although the questions mentioned above in which there is now a growing pluralism are comparatively few and not the most important considerations involved in moral theology, nevertheless, they do have some importance. Why is pluralism now beginning to arise in these questions? Once again the answer to this question attempts to give some intelligibility to the fact which has been observed and to understand better some of the reasons justifying such pluralism. In my judgment there is a common denominator which is present in all these questions, although it limps somewhat in the question of divorce, which in some ways is a different type of question and will be discussed in Chapter 3. In all these other questions there has been an identification of the moral or human aspect with the physical structure of the act itself. As mentioned earlier, I do not deny that at times, but not always, the moral act is the same as the physical structure of the act. When one does conclude that the moral or the human is identical with the physical, such an identification cannot be made with the same type of certitude that an older methodology claimed. It is precisely the possible questioning of this fact of identification which is the reason for the contradictory pluralism which is now existing on all these questions.

It is also interesting to note that in these limited questions, again excluding the question of divorce, the appeal in Roman Catholic theology has always been based on the natural law. In other words, the Roman Catholic Church has traditionally claimed that it is human reason by which one is able to arrive at these particular truths and conclusions. No great appeal has been made to scripture or revelation in determining these questions. It should only be natural then that changing understandings of humanity and changing perceptions of human reason might also have important effects in these areas. Again I want to underline that my own approach to such problems cannot be fully developed in the short space available here. Sometimes the human is identified with the physical, but even when such identification is made I cannot do it with the degree of certitude which excludes the possibility of error. Likewise, the hierarchical Church can and should teach on these issues. Roman Catholics must attach special importance to such teaching, but dissent cannot be excluded.

In conclusion, there has been a contradictory pluralism on many important specific moral questions within Roman Catholicism. There is a tendency today to extend this pluralism to a comparatively few other areas where it did not exist before, but the same epistemological reason justifies the pluralism in these new areas just as it did in the more numerous areas where pluralism has existed in the past.

A FOURTH CONSIDERATION

There are several other questions raised by Dubay, but I believe I have answered the most significant questions and at the same time responded to other comments he raised on the whole question of pluralism. There remains to be considered a comparatively large section of his article which begins with the heading—"Is Moral Theology Prophetic?" (pp. 493–500). This question has great importance and deserves attention, although Dubay himself develops this section not in terms of moral theology, but in terms of the moral theologian. Nonetheless, one should first say a few words about moral theology.

Dubay asks what the moral theologian says of the new creation and what is the place of the cross and self-denial in Christian morality. He goes on to point out that in the literature supporting premarital sexual relations, contraception, and abortion, little or nothing appears about common gospel themes such as carrying the cross every day, or renouncing all things to be a disciple or chastising our bodies lest we become castaways (pp. 504, 505).

In response to this it should be noted that even in the teachings of the manuals of moral theology on the same questions there are no similar quotations or references. As already pointed out, these moral teachings were based primarily on human reason, and the older manuals of moral theology refer to the scriptures in a very occasional and peripheral way.

One cannot deny the importance of these aspects mentioned by Dubay and the fact that they must be always integrated into a full development of moral theology. Moral theology as the systematic reflection upon the Christian life must always insist on the basic call to perfection and to the following of Christ. Christians are called to be perfect even as the heavenly Father is perfect. Catholic moral theology in the last few decades has overcome the former separation between moral and spiritual theology so that one can no longer talk about two classes of citizens in the kingdom of God. However, in the light of the fact that the fullness of the eschaton is not yet here, the Christian will never fully live up to the complete gospel teaching. We are often made aware that in the times in between the two comings of Jesus we experience ourselves as being *simul justus et peccator.* The radical ethical teaching of Jesus challenges us with the gospel call to perfection, reminds us of our own continued need for the mercy and forgiveness of God, and calls us to change of heart and conversion. A true moral theology can never neglect or omit these most significant considerations.

The paschal mystery calls for the Christian, who is united in baptism with the risen Lord, to live the Christian life by dying to self and rising in the newness of life. The Christian knows that in union with Jesus suffering and tragedy will always be a part of the Christian life. The paschal mystery remains our hope because in Jesus the Father has changed death into life, and we as Christians are called to share in the promise of that same risen life. However, one must be extremely careful in applying the very important but broad theme of the paschal mystery to particular moral questions.

In response to Dubay's contention that mention of the cross does not appear in literature on these questions, I might refer to an article I wrote over ten years ago in which I first urged a change in the Catholic teaching on contraception. The article began by saying that my previous arguments in favor of the official teaching of the Church developed along the lines of the controlling influence of love with regard to sexuality. Sacrificing love and self-control will always form part of human existence. True Christian asceticism does not constrain the individual; rather it enables the Christian to participate ever more in the freedom of the children of God which only the life-giving Spirit can produce. Like Christ, we die to self and rise in the newness of life. But then my consideration went on to indicate that such an argument was more of a defense of an already accepted position rather than an argument for the truth of that position. The reasoning assumes the official teaching of the Church and then tries to explain it within the whole context of the paschal mystery. But then, as now, theologians cannot merely assume the truth of the official teaching of the Church.[12]

The above paragraph illustrates that very often the paschal mystery or the cross has been used in a pastoral way to help the Christian find some meaning in the midst of a moral crisis or of suffering. In fact, reference to the cross or suffering in the Christian life is often in terms of such a pastoral approach. The Christian has no obligation to look for suffering or even to avoid the possible means of overcoming suffering. For example, in the case of a person who is sick, one immediately recommends that such a person try to be cured. However, if the best of medical knowledge testifies that the disease is incurable and that the individual person will suffer and die, then one understands this in the light of the cross and of the paschal mystery. The paschal mystery also has direct moral implications, but great prudence is required in applying it. Catholic moral theology in its history has tried to avoid the extremes of laxism and rigorism. A moral theologian cannot forget the new life in Jesus or the paschal mystery, but particular moral questions must be considered in the light of the total Christian perspective. For example, if one wanted to solve every ethical problem by appealing to the biblical text of the need to deny oneself, then there would be no room for legitimate self-love or pleasure which

12. "Personal Reflections on Birth Control," *The Current,* V (1965), 5–12. This was later reprinted in a number of places including my book *Christian Morality Today* (Notre Dame, Indiana: Fides Publishers, 1966), pp. 66–76. For a more extended treatment of the paschal mystery in Christian life, see my *Crisis in Priestly Ministry* (Notre Dame, Indiana: Fides Publishers, 1972), pp. 51–102.

Roman Catholic theology has always upheld. One thus must be very careful in the way in which such texts and the ideas behind them are applied in moral theology.

Also, from the strictly moral perspective, the paschal mystery itself does not always call for self-renunciation and self-denial. The paschal mystery involves us in the dying and the rising of Jesus. We as Christians do not yet participate in the fullness of the resurrection; but, nonetheless, through baptism we already have the first fruits of the resurrection. Roman Catholic moral theology, to its great credit, has never seen the paschal mystery as indicating an incompatibility between gospel values and human values. Catholic moral theology with its acceptance of the natural law and the goodness of man has seen that the values of the "supernatural order" do not deny or contradict the values of the "natural order" but rather build on them and thus surpass them. The cross does not stand as a denial and refutation of all that is truly human. In my judgment, the relationship should be seen in terms of the transforming of the human in the light of the paschal mystery itself.

In conclusion, any Catholic moral theology must give due place and importance to the new life which we share in Jesus. This constitutes the fundamental attitude, disposition and value in the Christian life. On specific moral questions such as cigarette smoking or the drinking of alcohol, one really cannot always appeal directly to the cross and paschal mystery alone to find a solution to such a question. Often on particular questions, once one realizes the difficulty and suffering involved, then the Christian seeks to understand it in view of the paschal mystery itself. The paschal mystery does have a meaning and intelligibility from the strictly moral viewpoint, but even here the cross of Jesus in the Catholic tradition does not always stand in contradiction to human values so that one cannot always interpret the meaning of the cross in moral theology in such a way.

Dubay in this section of his article concentrates his attention on the Catholic theologian and tries to see if the Catholic moral theologian fulfills the six traits of the prophet which he describes. I can agree with some of the six characteristics provided they are properly interpreted. The second characteristic maintains that "the prophet does not conform his message to popular morality or to what men will accept" (p. 495). No one should affirm that a majority belief in a particular teaching makes it correct.

However, an ethics which in the past has claimed that most of its teaching is based on human reason which is common to all human beings and an official teaching which has lately been addressed to all men of good will must recognize that at times one can and should learn from the experience of others. Likewise, the recognition that the Spirit dwells in the hearts of all men of good will also gives an important theological significance to the experience of people, although this can never be the absolute or ultimate determining factor any more than the noninfallible teaching of the hierarchical magisterium. The fact that a majority of practicing Catholics in France do not accept the teaching of the Church on divorce does not make their opinion correct; but a theologian must consider this data as well as other important aspects, especially the hierarchical teaching, in arriving at his conclusions.

Other criteria of the true prophet proposed by Dubay have some truth for the moral theologian but they cannot be accepted absolutely. The third criterion is that "the prophet is rejected by the majority" (p. 497). Often the prophet is rejected, but not always. Think of the universal acclaim given to Pope John XXIII on the occasion of his encyclical *Pacem In Terris*. At times though the prophet should speak out against the sinful conduct of the majority such as the consumerism so present in our society. The fourth criterion is that the prophet proclaims absolute precepts (p. 498). Dubay

ends his whole section on the prophet by remarking that
Pope Paul VI best exemplifies the biblical traits of a prophet
in his person (p. 501). However, take the example of the very
moving speech of Pope Paul VI to the United Nations in
which he uttered those very memorable words—"War - never
again." Was this an absolute precept? Did the pope require all
nations of the world immediately to put down all their arms
and destroy them? No, the prophetic utterance in this case
was a moving prayer and not an absolute precept.

The other three criteria proposed by Dubay ["1) The
prophet is a man sent, a man commissioned to proclaim the
Lord's holy will" (p. 494); "5) The prophet is faithful to his
tradition" (499); "6) The true prophet proclaims authentic
teaching" (500).] all can be accepted by me but not with the
interpretation given them by Dubay. What is the criterion of
this being sent, of being faithful to the tradition and of
proclaiming authentic teaching? Dubay explicitly and implicitly makes agreement with all the teaching of the hierarchical
magisterium, including the authoritative, noninfallible, hierarchical teaching, the criterion in all these cases. "Insofar as
theologians are at odds with the magisterium they are not
sent. They lack the first note of a prophet among God's
people" (p. 495). The faithful are "those who accept the
whole Gospel, who are willing to carry the cross every day,
who lead a serious prayer life, who accept the teaching
magisterium commissioned by Christ" (p. 500). Finally,
Dubay cites scriptural warnings about false prophets and
concludes that any theory of pluralism which neglects an
honest confrontation with these texts cannot be considered
adequate (pp. 500–1).

In all these cases, Dubay thus presupposes that true authentic teaching is identified with the teaching of the hierarchical
magisterium even when it is a question of authoritative,
noninfallible teaching. Catholic theology and the hierarchical

teaching office do not make such claims today. As I have pointed out in my earlier article, the fathers of Vatican II purposely rejected the simple application of the biblical phrase, "He who hears you hears me," to the authoritative, noninfallible, hierarchical teaching function. Dubay's argument is vitiated because he is presupposing what he wants to prove—that the proclamation of a teaching by the authentic, noninfallible teaching office is an absolute guarantee that such a teaching is truly the will of God.

One could make a very strong case on the basis of the prophetic function of the theologian for the fact that at times the theologian will have to stand up and disagree with authentic, noninfallible teaching. There can be no doubt that at times in the Old Testament the prophets did speak against what was proposed by the duly constituted religious authorities. The Constitution on the Church explicitly recognizes the existence of the prophetic office in the Church as separate from the hierarchical teaching office, thus indicating the existence of a possible friction between the prophet and the hierarchical teaching office. In the light of the whole understanding of the response due to authentic, noninfallible Church teaching one cannot deny that at times the theologian as prophet must speak in a way contrary to that proposed by the teaching office. The theologian should never do this lightly but must try to discern what God is truly asking of us. The rules for the discernment of spirits and the recognition of true prophets from false are very important, but their very complexity is such that they can never be reduced to the one criterion of the ordinary, noninfallible hierarchical magisterium as important a criterion as this is.

One must consider the prophetic aspect not only of moral theology itself and of the moral theologian but also the prophetic role of the hierarchical teaching office in the Church. Granted that the prophetic function and the hierarchical teaching function are not identical, nonetheless there should be a prophetic aspect, along with other aspects, to the hierarchical magisterium.

In the past few years it is precisely this prophetic element in the hierarchical teaching function which has been lacking in the opinion of many. The American bishops have often been criticized for speaking publicly and often on such questions as abortion but keeping silent on many other questions facing our society. Today it seems that the American bishops are beginning to speak up more on other issues (e.g., going on record against capital punishment at their November 1974 meeting in Washington); but for a long time the American bishops were silent on the issue of the Vietnam War which was probably the most significant moral issue which arose in the United States in the decade of the 1960's.

Why such silence on so important a moral question? In fairness, I believe there is a very plausible explanation. Although the American bishops frequently and loudly spoke on the question of abortion, they were for a long time silent on the war in Southeast Asia. On questions such as abortion the bishops were convinced that Church teaching was certain, so they had a duty to speak out and inform their people what is the certain teaching of the Church in this matter. In other areas where they realized that such certitude cannot be obtained, they tended not to speak out. They did not want to place any unnecessary burdens on the Catholic people; and, therefore, where a freedom of opinion exists, they felt it better not to speak.

In a true sense the need for absolute certitude has become an albatross around the neck of the teaching office of the hierarchical magisterium. If one waits for such certitude before speaking in today's fast-changing world, one can be certain of only one thing—by the time an utterance is made, it will be irrelevant. The problem will long since have gone by and no longer be a pressing, urgent contemporary problem.

The prophetic voice addressing the complexities of modern existence must be willing to accept the risk of being wrong but still speak out in the light of the best possible understanding of the gospel, of human experience, and of the concrete facts of the situation. Again, it is the epistemological reason which will prevent the possibility of certitude in these cases, but still some type of direction and guidance on some important issues should be given by the hierarchical teaching office in the Church. Such teaching should stress the general Christian attitudes, goals and ideals and then descend into the particularities with the recognition that specific proposals cannot claim to be absolutely certain.

In an earlier period it seems that the American bishops did exercise a more prophetic role in questions of social justice. The administrative committee of the National Catholic War Council in 1919 issued a call for a reconstruction of the American social order which was called "The Bishops' Program of Social Reconstruction: A General Review of the Problems and Survey of Remedies." Aaron A. Abell, one of the foremost historians of the Catholic social movement in the United States, mentions that some charged that this document was socialistic and revolutionary, even Marxist, rather than Christian in its approaches.[13] In 1940 the administrative board of the American bishops issued a statement entitled "The Church and the Social Order," which called for far-reaching reforms in the American economic system.[14]

In a sense these were not official statements of the whole American hierarchy exercising its teaching office, but they were truly prophetic utterances. There is a continued need

---

13. *American Catholic Thought on Social Questions,* ed. Aaron I. Abell (Indianapolis: Bobbs-Merrill Company, 1968), pp. 325–348.

14. Francis L. Broderick, *Right Reverend New Dealer John A. Ryan* (New York: Macmillan, 1963), pp. 256–257.

today for official statements by the bishops as hierarchical Church teachers on important issues of our day, but such teachings will be possible only if the hierarchical teaching office recognizes that its teaching might be wrong; but with the best insights of the gospel, human experience, and the assistance of the Holy Spirit it should nevertheless speak out on some of the important moral issues facing society and the world. Note that the bishops cannot and should not speak out on every issue, but they should strive to discern the most important moral issues and must always acquire a competent knowledge before speaking out.

In conclusion, the prophetic is an important aspect of moral theology, of the role of the moral theologian, and of the role of the hierarchical magisterium. But a proper understanding of the prophetic aspect coincides with the accepted Catholic teaching that at times and for sufficient reasons dissent from authoritative, authentic, noninfallible Church teaching is permitted. The prophetic aspect of the theologian's role at times might require the theologian to dissent from such teaching. The prophetic aspect of the hierarchical teaching office will be better accomplished if one acknowledges that such a teaching on specific questions cannot achieve the degree of certitude which excludes the possibility of error.

CONCLUSIONS

Two final points deserve brief mention. Some would argue that only the theologian is competent to dissent or disagree with the authentic, noninfallible teaching of the hierarchical magisterium. Such a proposition harbors a poor understanding of the function of the moral theologian. The moral theologian studies Christian decision making in a thematic, reflexive and systematic way. Every single Christian is called upon to make moral decisions and try to follow the gospel call in a nonthematic, nonreflexive and nonsystematic way (these are nonpejorative terms).

Perhaps a comparison might be helpful. The psychiatrist is the person who professionally studies in a thematic, reflexive and systematic way the questions of human maturity and emotional balance. One can ask the question—are psychiatrists the most emotionally mature and balanced human persons in the world? Without any degrading of a profession as such, I think most people would conclude that psychiatrists are not necessarily the most mature and balanced persons. There are many people who have never heard of Freud who are much more emotionally mature and balanced than those who have read his complete works. This is not to belittle psychiatric knowledge, but it is to show the difference between the more reflexive role of the theorist and the practical day to day life situation. There are many Christian people who have never read Thomas Aquinas who are "better Christians" than many theologians. All Christians are called to follow out the gospel and respond to it with conscientious decisions. One does not need the type of thematic, reflexive and systematic theological knowledge in order to make such decisions, but a prudent person would give some consideration to this particular source of knowledge.

The second point concerns the teaching function of the Church and the conscience of the individual Roman Catholic. There are many different ways in which the Church can and should exercise its teaching function. The liturgy remains a very important teaching instrument of the Church, although not the only one. The Church also teaches by the witness of its individual members and the corporate witness of the institution. The Church in so many different ways, in season and out of season, should exercise its teaching function. Likewise, the hierarchical teaching office has many different ways of exercising its teaching function in addition to those mentioned above. Sometimes it might raise a challenging question or point to the danger of motivation which is not truly Christian. At other times it might speak out on specific matters with the limitations we have already discussed.

In traditional Roman Catholic moral theology the ultimate moral decision rests with the properly formed conscience of the individual. Every individual must acknowledge the two-fold limitation of finitude and of sinfulness which affect all human beings. The individual person is limited and thus can never see the total picture but only a part of it. Likewise, sin affects all of us and impairs the possibility of complete objectivity. In making ethical decisions the individual thus seeks help from other sources. The community of the Church strives to overcome the twofold limitations of finitude and sinfulness which can affect the individual conscience. The believing Catholic recognizes the God-given role of the hierarchical magisterium but also realizes that the teaching on specific moral questions cannot absolutely exclude the possibility of error. The prudent person will pay significant attention to this teaching and only act against such teaching after a careful and prayerful investigation.

The hierarchical teaching office must also recognize its God-given function as well as its limitations. The authentic or authoritative teaching of the hierarchical magisterium on specific moral questions receives the assistance of the Holy Spirit. In the future the hierarchical magisterium must operate more in accord with the newer theological methodologies and with the ecclesial self-understanding as proposed in the Second Vatican Council.

However, even recognizing newer theological methodologies and following an ecclesiological search for moral truth as described in the documents of the Second Vatican Council, the authoritative, noninfallible, hierarchical teaching on specific issues can never claim to exclude the possibility of error. The Catholic can never hope to have that type of certitude because of the complexities involved in specific moral questions but must be content with the moral certitude and risk involved in such specific decisions. The Catholic should gratefully receive the teaching of the hierarchical magisterium and only for serious reasons and after commensurate reflection make a conscience decision in opposition with it.

3

Divorce in the Light

of a Revised Moral Theology

The scope of this study is to examine the question of divorce from the perspective of moral theology. The emphasis will be on the self-understanding and methodological approaches present in contemporary Catholic moral theology and how these relate to the specific question of divorce. In another study I have tried to assemble and critically evaluate the data which has been published on the question of divorce itself.[1] The present paper should serve as a companion to that earlier study and from this different perspective reinforce the conclusion that the Roman Catholic Church should change its teaching on divorce.

In particular, the topic will be considered under the following headings: (1) identification of the principal signs of the times and an evaluation in the light of contemporary moral theology; (2) the methodological use of the scriptures in moral theology; (3) the influence of the shift to historical consciousness; (4) the effect of a more personalist approach; (5) the implications of eschatological considerations.

---

1. "Divorce: Doctrine at pratique catholiques aux États-Unis," *Recherches de Science Religieuse* LXI (1973), 575–624. English version: "Divorce: Catholic Theory and Practice in the United States," *American Ecclesiastical Review* CLXVIII (1974), 3–34; 75–95; *New Perspectives in Moral Theology* (Notre Dame, Indiana: Fides, 1974), pp. 212–276.

SIGNS OF THE TIMES

The Pastoral Constitution on the Church in the Modern World adopted the ethical methodological approach of beginning its consideration of particular topics with an examination of the signs of the times. The most outstanding sign of the times in the study of the question of divorce is the quantity of the literature which has emerged on this subject in Roman Catholicism within the last few years. Major contributions were made and even pioneered by the theory and practice proposed in the United States. In the last issue of 1973 and the first issue of 1974, the French theological journal *Recherches de Science Religieuse* considered the question of divorce in the Catholic world today and began with a critical appraisal of the literature and pastoral practice in three different countries—France, West Germany, and the United States. According to the editor, the United States was chosen because it is the country in which the ecclesiastical processes of annulling marriages are the most numerous as well as the most troublesome and because in the United States the most advanced juridical and pastoral solutions have been evolved to regularize the position of divorced and remarried Catholics.[2] This comment reflects favorably on the pioneering work which has been done in the United States, especially by the Canon Law Society of America in the whole question of divorce.

A survey of the recent literature reveals that the symposium has frequently been employed as the way of addressing the question of divorce.[3] The first major symposium which discussed this question and then published the papers

2. "Avant-propos," *Recherches de Science Religieuse* LXI (1973), 487,488.

3. Wilhelm Breuning, "Discussion sur le divorce en Allemagne," *Recherches de Science Religieuse* LXI (1973), 552.

4. *The Bond of Marriage*, ed. William W. Bassett (Notre Dame, Indiana: University of Notre Dame Press, 1968).

prepared for the discussion was sponsored by the Canon Law
Society of America in October of 1967. The results of this
Symposium were published under the title *The Bond of
Marriage* in 1968.[4] Since that time many different symposia
have been held throughout the world on this subject, and
many collective volumes have been published in which different authors treat particular aspects of the problem. Articles
on the subject of divorce and remarriage were assembled in a
book edited in Germany by Jakob David and Franz Schmalz
in 1969.[5] A later symposium under the auspices of Katho-
lische Akademie in Bayern was edited by Franz Heinrich and
Volker Eid and published in 1972.[6] In May of 1970 a
conference on the bond of marriage was sponsored at the
University of Strasbourg and published under the title *Le lien
matrimonial.*[7] In March of 1971 a colloquim on this subject
was held at the Catholic University of Louvain.[8] A meeting
of the moral theologians of France in September of 1970
discussed the question of divorce and the indissolubility of
marriage, and the proceedings of this congress were published
in the following year.[9] Special issues of canonical and theological journals have been devoted to this question—e.g.,
Concilium,[10] *Perspectiva Teológica,*[11] *Theologische Quartalschrift.*[12] The very nature of the question involving the

5. *Wie unauflöslich ist die Ehe?* ed. Jakob David and Franz Schmalz (Aschaf-
fenburg: Pattloch Verlag, 1969).
6. *Ehe und Ehescheidung,* ed. Franz Henrich and Volker Eid (München: Kösel-
Verlag, 1972).
7. *Le lien matrimonial,* ed. René Metz and Jean Schlick (Strasbourg: Cerdic,
1970).
8. Francis V. Manning, "Divorce and Remarriage: Considered from an Interdis-
ciplinary Perspective," *Louvain Studies* III (1971), 243–258.
9. *Divorce et indissolubilité du marriage,* Congrès de l'Association de théolo-
giens pour l'étude de la morale, Chevilly-la-Rue, 18–20 Septembre 1970 (Paris:
Cerf/Desclée, 1971).
10. *Concilium* VII, n.9 (September 1973).
11. *Perspectiva Teológica* IV, n.7 (julho-dezembro 1972); 225–287.
12. *Theologische Quartalschrift* CLI (1971), 1–86.

different disciplines of scripture, history, sociology, psychology, theology, etc., has apparently favored the symposium format.

Monographs on divorce are comparatively few, at least in the context of the many symposia and individual articles which have been published on the subject. The pioneering monograph by Victor Pospishil published in the United States in 1967 has exerted a great influence on subsequent discussions.[13] Similar monographs have appeared in other languages—e.g., Michel Leclercq in French,[14] R. Gall in German,[15] and G. Cereti in Italian.[16]

To deal with the very abundant periodical literature one needs to employ the available bibliographical resources in this area. As usual, the bibliographies given in the *Ephemerides Theologicae Lovanienses* are generally complete and comprehensive. In addition, two other bibliographical sources deserve mention. J. Marcus Bach supplies a well annotated bibliography of the most important books and articles which have appeared in all languages since the debate on divorce began in the Catholic Church in the last few years and extending through the year 1971.[17] RIC Supplement from the University of Strasbourg published a computer indexed bibliography on marriage and divorce which includes 365 entries for the period from January 1970 to December 1972.[18] This bibliography is a supplement to the bibliog-

13. Victor J. Pospishil, *Divorce and Remarriage: Toward a New Catholic Teaching* (New York: Herder and Herder, 1967).

14. Michel Leclercq, *Le divorce et l'Église* (Paris: Fayard, 1969).

15. Robert Gall, *Fragwürdige Unauflöslichkeit der Ehe?* (Zürich-Würzburg: Echter, 1970).

16. Giovanni Cereti, *Matrimonio e indissolubilità: nuove prospettive* (Bologna: Edizioni Dehoniane, 1971).

17. J. Marcus Bach, S.J., "A Indissolubilidade do Matrimônio no Pensamento Teológico Moderno," *Persepectives Teológica* IV (1972), 255–281.

18. *Marriage and Divorce,* RIC Supplement under the direction of René Metz and Jean Schlick (Strasbourg: Cerdic Publications, 1973).

raphy contained in the symposium *Le lien matrimonial* published by the same university in 1971.

Call for a New Pastoral Practice

This paper will make no attempt at assessing and criticizing the vast theological literature on the question of divorce. Many, including myself, have called for a change in the teaching of the Roman Catholic Church on indissolubility. However, the most striking fact in the current literature is the emerging consensus that the Roman Catholic Church should at least change its practice with regard to the participation of divorced and remarried people in the sacraments of penance and eucharist. There are ever increasing calls for such a change in pastoral practice.

In May of 1974 the General Synod of the Dioceses of the German Federal Republic approved a document on marriage which among other things called for divorced and remarried people to be readmitted to the sacraments under certain precise conditions. The document was modified in the course of the debate but eventually approved by a vote of 219 to 34 with 14 abstentions although the bishops as a whole were somewhat opposed to the document in general and to the section on the sacraments for divorced and remarried Catholics in particular.[19]   In preparation for an earlier plenary assembly of the Synod in 1972, a document was prepared entitled "Guidelines for Pastoral Assistance for Divorced Persons who have Remarried and Wish to Share in the Sacramental Life of the Church." The plenary session of the

19. Manuel Alcala, "Évêques et synode en Allemagne Fédérale," *Études* (Août-Septembre 1974), 298,299; "Testfall oder Bewährungsprobe? Zur Ehe-Discussion auf der Gemeinsamen Synode," *Herder Korrespondenz* XXVIII (August 1974), 426–434.

Synod in 1972 asked that this comparatively short statement be incorporated into the context of a longer, more fundamental, statement about Christian marriage in general.[20] This is the genesis of the document which was finally approved by the general assembly in May of 1974.

The action of the German Synod is not unique. A similar proposal was submitted by the Commission on Marriage and the Family in a Changing Society for discussion by the regional meetings that are part of the ongoing project of the Swiss Synod.[21] There has just come to light the fact that the French moral theologians some years ago petitioned the French bishops to allow divorced and remarried Catholics to participate in the sacramental life of the Church. In September of 1970 the A.T.E.M. (The Association of Theologians for the Study of Moral Theology) discussed the matter of indissolubility and divorce in their annual meeting and published the papers from that symposium.[22] A great majority of the participants expressed their conviction that the Church should at least reconsider its pastoral practice of excluding divorced and remarried Catholics from the sacraments. In February of 1972, under the signature of the majority of French moral theologians, a document giving the rationale for such a change was sent to the French bishops. As of May 1974, the French theologians have received no official response to their petition. The journal *Le Supplément* obtained a slightly earlier draft of the document which was sent to the French bishops and published it in the May 1974 issue. The editor decided to publish this document because of the importance of the subject matter, the fact that the question is of extreme significance for many people, and because of

20. Karl Lehmann, "Indissolubility of Marriage and Pastoral Care of Divorced who Remarry," *International Catholic Review Communio* I (1972), 239.
21. *Ibid.*
22. *Divorce et indissolubilité du mariage* (Paris: Cerf/Desclée, 1971).

the reputations of those who associated their names with the statement.[23]

Again, pioneering work on this subject was done by the Canon Law Society of America which set up a committee to study the question in October of 1968. The committee gathered together and published in the *Jurist* XXX (1970) four significant articles as well as its own committee report. The committee report recommended that if the parties believe in good conscience that their previous marriage was invalid but it cannot be proven so in the legal forum, such couples can be admitted to participate in the sacraments. In the case of those who had a previous true marriage, the committee acknowledged that the matter was not mature for any legal conclusions but recommended that, if a priest by way of counsel in the forum of conscience permits a person living in such a marriage to have access to the eucharist, no legal action should be taken against such a priest.[24]

In June 1972 a committee of the Catholic Theological Society of America reported its recommendations on the same issues. If a couple judges in good conscience that a previous marriage was not a true marriage but this fact cannot be proven in the external forum, the community should respect their consciences in entering a second marriage and people already involved in such a second marriage should be able to frequent the sacraments of the Church. Those involved in second marriages even after a true first marriage can receive the sacraments on the basis of the mercy and forgiveness of God and their need to continue living together as a result of the obligations they have contracted, if they are showing in their lives a true reflection of the Christian gospel. Note that the committee does not consider the case of those

23. "Le problème pastoral des chrétiens divorcés et remariés," *Le Supplément* XXVII, n.109 (March 1974), 125–126.
24. *The Jurist* XXX (1970), 12,13.

who had a previous true marriage and are now contemplating a new marriage. It is obvious that this omission was intentional.[25]

The above paragraphs have consciously avoided mentioning the vast theological literature and have only tried to indicate how extensive and urgent is the call for a change in the pastoral practice of excluding all divorced and remarried Catholics from penance and the eucharist. Such a position advocating a change in the pastoral practice is also adopted by some Catholic theologians who have strenuously opposed any change in the teaching of the Church on the indissolubility of marriage. Henri Crouzel, in an article which appeared in different places, sharply rejects both the methodology employed and the conclusions proposed by Victor Pospishil in the section of his book dealing with the historical tradition of the Catholic Church. In the fourth and fifth centuries, according to Crouzel, only Ambrosiaster explicitly allowed the possibility of remarriage after divorce.[26] Crouzel himself has been answered by P. Nautin, who seems to convincingly disagree with Crouzel's conclusions on this matter.[27] But the substantative debate is not the primary concern for the moment. In his detailed monograph on the question of divorce in the primitive church published in 1971, Crouzel adopts a more moderate tone in general but still acknowledges only Ambrosiaster as explicitly permitting the possibility of remarriage after divorce. However, both

25. "The Problem of Second Marriages: An Interim Pastoral Statement by the Study Committee Commissioned by the Board of Directors of the Catholic Theological Society of America," *Proceedings of the Catholic Theological Society of America* XXVII (1972), 233–240.

26. Henri Crouzel, "Nuove nozze dopi il divorzio nella Chiesa primitiva? A proposito di un libro recente," *La Civilta Cattolica* CXXI, n.4 (1970), 455–63; 550–61. The same article appeared in English in *The Irish Theological Quarterly* XXXVIII (1971), 21–41.

27. Pierre Nautin, "Divorce et remariage dans la tradition de l'Église Latin," *Recherches de Science Religieuse* LXII (1974), 7–54.

with regard to the early church and to contemporary circumstances, Crouzel explicitly distinguishes between the acceptance and blessing of a marriage after divorce and the toleration by way of mercy and forgiveness of a second marriage
which is only civilly valid and cannot now be dissolved
because of the new responsibilities of the spouses. Such an
accommodation was sometimes accepted in the primitive
church.[28] In practice today Crouzel acknowledges that the
Church can and should try to hold in tension both the
teaching on the absolute indissolubility of Christian marriage
and at the same time show pastoral indulgence and tolerance
to those who are now involved in a second marriage.[29]

Karl Lehmann accepts the same general approach but spells
it out in greater detail. Lehmann's opinion is important
because he, too, strenuously upholds the teaching about the
indissolubility of marriage and because his article appears in
the journal *Communio* of which he is an editor.[30]

Lehmann sets forth the following criteria for readmittance
to the sacraments of divorced and remarried people, which in
his view are the standards generally agreed upon by most
authors. Such pastoral practice should not call into question
the teaching on indissolubility. If grave fault was involved in
the breakdown of the first marriage, it must be acknowledged
and repented. The first marriage has irreparably broken
down. The second marriage must have proved itself as a
moral union and the partners must have demonstrated their
witness to the Christian faith. It should also be examined
whether the maintenance of this union has become a new
moral obligation in relation to the partner or children of the

28. Henri Crouzel, *L'Église primitive face au divorce: Du premier au cinquième
siècle* (Paris: Beauchesne, 1971), pp. 372–374.
29. *Ibid.,* pp. 382,383.
30. Lehmann, *International Catholic Review Communio* I (1972), 238–250.

second marriage. Finally, no justified scandal can be caused in the Christian community.[31]

If the above reading of the signs of the times is accurate, there will soon be a change in the pastoral practice of the Catholic Church concerning the participation of divorced and remarried Catholics in the sacramental life of the Church. Even without any hierarchical sanction, today many Catholics in this situation are participating in the sacramental life of the Church. It seems that this will become the regular practice whether it is officially sanctioned by the hierarchical Church or not.

Is a New Pastoral Practice Enough?

How should one evaluate such a fact from the perspective of contemporary moral theology? In my judgment such a pastoral approach does not go far enough. I believe that the Catholic Church should change its teaching on the absolute indissolubility of marriage. Perhaps it could be argued that from a logical viewpoint one could propose an argument for a change in the pastoral practice towards divorced and remarried Catholics which does not involve any change in the teaching of the indissolubility of marriage. However, in the light of the data on the question of divorce itself and in the context of the self-understanding of contemporary Catholic moral theology, I argue that a change in the pastoral practice really involves and should lead to a change in the teaching on the absolute indissolubility of marriage.

Before developing the various reasons one most important point must be underscored. Although I believe there should be a change in the teaching on divorce, I also recognize the

31. *Ibid.,* pp. 249, 250.

great importance of impressing on Christian people the fact
that indissolubility remains the imperative goal of every true
Christian marriage. Selfishness and sinfulness will often
hinder the achievement of such a goal, but the Christian is
called to overcome such obstacles. In my judgment selfishness and sinfulness are not the only reasons why indissolubility is not attainable, but it would be foolish not to acknowledge that these elements are often present. My position does
not glory in the fact of divorce but acknowledges that divorce can occur without sin on the part of the parties
involved. Nonetheless, the Church must constantly strive by
all means possible to bring Christian couples to a realization
of the importance of indissolubility and to the practice of a
faithful love as the basis of Christian marriage.

What are the different reasons for asserting that a change in
pastoral practice does not go far enough and ultimately there
should be a change in the teaching on indissolubility itself?
The first reason comes from a realistic assessment of the
self-understanding of the Roman Catholic Church. It is very
difficult for the Roman Catholic Church to publicly change a
teaching that has been proposed by the hierarchical teaching
office in the Church. The contraception issue stands as an
outstanding example of this fact. In practice many, and
probably the vast majority of, Catholic lay people and writing theologians dissent from the official teaching of the
Church. Likewise, many Bishops' Conferences have acknowledged the possibility of dissent from the papal teaching, but
there has been no official change in that teaching.[32] The last
two centuries have shown the long and tortuous development
before the Catholic Church could change its teaching on
religious liberty.[33] Earlier, there was the question of usury in

32. William H. Shannon, *The Lively Debate: Response to Humanae Vitae* (New
York: Sheed and Ward, 1970).

33. Pius Augustin, *Religious Freedom in Church and State* (Baltimore:
Helicon, 1966); John Courtney Murray, *The Problem of Religious Freedom*
(Westminster, Md.: Newman, 1965).

which the teaching gradually was changed.[34] These are only illustrations to indicate that one has a better chance of obtaining a change if it is proposed as involving little or no discontinuity with the past.

The recent debate on contraception within the Roman Catholic Church itself illustrates how even Catholic theologians have tended to propose changes in as minimalistic a manner as possible. The first pioneering article of major importance calling for a change in the Catholic teaching on contraception was published by Canon Louis Janssens in the December 1963 issue of *Ephemerides Theologicae Lovanienses.* Janssens then called just for a change in the teaching on the pill while still condemning other forms of contraception.[35] Later he and others recognized that logically one could not approve the contraceptive pill and condemn other forms of contraception. The same stance was proposed somewhat earlier in a nontheological way by John Rock in his book, *The Time Has Come.*[36] The tendency even among pioneering Roman Catholic theologians to play down the radicalness of change in Church teaching is illustrated by another aspect of the contraceptive debate. Many of those who wrote against changing the teaching on contraception pointed out that a change here would lead to changes in many other areas of Church teaching.[37] The general tendency of those arguing in favor of the change was to minimize the possibility of other future changes and to insist that only the area of contraception was involved. History has

34. John T. Noonan,Jr., *The Scholastic Analysis of Usury* (Cambridge: Harvard University Press, 1957); Noonan, "Authority, Usury and Contraception," *Cross Currents* XVI (1966), 55–79.

35. L. Janssens, "Morale conjugale et progestogènes," *Ephemerides Theologicae Lovanienses* XXXIX (1963), 787–826.

36. John Rock, *The Time Has Come: A Catholic Doctor's Proposals to End the Battle Over Birth Control* (New York: Alfred A. Knopf, 1963).

37. Francis Canavan, "Reflections on the Revolution in Sex," *America* CXII (1965), 312–315.

clearly shown that those who were afraid that a change in the teaching on contraception would lead to other changes were quite accurate. A need to change the teaching on contraception was only indicative of the other areas in which change would occur.

There exists another subtle pressure against proposing radical change or discontinuity in the matter of divorce. Catholic moral theologians through their teaching exercise an important pastoral function in the Church and in the lives of Catholic people. This pastoral sense at the present time is calling upon many theologians to urge a change in the pastoral approach to divorced and remarried couples. I am quite confident that the idea does not consciously surface in the minds of most theologians, but no one can deny the reality that such proposals for helping divorced and remarried people stand a much better chance of acceptance in the Church if they do not involve any type of radical change or questioning of the past teaching of the Church. It should not be surprising, then, that proposals for a change in the matter of divorce in the Roman Catholic Church will stress that only the pastoral practice and not the teaching on indissolubility is involved. But this essay will attempt to show that the change must involve the teaching and not just the practice.

Can we learn anything from the process of change which has occurred in other moral questions? History is most instructive here because it indicates that change is usually begun by the practice of a growing number of people in the Christian community. Change is frequently justified on the practical level and then is accepted on a more theoretical level. Very often through confessional practice and other means the moral theologian becomes aware of the fact that the pastoral reality does not agree with the theoretical teaching. This disparity between the official teaching of the Church and the practice of many people calls for some response. Perhaps the practice is wrong and must continue to be condemned as wrong, but often it seems that the individual Christian might not be sinning in this matter. The prudent theological approach in such a case is to invoke the theological distinction between the objective order and the subjective order. In this way one can attempt to meet the needs of the individual person or persons here and now and at the same time uphold the traditional teaching of the Church.[38]

Such an "objectively wrong but not subjectively sinful" approach as a first step in ultimate change can be illustrated in the development of Catholic teaching on the question of masturbation. According to the traditional teaching masturbation always involves grave matter, but in practice especially with adolescents the confessional approach was willing to recognize that grave sin was often missing because of subjective conditions. However, it did take some time even for this milder confessional practice to take hold. Then the more radical question was raised that perhaps even in the objective order masturbation does not involve grave matter and at times is not wrong. Today a good number of Catholic theologians would accept such an opinion, but one can see how it slowly developed from the first step of saying that subjectively it might not be gravely sinful.[39] Another area in which the practice of Catholic people has changed the objective teaching is in the question of mixed marriages. Canon 1060 of the Code of Canon Law states that the Church everywhere and most severely prohibits mixed marriages, that is, marriages between two baptized persons one of whom is Catholic and other is non-Catholic. In practice the dispensation for such an impediment became increasingly more routine. Fi-

38. I willingly acknowledge that my own approach to contraception followed this approach as a first step before proposing more radical change. See my *Christian Morality Today* (Notre Dame, Indiana: Fides Publishers, 1966), pp. 47–76.

39. Felix M. Podimattam. *A Difficult Problem in Chastity: Masturbation* (Kotagiri, India: Assisi Press, 1972).

nally the pastoral practice of mixed marriages in the light of
the development of ecumenism and pluralism has become
such that one seldom hears papal documents or theologians
speaking about the most severe prohibition of mixed marriages.[40]

Karl Lehmann in the question of divorce speaks of maintaining both the absolute precept of Jesus and the toleration
of other situations in practice. Here the terminology is very
reminiscent of another situation in which change occurred in
the Church teaching through the stages of the acceptance of
something in practice and finally its acceptance in theory. In
the case of the relationship between Church and state and the
acceptance of religious liberty the first break from the older
teaching came in the famous distinction between thesis and
hypothesis which Archbishop Dupanloup employed to interpret the teaching of Pope Pius IX in the Syllabus of Errors. In
the ideal realm there should be a union of Church and state,
but in the contemporary historical circumstances the opposite can be tolerated.[41] Only much later was Roman Catholicism able to assert that the older approach was truly not an
ideal, but one could and should justify as good what was
formerly merely tolerated in practice. The Declaration on
Religious Freedom of Vatican Council II (n.1) recognized the
desire for religious liberty already existing in the minds and
hearts of people of good will and declared this to be greatly
in accord with truth and justice.

One cannot conclude from this line of reasoning that every
time a pastoral change is proposed or a situation is tolerated

40. For a brief discussion of recent writing on this subject in the light of new
norms proposed by the pope, see Leandro Rossi, "Morale matrimoniale e pluralismo teologico," *Rivista di teologia morale* V (1973), 127,128. For a detailed
theoretical study and compilation of the data about contemporary practice, see
John E. Lynch, "Ecumenical Marriages," in *Canon Law Society of America:
Proceedings of the Thirty-Fifth Annual Convention* (1973), pp. 33–54.

41. Roger Aubert, *Le pontificat de Pie IX* (Paris: Blond and Gay, 1952) pp.
224–261.

in practice that ultimately it will lead to a change in teaching in the objective order. However, in any evaluation of possible change one must learn from the history of Roman Catholicism that change often does follow this particular route. Contemporary Catholic moral theology realizes the importance of pastoral practice and the experience of Christian people. The whole Church can and often does learn through the experience of Christian people as a *locus theologicus*, [42] but one can never determine morality merely from what people do. The discernment of the spirit is not reducible to a Gallup Poll with moral truth decided by a majority vote. Our human experience is conditioned by the limitations and sinfulness which form a necessary part of our existence. Experience then cannot be absolutely accepted without a critical discernment. But when a large number of apparently good Christian people are involved in a particular mode of acting, at least the Church and the theologians must take them seriously and be willing to reexamine the teaching.

In this broader context one must examine both the explicit and implicit arguments which have been proposed to indicate that a new pastoral approach allowing some divorced and remarried Catholics to participate in the sacramental life of the Church will not entail a change in the Church's teaching on the indissolubility of marriage. The proposals along this line usually require that the couple show signs of a Christian and human way of life in their second marriage. One of the reasons frequently mentioned for readmission to the sacramental life is the fact that the couple in the new marriage has acquired obligations to one another which they can not now neglect. For such a couple separation would be wrong. [43] If such a condition is absolutely required for readmission to the

---

42. Bernard Quelquejeu, "La volonté de procréer," *Lumière et Vie* XXI, n.109 (Août-Octobre 1972), 57–62.
43. E.g., Lehmann, *Communio* I (1972), 249.

eucharist, there is present a barrier preventing any further change in the proposed pastoral practice. However, there are many indications even in the arguments proposed for a pastoral change that such a condition (i.e., that the couple in the second marriage has contracted new moral obligations to one another) is not necessary for readmission to the sacraments.

What are the primary arguments proposed to show that the readmission of divorced and remarried Catholics to the sacraments does not call for a change in the teaching of the Church on indissolubility? Great importance is given to the reason that a sin against indissolubility cannot be an unforgivable sin. The Church reconciles the adulterer, the thief and murderer so why not the divorced and remarried person?[44]

Such a reintegration into the community with participation in the sacramental life of the Church will not contradict the teaching on indissolubility. The first marriage no longer exists in reality so that indissolubility cannot be considered as a property of what does not now exist. Even in the contemporary practice the Church allows people in a second marriage to continue living their union of life together provided they live as brother and sister. The Church admits that people can live Christianly and humanly in the second marriage in all things save sex and have no real obligation to renounce their second union because of the indissolubility of the first marriage. Any change in the pastoral practice would not affect the teaching on indissolubility any more than the present practice does. Also from the viewpoint of the Church and what the Church stands for, a reconciliation of the divorced and remarried person will be a sign of the forgiving and reconciling work of the Church in the world. Thus not only motives based on the good of the individuals involved but also

44. This and the following paragraphs will rely on the argumentation proposed in the statement of the French moral theologians, *Le Supplément* XXVII, n. 109 (Mai 1974), 142.

reasons stemming from the understanding of the Church as the sign of forgiveness and mercy urge a change in the present pastoral practice.[45]

In my judgment the actual circumstances as well as the arguments proposed will lead to even further change in the proposed pastoral practice. The obvious problem now concerns the many divorced and remarried Catholics who do not participate in the sacramental life of the Church. However, once this problem is solved, then the spotlight will shift to the many divorced Catholics who are now contemplating second marriage. Lawrence Wrenn indicates that there were something like 120,000 valid Catholic marriages ended by civil divorce in 1971 in the United States.[46] How are such people to make up their consciences? Can they in good conscience now enter a second marriage?

At the very least a pastoral practice which allows divorced and remarried people after some time in the second union to receive the sacraments will have some influence on the decision of Catholics entering such a second marriage. Until recently, many Catholics did not remarry after divorce because they thought it would mean their exclusion from the sacramental life of the Church for the rest of their lives. If they know such an exclusion is not necessary, then there would be less reason for them to abstain from entering such a second marriage in the first place. The first basic reaction of "the ordinary Catholic" would find great difficulty in accepting a position acknowledging the later possibility of readmission to the sacraments but not allowing people to enter such a second marriage. Likewise, from a theoretical viewpoint it seems very difficult to say that sometime during the second

---

45. *Ibid.*, pp. 143–151.
46. Lawrence G. Wrenn, "Marriage—Indissoluble or Fragile?" in *Divorce and Remarriage in the Catholic Church*, ed. Lawrence G. Wrenn (New York: Newman Press, 1973) pp. 144,145.

marriage a couple can be reconciled with the sacraments of the Church, but it is wrong for them to enter the second marriage.

An analysis of the arguments proposed to allow the read-mission to the sacraments of those already involved in such a marriage indicates that many of the same arguments can be used to allow the second marriage to take place. First, the sin against indissolubility is not unforgivable. Forgiveness can take place any time after the sin has been committed. Sec-ondly, the teaching on indissolubility itself will not be af-fected because the first marriage is already dead. Divorce and not the remarriage constitutes the sin against indissolubility. Thirdly, the Church will be seen in its role of showing mercy and forgiveness especially if it now allows such people to enter a second marriage. True repentance demands that indi-viduals involved are sincerely sorry for whatever sin or faults they have committed and do their best to make amends. If the marriage itself is irreparably broken, then there is nothing that they can do to put it together again. One must willingly accept the obligations from that first marriage especially in terms of care and concern for the children involved, but true repentance would require no more than what has just been described. So under these conditions a person could then in good conscience enter a second marriage.

I believe that a pastoral practice which allows divorced and remarried Catholics to frequent the eucharist for the reasons given will also lead to the recognition that such Catholics, having confessed their sinfulness for the breakdown of a first marriage, will be allowed in good conscience to enter a second marriage. Some could say that this in itself is still just a pastoral approach and in no way involves a change in the teaching of the Church on indissolubility. The breakdown of the first marriage is wrong, but there is forgiveness for the wrong done and repentance insofar as this is possible. The

Church would thus continue to uphold the indissolubility of marriage but at the same time have a pastoral toleration of second marriages. Authors have noted the definite similarity of such an approach with the concept of *economia* (economy) invoked in the Eastern Church.[47] According to Alexander Schmemann, *economia* maintains in a paradoxical way the two important strains of the Christian tradition—the absolute indissolubility of Christian marriage and the practical and pastoral toleration of second marriages.[48] The practice of *economia* does not involve the Church's acceptance of divorce but merely its toleration.

In my judgment the objective teaching on indissolubility and the pastoral practice of toleration of second marriages should not be combined in a paradoxical manner which still claims to uphold the absolute indissolubility of Christian marriage. Both aspects are present because of the objective reality of the world in which we live. The Christian understanding of the world is that of existence between the two comings of Jesus. The fullness of the kingdom is not yet here although the kingdom has already begun. In this world there will always be the call to gospel perfection, but there will also be both the limitation and the sinfulness which at times will not allow the fullness of the gospel to come through. This eschatological understanding will be developed in greater detail later. In this view of the world the paradoxical linking of indissolubility and pastoral toleration of second marriages no longer seems to be fitting; rather, these two aspects must be brought closer together because they are both aspects

47. Archbishop Zoghby, "The Indissolubility of Marriage," *Diakonia* IV (1969), 155–161; William W. Bassett, "Divorce and Remarriage—The Catholic Search for a Pastoral Reconciliation," *The American Ecclesiastical Review* CLXII (1970), 20–36; 92–105.
48. Alexander Schmemann, "The Indissolubility of Marriage: The Theological Tradition of the East," in *The Bond of Marriage,* pp. 97–105.

corresponding to the realities of our life in the times in between the two comings of Jesus. The objective order in which we live is also marked by human limitation and by human sinfulness, since we are a pilgrim people trying to respond evermore to the call of God in Jesus. The last section of this paper will discuss at much greater length the understanding of indissolubility as the goal and ideal which is a true imperative of every Christian marriage, but which unfortunately might not always be possible in practice.

Such an understanding of indissolubility seems to correspond with the understanding of an *economia* as proposed by others in the tradition of the Orthodox Church. Some do not seem to accept the paradoxical understanding which holds in tension the absolute indissolubility of marriage and a more tolerant pastoral acceptance of second marriages. In 1966, Archbishop Iakavos listed ten cases in which the Orthodox Church accepts divorce and remarriage. This interpretation of accepting divorce and remarriage in practice does not seem to stress the paradoxical tension of also maintaining the absolute indissolubility of marriage in theory.[49]

Another factor which will also exert pressure for a change in the teaching of the Roman Catholic Church to a more radical approach comes from the growing recognition that the failure in marriage does not always involve a sin for the individual. In practice it is always a difficult question to judge if there is fault or guilt in the breakdown of a marriage. Very often one accepts the general human adage that there is guilt on both sides. However, in some cases there does seem to be a growing acceptance of the fact that at least for one

49. "Professor P.N. Trembelas on Divorce in the Orthodox Church," tr. George A. Maloney, *Diakonia* IV (1969), 44–46; Lewis J. Patsavos, "The Orthodox Position on Divorce," *Diakonia* V (1970), 4–15.

For an acknowledgement of the confusion in trying to interpret the meaning of *economia,* see Pierre Adnès, "De Indissolubilitate Matrimonii apud Patres," *Periodica de Re Morali, Canonica, Liturgica* LXI (1972), 220.

person and perhaps for both there might be no sin in the fact that their marriage broke down. What does this say about the indissolubility of marriage?

The moral reasoning proposed in this section by itself does not constitute a totally convincing argument for changing the teaching of the Church on indissolubility. However, in the light of the general tendency within Roman Catholicism to propose at the beginning the least change possible and in the light of the arguments for that change in pastoral practice only, there are strong indications that a more radical change in the teaching on indissolubility should be forthcoming.

USE OF SACRED SCRIPTURE

One of the significant changes in Catholic moral theology in the last decade or more has involved a greater emphasis on the role of the scriptures. The Decree on Priestly Formation of Vatican II declared that the scientific exposition of moral theology should in the future be more thoroughly nourished by scriptural teaching (n. 16). Previously the scriptures had a very minor role in the formulation of moral theology and often merely supplied a proof text for a particular teaching which was arrived at on other grounds.[50]

The teaching on the indissolubility of marriage, unlike many particular moral teachings in Roman Catholic moral theology, did appeal primarily and directly to the words of Jesus as recorded in the synoptic gospels and to the teaching of Paul in 1 Corinthians 7. These texts seem to clearly condemn divorce, although there was the perennial problem

50. J. Etienne, "Theologie morale et renouveau biblique," *Ephemerides Theologicae Lovanienses* XL (1964), 232–241; Édouard Hamel, "L'Usage de l'Écriture Sainte en théologie morale," *Gregorianum* XLVII (1966), 53–85; Tullo Goffi, "L'uso della parola di Dio in teologia morale," *Rivista de Teologia Morale* III (1971), 13–23.

88 Ongoing Revision

of interpreting the famous incision clauses (except for the case of *porneia*) in Matthew. The traditional Catholic response to this difficulty followed Jerome and Augustine in allowing separation but no remarriage after divorce, although lately some have followed Bonsirven in interpreting *porneia* as a marriage which was invalid from the beginning.[51]

The call to renew moral theology by a greater emphasis on the scriptural aspects raises the question about the proper role and use of the scriptures in moral theology. Especially in the area of specific moral teachings it has become evident that Christian ethics is not necessarily the same as biblical ethics.[52] The teaching of the scriptures on specific issues is colored by the historical and cultural circumstances of the times and by the eschatological orientation of Jesus and the early Christian community. In addition, many contemporary moral questions are not discussed in the scriptures. The ever present hermeneutic problem involves the process of interpretation by which one goes from the biblical teachings to the present reality.[53]

Roman Catholic theology with its traditional emphasis on scripture and tradition and not merely scripture alone, together with its understanding of the role and function of the Church, possesses the theoretical basis for appreciating that the Church must always strive to understand the scriptures in

51. Pierre Adnès, *Le Mariage* (Tournai, Belgium: Desclée, 1963), 20–28; 160.
52. Paul Lehmann, *Ethics in a Christian Context* (New York: Harper and Row, 1963), pp. 26–32.
53. For a more detailed and generally satisfying analysis of the question, see James M. Gustafson, "The Place of Scripture in Christian Ethics: A Methodological Study," *Interpretation* XXIV (1970), 430–455.; also Gustafson, "Christian Ethics," in *Religion,* ed. Paul Ramsey (Englewood Cliffs: Prentice-Hall, 1965), pp. 309–316. For an extreme position which sees no relationship between Christian ethics today and the teaching of Jesus because of the mistaken eschatology of Jesus, see Jack T. Sanders, "The Question of the Relevance of Jesus for Ethics Today," *Journal of the American Academy of Religion* XXXVIII (1970), 131–146.

the light of the present reality and the total historical tradition. In other words, one cannot always solve a moral question for the Christian today by just citing a scriptural passage.
If this were true, one could prove that taking oaths is always
wrong and that slavery is acceptable. The scriptures must
always be understood in the context of tradition and of the
living Church.

The present teaching and practice of the Roman Catholic
Church with regard to the indissolubility of marriage well
illustrate this understanding of the role of the Church. The
words attributed to Jesus seem to absolutely deny the possibility of divorce and refer such teaching not to redemption
but rather to creation and the original will of God, despite
Moses' concession because of hardness of heart. But the
Church in its present discipline and teaching has interpreted
the teaching on divorce in a way which is not totally consonant with the teaching found in the scripture alone and
which even seems to contradict the scriptures. Why is only a
ratum et consummatum marriage indissoluble? How can the
pope dissolve a marriage between a baptized and a nonbaptized person in favor of the faith? How can the Church
distinguish between an indissoluble sacramental bond and a
natural bond that can be broken? The Church has so interpreted the teaching of Jesus throughout the years that now
less than twenty percent of the marriages in the world are
absolutely indissoluble. (The only absolutely indissoluble
marriages are those that are *ratum et consummatum,* but this
involves at most twenty percent of the marriages in the
world).

Catholic theory and practice have traditionally acknowledged the role of the Church in interpreting the scriptures,
but Catholic biblical scholarship itself in the last decades has
appreciated the role of the Church in the formation of the
scriptures themselves. The written New Testament is truly
the product of the early faith community which in different

ways was interpreting the meaning of Jesus for their times. We can no longer accept the fact that the synoptic gospels, for example, were attempting to give us an historical reconstruction of the life of Jesus although Catholic scripture scholars rightly reject any attempt to drive a complete wedge between the Jesus of history and the Christ of faith.[54]

Rudolf Schnackenburg's book, *The Moral Teaching of the New Testament*, has exercised a significant influence in the field of moral theology, but in a sense it is also now showing its age. Schnackenburg treats in the first section the moral teaching of Jesus but does not seem to give enough importance to the fact that the synoptic gospels came from the faith of the early community.[55] One cannot always accept the synoptic teaching as merely recording the words of Jesus because very often the authors have adapted and interpreted the words of Jesus in terms of their own purposes. On that particular question of divorce, J.L. Houlden remarks that, assuming there was a logion of Jesus opposed to divorce, we cannot tell what its context was and already by the end of the first centuries Christians had contextualized it in writing in four quite distinctive ways.[56] Houlden goes on to say that in practice four distinct policies were available[57] —a point which I think is exaggerated, but the thrust of his earlier remarks is quite acceptable.

54. Édouard Hamel, "L'Écriture, âme de la théologie morale?" *Gregorianum* LIV (1973), 417–444.

55. Rudolf Schnackenburg, *The Moral Teaching of the New Testament* (New York: Herder and Herder, 1965), pp. 15–167. It should be pointed out that this volume first appeared in 1954—*Die Sittliche Botschaft des Neuen Testamentes* (München: Max Hueber, 1954). Later editions, such as the English translation, do acknowledge in the Introduction (p. 14) that the synoptic gospels were not uninfluenced by the theological concepts of the early Church, but the book itself is not changed in any way.

56. J.L. Houlden, *Ethics and the New Testament* (London: Penguin, 1973), 73–80.

57. *Ibid.*, p. 80.

This appreciation of the role of the Church, even in the formation of the scriptures, together with the recognition of an early eschatological anticipation coloring the thought of Jesus and of the early Church, has opened up new ways of interpreting the teaching on divorce. I agree with the interpretation that the early Church, as exemplified in the exception clauses in Matthew and in 1 Corinthians, made some accommodation in the absolute teaching on divorce.[58] Indissolubility is an imperative goal and ideal, but in different times and circumstances the Church is able to make accommodations in the teaching on indissolubility. The fact that this was done in the early Church is indicative of the power of the Church to continually understand and interpret the goal of indissolubility in the light of the signs of the times. Thus, a better understanding of the formation of the scriptures and their role in moral theology provides the framework that some have used to assert even on the basis of the scriptures a need to change the Catholic Church's teaching on divorce.

HISTORICAL CONSCIOUSNESS

Bernard Lonergan has described the shift from classicism to historical mindedness and its decisive importance for Catholic theology today. The historical, the concrete, the individual, and the changing, rather than the eternal, the abstract, the

58. It lies beyond the scope of this essay to develop the scriptural data on the question of divorce. For two pioneering articles which adopt the approach mentioned in the text, see Bruce Vawter, "The Biblical Theology of Divorce," *Proceedings of the Catholic Theological Society of America* XXIII (1967), 223–243; Dominic Crossan, "Divorce and Remarriage in the New Testament," in *The Bond of Marriage,* pp. 1–33. Many of the symposia mentioned earlier also have articles on the scriptural data. For a survey of recent literature, see Seamus Ryan, "Survey of Periodicals: Indissolubility of Marriage," *The Furrow* XXIV (1973), 150–159.

essential, and the unchanging, receive much more attention from the perspective of historical mindedness.[59] John Courtney Murray invoked historical mindedness to explain the change in the teaching of the Church on religious freedom. The evolving role and function of the state call for a different teaching on religious liberty.[60] In the debate about contraception great emphasis was given to the changing historical and cultural realities—the modern demographic problem, the inadequate biological knowledge on which the older teaching was based, the changes brought about by medical advances allowing many more children to live, the different sociological demands in an urban society. Earlier when these and other realities were not present, there did not seem to be such a need for contraception.[61]

Historical change and development are evident in the past history of the Catholic teaching on marriage and thus reinforce the realization that the Church is constantly interpreting the gospel and its tradition in the light of the signs of the times. For the most part of its existence the Roman Catholic Church has not reflexively and explicitly acknowledged the sacramentality of marriage. This development only occurred well into the second millenium of Christian history. Then there was the controversy about what constitutes the sacramentality of marriage. There has also been much debate about theological questions such as the identity and insepar-

59. Bernard Lonergan, "The Transition from a Classicist World View to Historical Mindedness," in *Law for Liberty,* ed. James E. Biechler (Baltimore: Helicon, 1967), pp. 126–33.

60. Murray, *The Problem of Religious Liberty,* pp. 17–45; Raymond O. McEvoy, "John Courtney Murray's Thought on Religious Liberty in Its Final Phase," *Studia Moralia* XI (1973), 201–264.

61. These reasons can be found in the voluminous literature on the subject in the middle and late 1960's. For a convenient summary containing articles by leading Catholic thinkers, see *The Catholic Case for Contraception,* ed. Daniel Callahan (New York: Macmillan, 1969).

ability of the sacrament and the contract, what constitutes the matter and form of the sacrament of marriage, and the minister of the sacrament.[62]

More closely associated with the specific question of indissolubility has been the development concerning the papal power to dissolve a marriage between a nonbaptized person and a baptized person. The discussions about this question and the opinion favoring such power as adopted and encouraged by Gasparri are well known in canonical circles. Such power has been recognized and used widely only in the twentieth century.[63] Interestingly, in the manuals of theology and canon law (e.g., Cappello) the primary theological argument for the existence of this power is the fact that the pope has exercised such power. The changing historical situation and the de facto exercise of the power constitute the first theological reason to justify it.[64] In the summer of 1970 there was another change, for such privileges were not given without the conversion of one of the parties, but the more lenient policy has recently been reintroduced.[65] Without doubt there have been historical developments and changes in the theory and practice of marriage affecting many aspects of the question, including indissolubility.

A historically conscious methodology gives greater (not necessarily exclusive) emphasis to an inductive methodology. Such a process is well illustrated in the Pastoral Constitution

---

62. Manuals of theology on marriage, such as Adnès, *Le Mariage,* develop these points in great detail.

63. John T. Noonan,Jr., *Power to Dissolve: Lawyers and Marriages in the Courts of the Roman Curia* (Cambridge, Mass.: Belknap Press of Harvard University Press, 1972), pp. 341–392; Heinrich Molitor, "Die Auflösung von Naturehen durch papstilchen Gnadenakt," in *Ecclesia et Ius,* eds. Karl Siepen, Joseph Weitzel and Paul Wirth (Paderborn: Ferdinand Schöningh, 1968), pp. 513–535.

64. Felix M. Cappello, S.I., *Tractatus Canonico-Moralis De Sacramentis,* Vol. V: *De Matrimonio* (Turin: Marietti, 1961), pp. 720–728.

65. Noonan, pp. 391,392.

on the Church in the Modern World which begins each chapter in the second part by examining the signs of the times. What are the signs of the times in the matter of the indissolubility of marriage? There is no doubt that divorce and remarriage is becoming much more common both in the general population and also among Catholics, not only in this country but throughout the world. As mentioned above, Lawrence Wrenn has estimated that in the United States "something like 120,000" valid Catholic marriages ended in civil divorce in the year 1971.[66] Polls and surveys indicate that many and perhaps a majority of Roman Catholics do not now approve the present teaching of the Church prohibiting remarriage after divorce. Fifty percent of practicing adult Catholics in France disagree with the teaching of the Church. Sixty-one percent of practicing Catholic youth in France disagree with the teaching.[67] A 1973 survey of 883 engaged people planning to marry in the Catholic Church taken in the United States by Lawrence Wrenn indicates that twenty percent expressly reject the Church's teaching on indissolubility, although preparing for marriage in the Church.[68] As mentioned above, a widely divergent practice among Catholics does not necessarily make something either right or wrong, but it remains an important factor in the discernment process.

To report properly the signs of the times is not too difficult, but an adequate evaluation involves many possible pitfalls. In general I reject an extreme interpretation which explains the present tendency to divorce only in terms of human sinfulness or which evaluates the change only in terms

66. Wrenn, *Divorce and Remarriage in the Catholic Church,* p. 144.

67. These and other statistics are cited by René Simon, "Questions débattues en France autour du divorce," *Recherches de Science Religieuse* LXI (1973), 496 and 503–505.

68. Lawrence G. Wrenn, "A New Condition Limiting Marriage," *The Jurist* XXXIV (1974), 292–315.

of positive factors. Selfishness, lack of a true sense of commitment, immaturity, and utopian expectations obviously must be exerting some influence. But, on the other hand, there are also neutral and even positive factors that are influencing the changing reality of growing divorce and remarriage in our time.

Marriage, with much help from the Christian tradition, has become more and more a personal community of love. A marriage which rests on the free choice and the true love of the parties reveals more truly human and personal characteristics than the type of arranged marriage or marriage of convenience which characterized marriage in the past. There has been an evolution toward a more personal understanding of marriage, but such a marriage is also more fragile and subject to breakdown. There are no longer the outside supports keeping it together as there were in the past when marriage was often a way of joining families together, or of serving other purposes. Also in our society today there is little or no place for the single adult who previously could live as a part of the extended family. Likewise in our contemporary society it is often very difficult for a single Catholic after the age of twenty-five to find a marriage partner who has not previously been married.

A greater emphasis on historicity makes a permanent type of commitment difficult. In a more stable society with less change such a commitment is easier. In the midst of much greater complexity and change it is more difficult to make a choice which will still have meaning in vastly changed circumstances. Today there are so many new and different circumstances which can threaten the meaning that came from such a commitment. Even a thomistic hylomorphic theory supports such an argument. The more complex the matter, the stronger and the more intense is the form needed to inform that matter. Since contemporary human existence is enmeshed in great historical complexity, a very intensive commitment is needed to give meaning even in the midst of the present complexity but above all to continue to supply meaning in the many contingencies of the future. This problem is but one facet of the very pervasive and basic cultural problem for human beings today to find meaning and intelligibility in the midst of such great complexity and change.[69]

Historical consciousness has emphasized the importance of the study of the historical development of a particular moral teaching. In the last few years a number of such studies have been made on the question of divorce.[70] In my judgment there is good evidence that the Church has accepted at times a different teaching and practice, but evaluation of the historical data lies beyond the scope of this study. Nonetheless, one can point out that there is greater historical variation on the question of divorce than on other questions such as contraception, usury, and religious liberty in which change of one type or another has taken place in Church teaching and practice.

Historical consciousness has not only occasioned the hermeneutic problem in the interpretation of the scriptures, but it has also focused attention on the statements of the hierarchical magisterium and underscored the need to study these in the light of their historical and cultural circumstances. At first sight the teaching of the seventh canon of the twenty-fourth session of the Council of Trent seems to propose the teaching of the Church on the indissolubility of marriage as an irreformable dogma of the Church. However, historical investigations, especially by Piet Fransen, have indicated that

69. *Collection: Papers by Bernard Lonergan,* ed. F.E. Crowe (New York: Herder and Herder, 1967), p. 266.

70. Seamus Ryan: "Survey of Periodicals: Indissolubility of Marriage," *The Furrow* XXIV (1973), 214–224. This particular article treats exclusively of the historical aspects of the question. For a later article which includes references to much of the earlier bibliography, see Pierre Nautin, *Recherches de Science Religieuse* LXII (1974), 7–54.

this is not so.[71] The Fathers of Trent themselves recognized that the Fathers of the Church and some well-renowned theologians accepted the possibility of divorce and remarriage. Likewise the Council Fathers wanted only to condemn the Lutheran assertion and not the practice of the Greek church. The hierarchical teaching of Trent on indissolubility is not irreformable Church teaching.[72] In concluding a recent monograph specifically on the teaching of Canon Seven, Luigi Bressan admits that the teaching and practice of the Catholic Church have gone beyond the affirmation of this Tridentine canon.[73] Thus, in many different ways the contemporary emphasis on historical consciousness in moral theology provides both a perspective and supporting reasons for a change in the teaching of the Church on the indissolubility of marriage.

PERSONALISM

Personalism has become a very important normative criterion in contemporary moral theology. The category of person has often taken over the primacy which the older manualist approach gave to the concept of nature. The person does not totally conform in a passive way to a given

71. Fransen's doctoral dissertation at the Gregorian University was on this particular question and he has developed his thesis in subsequent articles. Piet Fransen, *Die Formel "si quis dixerit ecclesiam errare" auf der 24. Sitzung des Trienter Konzils (Juli bis November 1563): Excerpta ex dissertatione ad Lauream in Pontificia Universitate Gregoriana* (Freiburg, 1951). A complete reference to all Fransen's articles on the subject may be found in the bibliography of Bressan in note 73.

72. Peter McEniery, "Divorce and the Council of Trent," *Australasian Catholic Record* CLXVII (1970), 188–201.

73. Luigi Bressan, *Il Canone Tridentino sul Divorzio per Adulterio e L'Interpretazione degli Autori,* Analecta Gregoriana, Vol. 194, Series Facultatis Iuris Canonici: Sectio B, n.33 (Rome: Università Gregoriana, 1973), p. 352.

nature, but rather all things are to be integrated into the good of the person. Many changes in contemporary thought illustrate the importance of personalism. The Declaration on Religious Freedom bases its teaching on the dignity of the human person as this dignity is known through the revealed word of God and by reason itself (n.1,2). No longer is objective truth the ultimate and controlling factor although it does have some importance. The call to reform canon law recognizes the danger of a one-sided emphasis on the institution and tries to safeguard the dignity and rights of persons in the Church as well as the participation of all persons in the life of the Church.[74] A criterion of person rather than nature has been at the heart of the call for change in the traditional Catholic teaching on contraception and sterilization.[75]

Contemporary theology in the light of Vatican II calls for a more personalist understanding of marriage.[76] A personalist rather than a more institutionalist understanding of marriage gives a different perspective to the question of indissolubility. If marriage is seen primarily as an institution, then one can talk about the various properties of marriage, such as indissolubility based on an unbreakable bond. From a more personalist perspective, if the marriage has unfortunately broken down irreparably, it is rather difficult to speak of the marriage as still existing in any truly meaningful way. Marriage is ultimately the relationship existing between two people and not the metaphysically conceived bond which comes into

74. This theme runs through the many symposia sponsored by the Canon Law Society of America in the last few years. See especially *The Case for Freedom: Human Rights in the Church,* ed. James A. Coriden (Washington: Corpus, 1969).

75. Warren T. Reich, "Medical Ethics in a Catholic Perspective: Some Present-Day Trends," in *Pastoral Care of the Sick,* ed. National Association of Catholic Chaplains (Washington: United States Catholic Conference, 1974), pp. 180–184.

76. Pastoral Constitution on the Church in the Modern World, Part Two, Chapter One. See *Marriage in the Light of Vatican II,* ed. James T. McHugh (Washington: Family Life Bureau, United States Catholic Conference, 1968).

existence through the consent of both parties to the matrimonial contract and continues in existence no matter what happens in their personal relationship.

Such a changing perspective supports the argument of those who speak about the spiritual death of the marriage. Just as natural death is now allowed to dissolve the bond (even though at one time in the history of the Church it did not), so spiritual death should be recognized as breaking the bond.[77] It is also important to point out that at times a purely personalist approach can be too narrow and fail to see the needs of others in the broader community. Again, there can be no question of an absolutely convincing argument for indissolubility from what has been said thus far, but a personalist perspective creates a climate more favorable to a change in the present teaching.

The personalist influence in contemporary moral theology is readily seen in the reconsideration of human acts and especially sin. Sin is not primarily an act in violation of a law, but the fundamental option theory views sin in terms of the basic personal decision directing and guiding one's life. The fundamental option gives meaning and intelligibility to the whole life of the person. This basic option involves one's orientation toward God and neighbor in love or else the opposite which an older theological parlance called the state of sin. Even as basic, primordial and fundamental a choice as this is not irrevocable. The sinner can always turn back to God and the person in the state of grace is always menanced by temptations to change the fundamental orientation. [78]

77. Bernard Häring, "Internal Forum Solutions to Insoluble Marriage Cases," *The Jurist* XXX (1970), 22.

78. E.J. Cooper, "A New Look at the Theology of Sin," *Louvain Studies* III (1971), 259–307; Josef Fuchs, *Human Values and Christian Morality* (Dublin: Gill and Macmillan, 1970), 92–111; John W. Glazer, "Transition between Grace and Sin," *Theological Studies* XXIX (1968), 260–274.

What is the ultimate explanation for this? Even so basic and profound an orientation never completely exhausts the depths of the human person. This choice can never absolutely be identified with the total reality of the person. The historical character of human existence with its accelerating rate of change in our day only makes the reversal of the fundamental option more possible.

In an analogous way one can and must evaluate other basic human choices and decisions which are not as fundamental as the basic option which gives meaning and direction to the entire life of the person. Other such choices would be vocational decisions or even the marriage or religious vows. Even in its older teaching and practice the Roman Catholic Church has somewhat recognized these personalist and historical factors as influencing the choices and decisions which people make and preventing them from being irrevocable. The Code of Canon Law mentions four cases in which a vow ceases to exist. Two of these cases concern a substantial change in the matter of the vow itself or a substantial change in the person making the vow (Canon 1311). In the case of vows of religious life the Church has been willing to dispense from such vows—a juridical response to the fact that such a vow might no longer be obliging and implying no fault involved for the individual person.

No particular human choice, even the commitment to marriage or to religious life, is totally identical with the reality of the person making such a decision. In such a choice a mistake is always possible, and it may only become apparent in the future. Especially where there are so many elements which are outside the control of the one making such a promise, it has to be admitted that this choice cannot be absolutely irrevocable. The mystery of the human person is ultimately deeper than any human choice can ever fathom. Every decision of magnitude such as that of embracing marriage or religious life must be made with great reflection and prudence because in such a decision one is trying to discover the meaning and direction of one's entire life. However, the fact that no one act can ever be totally identical with the person means that one cannot demand irrevocability in this matter. It is necessary to add that the marriage choice and promise involve another partner who is dependent on that choice. While such an important consideration adds another aspect to the question, it does not overcome the fact that the person can never be identified with a particular choice or decision.

Some Catholic theologians, recognizing the importance of personalism, argue that a personalist perspective does call for the indissolubility of marriage. Fidelity is the context within which marital love grows and develops. The fidelity of love is based on the "logic of the person"—fidelity to self and one's basic irrevocable choice is a demand of the human person. [79] In my judgment such arguments do not seem ultimately convincing because they fail to recognize the limitation involved in any human choice which can never totally exhaust the meaning of the person.

ESCHATOLOGY

The importance of eschatology has emerged in all contemporary theology and also in moral theology in the last few years. An eschatological perspective views our present existence as partaking in the kingdom which is already inaugurated but whose fullness is not yet here. The relationship between the now and the future is positive and there is continuity between the two, although I would insist that some contemporary theologians do not stress enough the aspect of discontinuity. Theologies of hope and liberation

79. Giannino Piana, "Il significato della indissolubilità matrimoniale nella riflessione personalistica," *Rivista di Teologia Morale I* (1969), 117–139.

show the significant influence of eschatology. The eschatological perspective is especially evident in Chapter Five of the
Constitution on the Church of Vatican II which calls the
whole Church to holiness. All the faithful of Christ of whatever rank or status are called to the fullness of the Christian
life and to the perfection of charity. This universal vocation
of all Christians to the fullness of the gospel message is
rooted in the call of all to be perfect as the Heavenly Father
is perfect.

In this world, however, no one will ever fully attain that
perfection of charity to which all are called. In the light of
this teaching of the universal call of all to holiness, Catholic
theologians have stressed the concept of continual conversion. In the light of the fullness of the eschaton the Christian
is called to strive continually for a more intimate union
through the Spirit with the risen Lord and for a constant
change of heart. Every Christian falls short of the fullness of
Christian love, but all must constantly realize the need for an
ongoing change of heart and a greater willingness to show
forth the fruits of love, mercy and forgiveness. This continual
conversion also has a social and cosmic aspect to it so that it
can never be reduced merely to the internal change of
heart.[80]

Eschatological considerations affect the approach to divorce in a number of ways. Theology has grappled with the
problem of the eschatological orientation of Jesus and the
members of the early church. In some of the seemingly
impractical moral teachings of the Sermon on the Mount
many theologians see the effect of a very imminent pa-
rousia.[81] Within the Catholic tradition the fact that such an

---

80. Bernard Häring, "La conversion," in Ph. Delhaye et al, *Pastorale du péché*
(Tournai, Belgium: Desclée, 1961), pp. 65–145.
81. Richard H. Hiers, *Jesus and Ethics: Four Interpretations* (Philadelphia:
Westminster Press, 1968).

eschatological coloration was present is not decisive, for the scriptures must constantly be interpreted by the living Church. In this light many scholars today interpret some of the moral teachings of the Sermon on the Mount in terms of our present day understanding of eschatology. We live between the two comings of Jesus. Often in the synoptic gospels the moral teaching points out the goal or ideal toward which we must strive, but pilgrim Christians will often fall short of that goal.[82] This general understanding of some of the moral teachings in the New Testament, as pointed out earlier, has also been applied to the question of divorce.[83] The very fact that Matthew includes his teaching on divorce in the context of the Sermon on the Mount gives added weight to such an interpretation.

The eschatological perspective reinforces what the historically conscious and personalist approaches teach about human choices and decision making. Christian marital love shares and participates in the love of God for his people and of Jesus for his Church. This is the truly imperative goal and ideal toward which all marital love must tend. The loving commitment of one person to another is not a restriction of one's freedom but rather a sign of transcendence by which the love of the couple tries to overcome the limitations of time and space which characterize our human existence. But this side of the fullness of the eschaton, the perfection of Christian love cannot always be attained. God's love for us remains the model and the ideal, but our love will at times

82. Josef Blank, "Does the New Testament Provide Principles for Modern Moral Theology," *Concilium* III, n. 5 (May 1967), 9–22; David Greenwood, "Obligation in the Sermon on the Mount," *Theological Studies* XXXI (1970), 301–309; Bernard Häring, "The Normative Value of the Sermon on the Mount," *Catholic Biblical Quarterly* XXIX (1967), 365–385; Rudolf Schnackenburg, *Christian Existence in the New Testament* (Notre Dame, Indiana: University of Notre Dame Press, 1968), pp. 128–157.

83. Crossan, *The Bond of Marriage,* pp. 29–33; Vawter, *Proceedings of the Catholic Theological Society of America* XXII (1967), 241–243.

fall short of that goal. Christian marital love in this world remains the love of pilgrim Christians who have not yet come to the fullness of love. The marital commitment of Christians shares in that hope which characterizes all human reality. In hope the couple prays that their love might be more and more transformed into the fullness of that love upon which it is modeled and toward which it strives.[84]

On other questions (e.g., homosexuality) I have proposed a solution in terms of the theory of compromise which rests on the theological premise that the presence of sin in this world (not the personal sin of individuals but sin incarnate in the structures of human existence) sometimes forces us to do things which under ordinary circumstances we would not do.[85] However, in my judgment there is a different rationale in the case of divorce.

In the light of the fullness of the Christian perspective on reality I see conflict situations arising from three different sources—the limitations of creation, the presence of sin and the imperfection stemming from the lack of eschatological fullness. In no way should all conflict situations be reduced to any one of these reasons although there may be overlapping reasons. The theory of compromise was never intended to cover all conflict situations but only those in which the presence of sin causes conflict. Many conflict situations come about because of creaturely limitations. Roman Catholic theological ethics has tried (in my opinion unsuccessfully) to come to grips with many of these conflict situations by the application of the principle of the double effect, which will be discussed in greater detail in Chapter 6. But in the case of the indissolubility of marriage it is precisely the

---

84. For a somewhat similar analysis of the marriage commitment, see Klaus Demmer, "Decisio Irrevocabilis? Animadversiones ad problema decisionis vitae," *Periodica de Re Canonica, Liturgica, Morali* LXIII (1974), 231–242.

85. Charles E. Curran, *Catholic Moral Theology in Dialogue* (Notre Dame, Indiana: Fides Publishers, 1972), pp. 184–219.

eschatological fullness of love which is not always able to be had in this pilgrim existence. Human limitation and finitude also play a role. Some people will obviously fall short in their marital commitment because of personal sin—a point which can never be forgotten; but even without personal sin it is not always possible for pilgrim Christians to live up to the fullness of love.

Finally, an eschatological perspective which tries to account for the tension which comes from our living between the two comings of Jesus argues against an approach which wants to maintain in paradoxical tension the teaching on the absolute indissolubility of marriage and a pastoral practice tolerating second marriages after divorce. The limitations coming from the fact that the fullness of the eschaton is not yet here need to be expressed in more than just the toleration of a pastoral practice. This limitation of the present affects the objective understanding of marriage in the only world that we know. Indissolubility of marriage in such a perspective can only be the goal which is imperative for all and which the couple promises to each other in hope; but which, without their own fault, might at times be unobtainable.

CONCLUSION

This essay has assumed that an approach which keeps the present teaching on indissolubility but merely changes certain theological and legal understandings because of which more marriages may be declared invalid is not an adequate solution to the present problem. Likewise the approach which accepts the absolute teaching on indissolubility but introduces a pastoral toleration of second marriages after divorce not only seems inadequate but in the last analysis can only be a temporary move which logically must go further. In the light of the self-understanding of moral theology today, perspectives and reasons have been proposed for changing the teaching of the Church on indissolubility. These reasons taken cumulatively, together with the interpretation of the various data about divorce which I have developed elsewhere, call for a change in the teaching on indissolubility. However, in one sense we are unfortunately expending our time and energies on what is not the primary question today. Yes, a solution must be found for the problem of divorce; in fact there already is a new pastoral practice growing with great rapidity in our country and elsewhere. But even more importantly, the whole Church must expend every effort possible to strengthen the loving marriage commitment of spouses, even if this eschatological ideal cannot always be fulfilled in our present and limited world.

4

Civil Law and Christian Morality:

Abortion and the Churches

The relationship between civil law and morality, especially Christian morality, continues to be a subject of great debate. The problem arises because, whereas most people admit a difference between civil law and Christian morality, nonetheless there is not a complete separation between the two. The overlapping between the two presents possible sources of tension. In the recent debates in England, Patrick Devlin underscores the complexity of the relationship as illustrated in how contemporary society adopts monogamous marriage as part of its social structure. The historically Christian roots of England explain how monogamous marriage came into the structure of society, but such marriage remains there now not because it is Christian but because it is built into the house in which we live and could not be removed without bringing the whole house down.[1] Basil Mitchell accepts and develops this metaphor of an old and rambling English house which has grown over the centuries and thus includes many things from the Christian ethos of the society.[2]

The question has been particularly acute for Roman Cath-

---

1. Patrick Devlin, *The Enforcement of Morals* (London: Oxford University Press, 1968), p. 9.
2. Basil Mitchell, *Law, Morality and Religion in a Secular Society* (London: Oxford University Press, 1967), pp. 131–136.

olicism. There is a close relationship between this question and the related matter of religious liberty. In the last few centuries one can recall the long and tortuous development within Roman Catholicism before the Second Vatican Council could accept the teaching on religious liberty.[3] At the present time the Roman Catholic hierarchy in the United States is generally, and rightfully, identified in the popular mind as opposed to liberalized abortion laws and now is seeking an amendment to the constitution to overturn the recent ruling of the Supreme Court. In fairness, however, it must be pointed out that Roman Catholics are by no means the only ones who are opposed to abortion, and at the same time one must also signal the incipient dissent within Roman Catholicism itself on the morality of this particular issue, although that dissent is quite minimal at the present time.

This mode of action by the Catholic bishops of the United States is reminiscent to many of the Roman Catholic opposition to changing the laws of Connecticut which made the use of contraception a crime and also of the opposition to public policy promoting and distributing artificial contraceptives. In November of 1959, the American bishops condemned the use of foreign aid funds to promote artificial contraception in developing countries, since the logical answer was not to decrease the number of people but to increase the food supply. This statement raised a political storm especially in the light of the impending presidential candidacy of John F. Kennedy. Bishop Pike, the well known Protestant Episcopal bishop, asked if the statement was binding on Roman Catholic candidates for public office.[4] Although the Kennedy

3. Pius Augustin, *Religious Freedom in Church and State* (Baltimore: Helicon, 1966); Richard J. Regan, S.J., *Conflict and Consensus: Religious Freedom and the Second Vatican Council* (New York: Macmillan, 1967).

4. Norman St. John-Stevas, *Birth Control and Public Policy* (Santa Barbara, California: Center for the Study of Democratic Institutions, 1960), pp. 57,58. St.

presidency did much to alleviate the fears and questions about a Catholic president that had emerged in a somewhat divisive way in the context of the Smith candidacy of 1928, still the problem of the relationship of Christian morality, especially moral teachings held by Roman Catholics, to civil law still remains.

Efforts by the Roman Catholic hierarchy in the United States to influence legislation in the light of Christian moral teaching have not always met with ecumenical rebuff and suspicion. In 1919, the administrative committee of the National Catholic War Council issued a document entitled "Social Reconstruction: A General Review of the Problems and Survey of Remedies." As a program for social reconstruction after World War I, the document advocated both specific short term steps and long term goals. The short term strategies called for the state to pass laws on such things as child labor, a living wage and to make comprehensive provision for insurance against illness, unemployment and old age. The long term goals called for considerable modification of the existing system through cooperation and copartnership because of the existing defects of enormous inefficiency and waste in production, insufficient incomes for the majority of wage earners, and unnecessarily large incomes for a minority of privileged capitalists. It was more than a decade later that some of the short term goals were enacted into legislation although the more radical long-range plans were never met. Many people in American society applauded the leadership

---

John-Stevas wrote extensively on this question in the 1960's and argues against laws banning the use of contraception and also reasoned that private homosexual acts between consenting adults should not be legally prohibited. His reasoning, however, is not quite the same as the approach to be developed in this paper. For his most systematic study of the question, see Norman St. John-Stevas, *Life, Death and the Law: Law and Christian Morals in England and the United States* (Bloomington, Indiana: Indiana University Press, 1961).

exercised by the American bishops in this struggle for social justice at the time.[5]

One could call to mind many other instances similar to those already mentioned, but the point is clear. There is a distinction but also an overlapping between civil law and Christian morality, and especially from the Roman Catholic perspective there has been a tendency to see a rather close identification of the two. What has been the approach of Roman Catholic theology to this question? What explains this teaching within Roman Catholicism? What should be the proper understanding of the relationship between Christian morality and civil law today?

Until very recently there was one approach within Roman Catholic thought to the proper understanding of the relationship between civil law and morality. On the basis of some developments in Roman Catholic theology, especially as illustrated in the teaching on religious liberty proposed at the Second Vatican Council, a different approach to the question is required. This study will explain the basis for the older teaching and show its application to particular questions before arguing for a different approach judged to be more consonant with accepted developments in Roman Catholic thought. In the light of this approach the legal aspects of the abortion question will be discussed.

THE FOUNDATIONS OF THE OLDER APPROACH

To understand properly the older approach to the relationship of morality and civil law, it will be most helpful to consider three questions developed in Roman Catholic theology which have contributed to this approach—the relation-

5. Aaron I. Abell, *American Catholicism and Social Action 1865–1950* (Notre Dame, Indiana: University of Notre Dame Press, 1963), pp. 199–205.

ship of church and state, the origin and purpose of the state, and the role and function of positive law. These teachings all developed in the context of historical circumstances which are quite different from the contemporary historical context. The society at the time of the Middle Ages was not generally democratic. The idea of a unified Christendom was still an ideal in the mind of many. Much less importance was given to political and civil liberties of individuals. These historical circumstances understandably influenced the development of the teaching in Roman Catholicism on the subjects under consideration, but the basic tendencies in Roman Catholic thought also influenced such teachings. Roman Catholic moral theology in its historical development has insisted on the goodness of the human, the role of rationality and the existence of a hierarchical ordering in all aspects of God's creation with very little emphasis on the freedom of the individual person. A brief consideration of the three topics will indicate how both historical circumstances and traditional Catholic emphases influenced the development of the teaching.

Church and State. Catholic theorizing in the Middle Ages about the relationship between church and state took place in the context of medieval theocracy. Without attempting an exhaustive treatment of this question in Thomas Aquinas, a consideration of Chapter 14 of *De Regimine Principum* shows the general approach taken by him at least in this one place. Thomas here employs Aristotelian thought to explain the medieval theory developed earlier by the canonists and theologians. There is a twofold ordering of human beings in this world and thus a twofold governing power which the commentators often called the *Regnum* and the *Sacerdotium*. The temporal and the spiritual order are two different orders with two different ends, but the end of the temporal order is subordinated to the more important end of the spiritual order. (This hierarchical ordering is typical of thomistic thinking.) The temporal or earthly realm is committed to earthly kings. The object of human society is the virtuous life, but the person who tries to live virtuously is destined to a higher end—union with God. Such an end cannot be attained by human virtue alone but only by divine grace. The government of this higher order belongs to Jesus Christ and is delegated not to kings but to priests especially the Roman Pontiff who is the vicar of Christ and successor of Peter.[6]

According to one modern commentator, in Aquinas' theory the temporal power is subject to the spiritual as the body is to the soul, as philosophy is to theology, as the natural is to the supernatural. However, in comparison with Pope Boniface VIII, Aquinas' understanding of the subordination of the temporal to the spiritual is somewhat moderate. By giving a solid independent base to the temporal order, thomistic teaching does provide for a clearer distinction between the temporal and the sacred orders, but in practice Aquinas emphasized the subordination between them. The theory of St. Thomas is the theory of the orthodox state.[7]

In the light of such an understanding one can appreciate Aquinas' teaching on the proper attitude of the state toward those who do not profess the true faith. In general he is against conversion of infidels by force, but force can be employed against those who have left the true faith such as heretics and schismatics.[8] The question then arises about the rights of infidels to publicly practice their religion and have their celebrations. The response is in terms of toleration. Human government should imitate God's way of governing, but at times even Almighty God permits certain evils to occur

---

6. Thomas Aquinas, *De Regimine Principum,* Caput 14.
7. *Aquinas: Selected Political Writings,* ed. with an introduction by A.P. D'Entreves (Oxford: Basil Blackwell, 1954), pp. xxi–xxiv.
8. *Summa Theologica,* II^{a}II^{ae}, q. 10, a.9.

which could be prohibited, less greater goods would be prevented or greater evils would occur by taking away such evil. Thomas is willing to tolerate rites and celebrations of the Jews, which prefigure the truths of faith, and also at times the rites of infidels if it is necessary to avoid a greater evil. Heretics, since they have left the true faith, are not to be tolerated. By their own deeds they have merited not only to be separated from the church by excommunication but also to be excluded from the world through death. However, the church can mercifully extend a period for conversion, but if the heretic remains obstinate the twofold separation should occur.[9]

One can see how the thomistic teaching itself could serve as a basis for the position on the relationship between church and state and the question of religious liberty as these were developed in Roman Catholic theology. Modifications were made especially in the nineteenth and twentieth centuries to recognize that external religious liberty could be accorded to non-Catholics, but this was still in terms of toleration to avoid greater evil. It was only at the time of the Second Vatican Council that a more satisfactory approach to these questions was officially promulgated by the hierarchical magisterium of the Church.

The Origin of the State. The second question concerns the origin of the state and will necessarily include somewhat oblique references to the nature and purpose of the state. The Lutheran tradition and much of the Protestant tradition has seen the origin of the state in light of the sinfulness of human beings. The state is necessary to bring about order and

---

9. *Ibid.,* a.11. For a further development of the teaching of St. Thomas from the viewpoint of the rights of conscience of individuals in the question of religion, see Eric D'Arcy, *Conscience and its Right to Freedom* (New York: Sheed and Ward, 1961), pp. 87–180.

prevent the chaos that sinful human beings will wreak upon
one another and upon society. Coercion is the primary way
in which the state functions to prevent chaos and bring about
order. Such an approach with a heavy emphasis on sin also
tends to see opposition and discontinuity between what is
good for the individual and what is good for the society and
sees societal rules as constraints upon the freedom and liberty
of the individual person.[10]

Thomas Aquinas occupies a significant place in the historical development of the teaching on the origin of the state in
Christian thought. In the eyes of most commentators, he
signaled a break from the Augustinian tradition of the past to
a more Aristotelian understanding, but he himself only gradually came to this understanding. Thomas' understanding of
the origin of the state can be seen in his interesting discussion
of the question whether there would have been authority
(*prelatio seu dominium*) in the state of innocence. Is the state
a natural society in the sense that the very nature of human
beings calls upon people to band together in a political
society to work for the common good? Or is the existence of
political society due to the sinfulness of human beings which
must be kept in check? Does authority or political rule which
is characteristic of the state owe its origin to the nature of
human beings or to the sinfulness of human beings? Manv
earlier thinkers made a distinction between authority that
parents exercise over children and the authority that the state
exercises over its people. This latter type of dominion and
subjection like the subjection of a slave to the master would
be a result of sin. The authority of the state is coercive

---

10. For a general overview of the question, see John Coleman Bennett, *Christians and the State* (New York: Charles Scribner's Sons, 1958). For a Lutheran
approach, see Helmut Theilicke, *Theological Ethics,* Vol. II: *Politics,* ed. William
H. Lazareth (Philadelphia: Fortress Press, 1969).

authority which indicates its origin in human sinfulness and not in human nature as such.[11]

Thomas first discusses this question in his *Commentary on the Book of Sentences of Peter Lombard*—a context in which his contemporaries (e.g., Bonaventure and Albert the Great) also discuss the question. In responding to the question whether there would have been authority (*praelatio seu dominium*) in the state of innocence, Thomas distinguishes two modes of authority—one for the sake of government (*ad regimen ordinatus*) and the other for the sake of domination (*ad dominandum*). Relying on a citation from Aristotle, Thomas compares the first way with the king's authority when the king rules for the good of the subjects; whereas the second mode is compared to the tyrant, who rules for his own good and not the good of the subjects. The second mode could not have existed in the state of innocence because no human being would be subject to another for the other's good. Such a relationship of domination could exist only in the relationship of human beings to inferior beings whose finality is in the service of humans.[12]

After making this fundamental distinction, Thomas now considers further this dominion of the king over his subjects for their good and distinguishes three aspects of this ruling authority, only one of which would have been present in the state of innocence. The dominion of the king over his sub-

11. In what follows I am heavily indebted to R.A. Markus, "Two Conceptions of Political Authority: Augustine, *De Civitate Dei,* XIX. 14–15, and Some Thirteenth Century Interpretations," *The Journal of Theological Studies,* XVI (1965), 69–100. For an authoritative study of Augustine's thought with emphasis on the more negative aspects of the state, see Herbert A. Deane, *The Political and Social Ideas of St. Augustine* (New York: Columbia University Press, 1963). A contrary view is expressed by Etienne Gilson in St. Augustine, *The City of God,* foreward by Etienne Gilson (Garden City, New York: Doubleday Image Books, 1958), pp. 13–35.

12. *In Sent.* II, d. 44, q. 1, a.3.

jects insofar as it directs subjects to what should be done would be present in the state of innocence; but insofar as it supplies for defects as illustrated in the defense of the people against enemies or insofar as it involves the correction of morals in that evil persons are punished and forced to do the good, such dominion would not be present in the state of innocence. Since the first function of ordering involves direction by one who has a greater gift of wisdom and a greater light of intelligence, it would be present even in paradise. Aquinas employs the above distinction to respond to some objections that all dominion comes from sin. Nature makes all people equal in liberty, but not equal in natural gifts. When individuals are being directed to their own good, there is no restriction of their freedom, and in fact the ruler in this case is not incongruously called the servant of the people.[13]

In the *Summa Theologica* Thomas again turns to the question of the origin of the state in the same context of whether human beings in the state of innocence would have had authority and dominion over other human beings. After mentioning some arguments in favor of denying the possibility of such dominion in the state of innocence, Aquinas points out that the condition of human beings in the state of innocence would not be higher than the state of the angels. Even among the angels some had dominion and authority over others as is evident from the order existing among the angels. Thomas responds by recognizing that dominion or authority can be understood in two different senses—one sense in which it is connected with servitude and another sense in which it refers to any subject so that one who has the office of directing and governing children can be said to have dominion or authority. Obviously the first was not present in the state of paradise but the second could be present. The distinction proposed here by Aquinas, unlike

13. *Ibid.*

the distinction found in the *Commentary on the Sentences,* proposes a general concept of dominion related to any subjection and a particular type of subjection which is based on sin.[14]

In the instance of slavery, the slave loses freedom and is ordered to the utility and good of another. A subject is governed as a free person insofar as one is directed to one's own good or to the common good, and this dominion or authority would have existed in the state of innocence. Such dominion must have existed before the fall, for according to Aristotle the human being is by nature a social animal, and the social life of many would be impossible without someone directing all to the common good. As Aristotle says, when many are ordered to one, then there is found one who is the director. For a second reason, it would not be fitting for a person who has received a greater gift of knowledge or justice not to use these for the good and utility of others. This argument presupposes what Thomas had developed in the previous question; namely, there would have been differences and disparities in the state of innocence even with regard to knowledge and justice. Thomas then goes on to invoke the authority of Augustine in a passage from the *City of God* that the just rule not through a desire for power but through an obligation to give guidance; and this is what the order of nature prescribes, this is how God created man. There is irony in such a citation because Aquinas now uses Augustine for what Augustine himself did not admit—political authority is compared to the authority of the father of the family and not to the authority of the tyrant or the master over slaves.[15]

---

14. I^a, q.96, a. 4.
15. Ibid. For a development of Aquinas' teaching on dominion as a natural condition, see Thomas Gilby, *The Political Thought of Thomas Aquinas* (Chicago: University of Chicago Press, 1958), pp. 146–158.

There is a significant change and development in Thomas' thought on the question which shows the growing influence of Aristotle on his intellectual development. When Thomas wrote the *Commentary on the Sentences,* he did not as yet fully know the *Politics* of Aristotle, although he was familiar with many other writings, including the *Ethics.* Thomas gradually came to accept the Aristotelian notion that the human being is by nature political. Both Augustine and Aristotle could agree that the human being is by nature social; but for Augustine the ideal society was the communion of the blessed in heaven, whereas the only society Aristotle knew was the *polis.* By insisting that the human being is *animal politicum et sociale,* Aquinas came to accept the Aristotelian notion. Political life belongs to the very nature of human beings.[16]

The question which Aquinas was really confronting in the passage cited above was how political society can be natural to human beings when it restricts their freedom and forces them to do things. Surely such restrictions and coercion, which at times force people to act against their wills, could come only from sin, according to the Christian perspective. But, according to Aquinas, political authority merely directs human beings to do what by nature they should do and thus constitutes no violation of their freedom. Such an approach is possible for Thomas because he accepts the fact that there is no contradiction between the good for the individual and the common good. Also, individual persons have different gifts and qualities because of which they can work together doing different things to achieve the common good. The direction from political authority does not violate human nature but rather acts in accord with it. Sometimes the shortcomings of the agent cause one to feel coercion, but in so feeling one acts against the true self.

16. Markus, *The Journal of Theological Studies,* XVI (1965), pp. 88–100.

The relationship of the individual to the political order does not involve any restriction on the freedom of the individual, for by nature the human being is called to achieve one's own end and the end of society. Such a view of human nature and freedom has important ramifications for problems raised about the relationship between law and individual freedom. Civil law in no way involves a violation of the individual's freedom, for its purpose is to direct the individual to do what by nature he is meant to do. There is no dichotomy between political authority and the freedom of the individual, but only a harmonious interplay.

Positive Law. A third important teaching for our purposes concerns the very nature and function of positive or human law. Our discussion will be restricted to a brief overview of the teaching as proposed by Aquinas in the *Summa.* Although Aquinas does discuss law in other places, the manuals of moral theology were usually content just to refer to his teaching as found in the *Summa.* Thomas acknowledges that human civil law is derived from natural law. Thomas defines human law as the ordering of reason for the common good made by the one who has charge of the community and promulgated to the subjects. Human law depends primarily on the reason of the lawgiver, for the lawgiver's function is to order the people to the common good.[17]

This ordering of reason which is human law according to Aquinas is derived in two ways from natural law, which is the rational creature's participation in the eternal law. The first is by way of a conclusion from more general principles such as the condemnation of murder. The second way in which human law is derived from natural law is by way of specifying or determining what itself is general and undetermined in the natural law; e.g., by determining what penalty should be attached to a particular crime. The second way relates more

17. $I^a II^{ae}$, q. 90, a. 4.

to art than to science, as illustrated by specifying and determining in a particular way that which is general; e.g., the artist adapting the general concept of house to a particular type of house. The second type, which specifies for the common good what is left unspecified by nature, has the force only of human law, whereas the first type also has the force of natural law. This connection with eternal law and natural law explains the obligatory force of human law, but also furnishes a higher criterion by which human law can be judged. Thomas accepted the very basic axiom that an unjust law is no law and does not oblige. Human law always stands under the judgment of the eternal law and the natural law. [18]

However, Thomas also points out there is not an exact equation between natural law and the civil law or what others describe as the relationship between a sin and a crime. Law is ordered to the common good and therefore does not command all the acts of all the virtues, but only those which can be ordered to the common good either mediately or immediately. In this connection though there is no virtue whose acts cannot be commanded by laws.[19] Likewise, it does not pertain to human law to prohibit all evils because laws are imposed on people according to their condition. The majority of humans are not perfect; therefore, human law should not suppress all the vices, but only the more grievous vices from which the majority are able to abstain and especially those which are harmful to others, for such prohibitions are necessary for the preservation of society. Note the very close connection between moral law and civil law and also the moral obligation of civil law, but also Thomas recognizes there should not be an identity between the two.[20] In another discussion Aquinas approves of Augustine's toleration and regulation of prostitution.[21]

18. $I^a II^{ae}$, q. 95, a. 2.
19. $I^a II^{ae}$, q. 96, a. 3.
20. $I^a II^{ae}$, q. 96, a. 2.
21. $II^a II^{ae}$, q. 10, a. 11.

The manuals of moral theology in a somewhat truncated way base their teachings on Aquinas. According to the typical teaching found in the manuals, law is the objective norm and conscience is the subjective norm of morality. Over the entire universe there reigns the eternal law of God which is the plan of divine wisdom directing all toward a final end. The eternal law is thus the source of all other laws. Corresponding to the twofold participation in revelation and in creation, eternal law or divine law is distinguished into divine positive law and natural law, the latter being the participation of the eternal law in the rational creation. Eternal law as found in the natural law cannot cover all the particular questions and changing circumstances of the individual and the community. The natural law gives the basic unchanging laws which are of universal obligation. The application of these laws to concrete sociological and historical conditions is the task of human law. In adding new prescriptions human law cannot contradict natural law. All human laws thus depend for their obliging force on the divine law and are bound up with this fundamental law by reason of their content.[22]

FORMULATION AND APPLICATIONS
OF THE OLDER APPROACH

In the light of these three considerations, it is possible to understand better the formulation of the older approach to the relationship between civil law and morality. The civil law applies the natural law amid the changing and particular cultural circumstances of a particular region, either by di-

22. Franz Böckle, *Fundamental Concepts of Moral Theology* (New York: Paulist Press, 1967), pp. 45, 46; 63, 64. Note the date of this work which might no longer express the author's view of these questions, but such teaching is typical of the manualist approach.

rectly promulgating the conclusions of natural law or by specifying and making determinate what has been left undetermined (e.g., what side of the street cars should use). Civil law is not exactly the same as natural law, for civil law legislates what is necessary for the common good and at times may even tolerate moral evil in order to avoid greater evil. Notice that no mention is made of the freedom and the rights of conscience of the individual, for a just law never constitutes an infringement on the true freedom of the individual. The basic thrust of this approach is to see civil law in its relationship with natural law even though there is not a perfect identity.

History, especially more contemporary history, shows that Roman Catholicism has often, although not always, urged the existence of civil laws in such questions as contraception, divorce, homosexuality, abortion, as well as social justice. Even though the theory acknowledged that civil law, since it looks to the common good, is not identical with the natural law, nevertheless it was easy to argue that anything which is against the natural law as the plan of God will ultimately have bad consequences for society. Roman Catholics who urged the continuing validity of the Connecticut law making the use of contraceptives a crime maintained that contraception is corrupting to the individual and furthermore undermines political morality.[23]

William J. Kenealy in 1948 argued in favor of the Massachusetts law which forbade the sale, manufacture, exhibition and advertizing of contraceptives. He ended his remarks with the eloquent plea, "I urge all not to permit the majesty of our civil law to sanction a perversion of God's natural law."[24] In a later article in 1963, Kenealy continues to see

23. St. John-Stevas, *Life, Death and the Law*, p. 88. St. John-Stevas himself rejects this argument.

24. William J. Kenealy, "Contraception: A Violation of God's Law," *Catholic Mind*, XLVI (1948), pp. 552–564.

the civil law in relationship to the moral order and the natural law, but he distinguishes between private morality and public morality with the latter coming under the power of the state. Kenealy does not support the Connecticut law which forbids the use of contraception, but he approves of laws which prevent the public display of contraceptive devices in store windows. The use of public funds and public agencies to encourage and support artificial contraception is a matter of public morality, and hence he is opposed to it. [25]

The possibility of tolerating an evil to avoid a greater evil becomes an important consideration in this approach. A statement issued by the Roman Catholic Archbishop of Westminster (England), in response to the Wolfenden Report, which urged that there be no laws against homosexual actions between consenting adults in private, well illustrates how the older approach in Roman Catholic thought considers a question of morality and civil law. The Archbishop of Westminster argues that, since homosexual acts are morally wrong, the state could, in view of the harm which would result to the common good from the practice of homosexuality, make such acts crimes and in no way exceed its legitimate functions. However, two questions of fact arise: do worse evils follow if the law makes private acts of homosexuality a crime and would a change in the present law harm the common good by seeming to condone homosexual conduct? These questions of fact are not clear, and Catholics are free to make up their own minds on these two particular questions of fact.[26] This position tolerates some moral evils because of possibly greater evils that a law against them

25. William J. Kenealy, "Law and Morals," *The Catholic Lawyer,* IX (1963), pp. 200–210.

26. *The Tablet,* CCX (1957), p. 523. The previous Archbishop of Westminster established a committee to make suggestions to the Wolfenden Committee in the course of its work. This committee concluded there should be no law against homosexual acts in private between consenting adults. For their report, see *The Dublin Review,* CCXXX (1956), pp. 60–65.

would cause. Although the older approach in Roman Catholic thought sees the civil law primarily in the light of the natural law, there is no perfect identity between them.

TOWARD A REVISED UNDERSTANDING
OF CIVIL LAW

In my judgment the older approach in Roman Catholicism to the relationship between civil law and morality is no longer acceptable. In attempting a better understanding of the relationship between law and morality, it is necessary to revise some of the basic understandings of law that have existed in the Roman Catholic theological understanding. Changes have already occurred in the teaching on church and state and religious liberty, but there are still many who do not see the implications of such changes in the area of the relationship between law and morality. The change in the teaching on religious liberty and even more importantly the underlying changes in the basic understanding of the role and function of the state are most instructive for our purposes.

In any discussion of religious liberty it is important to recognize what precisely the term implies, for misunderstandings abound. Religious liberty means the immunity from external coercion in civil society in the worship of God, so that no one is forced to act contrary to religious beliefs and individuals are not restrained from acting in accord with their consciences in religious matters.[27] Two very important developments in Roman Catholic theology lay behind the change in the teaching on religious liberty. The first involved a better understanding of the rights of conscience of the individual human person. The older denial of religious liberty in theory accepted the fact that truth was to prevail and error has no

27. Declaration on Religious Freedom, n.2.

rights. However, in certain cases one could tolerate the public expression of such religious rites. "The duty of repressing moral and religious error cannot therefore be an ultimate norm of action. It must be subordinate to higher and more general norms which in some circumstances permit and even perhaps seem to indicate as the better policy toleration of error in order to promote a greater good."[28] This statement by Pope Pius XII in 1953 was as far as the older approach could go in terms of practical toleration of what was wrong.

Some Catholic thinkers reasoned that the whole question had to be put in a different context. Such an approach did not give sufficient attention to the rights of the individual person and the freedom of conscience. An examination of the understanding of conscience, including its development within the context of Roman Catholicism, came to the conclusion that "a person has a right to follow his conscience, with freedom from state interference, in matters of religious choice, profession, and worship."[29] As the Declaration on Religious Freedom of Vatican Council II phrases it: "In all his activity a man is bound to follow his conscience faithfully. . . . It follows that he is not to be forced to act in a manner contrary to his conscience; nor, on the other hand, is he to be restrained from acting in accord with his conscience, especially in matters religious" (n.3). Thus a greater awareness of the dignity of the individual person and the rights of conscience provided a different context from which to view the question of religious liberty.

In the debates within Roman Catholicism in the 1950's and 1960's and even in the conciliar debates among those favoring religious liberty, John Courtney Murray pointed out that one school regards religious freedom as formally a theological and moral concept which has juridical consequences and

28. Pope Pius XII, *"Ci riesce,"* *Acta Apostolicae Sedis,* XLV (1953), p. 799.
29. D'Arcy, p. 259.

begins from the single insight of the exigency of the free person for religious liberty. Among the problems with such an approach is the risk of setting afoot a futile argument about the rights of the erroneous conscience. Murray favors a second approach which begins with a complex insight—the free human person under a government of limited powers and thus recognizes religious freedom as formally a juridical or constitutional concept which has foundations in theology, ethics, political philosophy, and jurisprudence.[30]

According to Murray there are four principles on which constitutional government is based. The first principle is the distinction between the sacred and the secular orders of human life. The second principle concerns the distinction between society and the state. The state is an agency that plays a limited role in society, for the purposes of the state are not coextensive with the purposes of society. The public authorities are entrusted with certain limited powers using political means and the coercive force of law for the good of society, and these functions are defined by constitutional law in accord with the consent of the people. The third principle, following from the above consideration, is the distinction between the common good, which embraces all the social goods, spiritual and moral as well as material, which human beings pursue on earth, and the public order, which is a narrower concept whose care devolves upon the limited state as such. The fourth principle is freedom under the law which is the higher purpose of the juridical order itself. This principle can be formulated in the following way as the basic law of jurisprudence: "Let there be as much freedom, personal and social, as is possible; let there be only as much restraint

30. John Courtney Murray, *The Problem of Religious Freedom* (Westminster, Md.: Newman Press, 1965), pp. 19–22; John Courtney Murray, "The Declaration on Religious Freedom: A Moment in its Legislative History," in *Religious Liberty: An End and A Beginning,* ed. John Courtney Murray (New York: Macmillan, 1966), pp. 15–42.

and constraint, personal and social, as may be necessary for the public order."[31]

Two comments about Murray's position are in order. First, the Declaration on Religious Freedom of the Second Vatican Council affirms the teaching on religious liberty but wisely does not take a decisive stand on the underlying reasons for such teaching. The Declaration just lists the various reasons that have been proposed by the different schools as the basis for the teaching and does not take an ultimate position on which one provides the best basis for the teaching (n.3).

Second, it is important to recognize the changed understanding of the role and function of the state and consequently of the law which Murray explicitates. In his formulation there remains a danger that one does not give enough importance to the role of the state especially in areas of social and economic justice. Some Fathers at the Second Vatican Council expressed the same concern. The concept of public order reduces the role of the state to the role of the corner policeman after the fashion of nineteenth century liberalism and thus denies the positive role of the state in terms of social and economic justice. The second introductory report of the fourth draft of the Declaration on Religious Freedom (*Textus re-emendatus*) defended the concept of public order in matters involving religious freedom and pointed out that the text was not concerned with social questions. The right of the state to restrict personal freedom is qualitatively more limited than its right to redress social and economic injustices.[32] At the very minimum one should include here the concept of socialization which Pope John XXIII employed in his encyclical *Mater et Magistra,* to balance off the principle of subsidiarity and justify the positive

---

31. Murray, *The Problem of Religious Freedom,* pp. 28–31.
32. Richard J. Regan, *Conflict and Consensus: Religious Freedom and the Second Vatican Council* (New York: Macmillan, 1967), p. 124.

intervention of the state to bring about social and economic justice.[33]

These changes both in emphasizing the right to freedom of the individual conscience and in recognizing the different political structure of constitutional government, which came to the fore in the newer teaching on religious freedom, also affect our understanding of the role and function of civil law in society. The emphasis on a hierarchical ordering and a synthetic overall picture which see all the different pieces fitting together in perfect objective harmony under the direction of God and those who in some way are taking the place of God can no longer be the controlling concept in our understanding of the meaning of law. As a very first step, the present understanding calls for the secular order to stand on its own two feet with its own finality, and it cannot be subordinated to the sacred order as in the past.

Greater importance must be given to the individual person living in society. At the same time there has been a greater recognition of the pluralistic society in which many contemporary human beings exist, for not all are in agreement about what is morally good. The function of the state and of civil law is not to direct the lives of all its citizens to the common good, and likewise the lawgiver is not the one who sovereignly directs all the individuals for the good of the whole. Our present constitutional understanding of government sees the role of the state as limited. Individuals must enjoy the freedom and creativity by which in their own way and in many other groupings they can work for the good of the whole. The law does serve the good of society, but today this means especially in areas of personal morality that the state and the law safeguard the personal freedom of the individual and restrict that freedom only when necessary.

Our present discussion is confined to questions generally

33. Pope John XXIII, *Mater et Magistra,* n. 59–66.

associated with private morality as distinguished from social or public morality. It might be somewhat difficult at times to make an exact distinction between the two; but, in general, private morality embraces those actions of individuals which tend not to have that much effect on others, whereas social morality involves actions which do have a much greater impact on others. In the area of social morality past Catholic approaches have rightly accentuated the need for state intervention for the common good and denied the excesses of a laissez-faire capitalism with its distorted notion of freedom calling for no government interference in the economic life of society. However, in matters more closely associated with personal morality the action of the individual by definition does not have that much effect on others living in the society.

FORMULATION OF A NEWER APPROACH

The fundamental and primary criterion of the role and function of civil law in questions of personal morality is as follows: "For the rest, the usages of society are to be the usages of freedom in their full range. These require that the freedom of man be respected as far as possible, and curtailed only when and insofar as necessary." This is a direct quotation from the Declaration on Religious Freedom (n.7) of the Second Vatican Council and applies now in my understanding to the role of civil law in private morality just as the Fathers of Vatican II applied it to the question of religious liberty. John Courtney Murray exultantly sees in this sentence the culmination of a developing tradition in the Roman Catholic Church. This is a statement of the basic principle of the free society which has important origins in the medieval traditions of kingship, law, and jurisprudence, but its statement by the Church has an air of blessed newness. Secular experts may well consider this to be the most important sentence in the document on religious freedom.[34]

This principle, in my judgment, is the fundamental governing criterion in the relationship of civil law and personal morality. Unfortunately, many Roman Catholics do not realize that the two fundamental changes concerning the dignity of conscience and the limited nature of constitutional government must affect and change the understanding of the nature and function of civil law. One can understand this failure because the development has occurred so quickly and so recently that its ramifications have not been explicitly proposed in other areas. It is helpful to recall the slow and somewhat tortuous development that led to the newer understanding proposed in Vatican II.

In the nineteenth century the Roman Catholic Church opposed religious liberty and many of the new freedoms as illustrated in the condemnations found in the Syllabus of Errors. Undoubtedly there were excesses in the understanding of freedom proposed in the nineteenth century, as illustrated in the injustices found in laissez-faire capitalism, which called for governments to respect the freedom of the economic order and not to intervene. In the twentieth century the Roman Catholic Church was faced with the growing threat of Nazism, fascism, and communism. Papal teaching in this context emphasized the freedom and rights of the individual against encroachments from the totalitarian state. This marked an important stage in the development of Roman Catholic teaching on the freedom of the individual, but one can note even as late as the pontificate of John XXIII the dawning realization of the importance of the role of freedom

---

34. Declaration on Religious Freedom, *The Documents of Vatican II,* ed. Walter M. Abbott (New York: Guild Press, 1966), p. 687, fn. 21. This is not an official footnote of the text of the document but rather a comment made by Murray.

in human society.[35] In *Mater et Magistra,* issued in 1961, Pope John XXIII speaks of the reconstruction of social relationships in truth, justice, and love.[36] In 1963, in *Pacem in Terris,* the same pontiff adds a fourth to this triad—truth, justice, charity, and freedom.[37] Thus, one can see even as late as the early 1960's that Roman Catholic teaching did not give the importance to freedom in the social life of human beings that it now does attribute to it. It is only natural to realize that in the area of the role and function of civil law that Catholic theology even today might not give the importance to freedom that is necessary in the light of both the contemporary understandings of the rights of conscience in civil society and of the limited constitutional government in most contemporary societies.

What are the criteria to judge the intervention of civil law in matters of private morality? The first limit on any freedom is the responsibility of the individual person in the exercise of that freedom. We should all exercise our freedom in such a way as not to unnecessarily harm the rights and freedom of other people. However, in addition it might be necessary for the state itself to intervene and place limits on the freedom of individuals. The function of the state in these matters is to safeguard the public order, and the criterion of public order guides the intervention of the law. This is in keeping with the function of the limited constitutional state. The public order includes an order of peace, an order of justice and an order of morality.[38]

The Declaration on Religious Freedom proposes the same concept of public order with its threefold content as the criterion for legal limitations on the exercise of religious

---

35. Murray, *The Problem of Freedom,* pp. 47–84.
36. *Mater et Magistra,* n. 226.
37. *Pacem in Terris,* n. 35.
38. Murray, *The Problem of Religious Freedom,* pp. 29–30.

liberty.[39] Thus, for example, even in the matter of religious
liberty, the state certainly has the right to intervene for the
sake of domestic peace if one religion believes it is necessary
for its followers to gather at 4:00 a.m. on Sunday morning
and proceed with a hundred piece band to march around the
neighborhood. Since the state also exists to bring about
justice, an order of justice including the rights of innocent,
individual persons will be a sufficient and necessary criterion
for the intervention of the state. The third component of
public order is an order of morality, but it is important to
realize that the morality under discussion here does not
involve an agreement on all specifics of morality but rather is
that basic shared morality which is necessary for people to
live together in society.[40]

There is another important consideration in determining
the relationship between civil law and morality. This consideration involves the prudential, pragmatic, and feasible
aspects of law in a pluralistic society. Within a pluralistic
society one must recognize the rights of other people who
might be in disagreement about the morality of a particular
action. Respect for the rights of others, especially minorities,
is an essential part of a proper functioning of the democratic
process. If many other people in a society do not believe that
something is wrong and harmful to others, this fact definitely
must be taken into consideration in law making.

In this same connection one realizes the way in which
legislation is made allows for a great deal of political accommodation. For example, a legislator who believes that human
life is present from the moment of conception might think it
more prudent to work for a law which would make abortion

---

39. Declaration on Religious Freedom, n. 7.
40. *Documents of Vatican II,* p. 686, fn. 20. Again this is an unofficial
footnote expressing Murray's view of public order.

legitimate in the first twelve weeks of pregnancy but forbid it after that time, since in the judgment of such a legislator that particular law would be better than a law which would allow abortion on demand for a much longer period. In backing such a compromise piece of legislation, it might be possible to avoid the greater problem of no restriction at all on abortion.

Other considerations of a feasible and more pragmatic understanding of the function of law involve the divisive effect of law on society. Even more important are the questions of enforceability and equitableness. If a law cannot be enforced, then it does not fulfill the characteristics of a truly just law. The fact that many people in a particular society at a given moment are not observing the law would be a good argument for doing away with such a law. Likewise, a law which discriminates against the poor or a particular segment of society is also a poor law. In both these cases law really is not properly exercising its function and is a cause of a general disregard for law in a particular society.

The above three criteria—as much freedom as possible for the individual, the criterion of public order to justify state intervention by law, and the recognition of pragmatic, prudential and feasible aspects in the law—constitute the framework for the proper understanding of the relationship between law and private morality. Note that in this understanding of law there is what some have called an idealistic function of law insofar as it must support peace, justice, and an order of morality, but there is also the recognition of the rights of freedom of individuals and at the same time the recognition of prudential and pragmatic judgments about the effectiveness and function of law itself. In this way the danger of an idealistic approach, which does not give enough importance to freedom and considerations of feasibility, is avoided as is the danger of a purely pragmatic approach, which sees law as totally distinct from considerations of justice and peace and merely accepting the mores of a particular society at any given time.

APPLICATION TO ABORTION

The application of such criteria to particular questions will obviously allow for different possible interpretations, but it is important to recognize that these are the criteria by which civil law is to be judged. In the questions of the use of contraception or even of homosexual acts between consenting adults in private, I do not see how the criterion of public order, embracing as it does an order of peace, an order of justice, and an order of morality, justifies the intervention of civil law. However, one must admit that abortion is an entirely different case. For those who believe that human life is present from the moment of conception, or very early in pregnancy, then abortion involves the rights of an innocent human being, in addition to the rights of the mother. On the basis of the criterion of public order, one is totally justified in striving for a law which would prevent abortion, since this safeguards the rights of the innocent human being.

However, there are other considerations of feasibility which can be raised. What about the rights of very many people in our society (the exact number is impossible to determine) who do not believe that human life is present in the fetus or at least do not believe that human life is present immediately after conception? What about the fact that in most countries in which there has been a very restrictive abortion law which allows practically no abortions there has been the great problem of clandestine abortions? In other words, it seems that many people even now are flaunting laws prohibiting abortion. (In this connection it must be pointed out that many of the statistics that have been proposed as to the number of illegal abortions are often vulnerable to criticism.) There also arises the practical consideration that a law must be equitable. If a law prohibiting abortion prevents the poor from having abortions, while at the same time the rich are able to circumvent the law, then one can definitely question the equitableness of such a law. These are some of the considerations of feasibility which must enter into any discussion about a law on abortion in our contemporary society.

An understanding of the above criteria and their application to the question of legislation in the matter of abortion indicates that one who believes that human life is present even from the moment of conception could adopt a number of different approaches to the question of the law concerning abortion. In practical terms this means that for Roman Catholics there is no such thing as *the* one Roman Catholic approach to abortion legislation. The existence of the prudential and the feasible aspect in law argues against the possibility of any immediate and necessary translation of a moral teaching into a matter of law. Roman Catholics and those in society who believe that human life is present from the moment of conception can very well argue there should be a law against abortion. On the other hand, in light of some of the considerations of prudence and feasibility in a pluralistic society, one might argue that there should be no law against abortion. If such a large number of people in our pluralistic society do not accept the fact that human life is present in the fetus, then one might argue that there should be no law against abortion, for an abortion law would unnecessarily restrict their freedom.

My own approach to such questions is to attempt some type of accommodation. In the beginning I advocated a moderately restrictive law such as that proposed by the American Law Institute which would allow abortion in certain particular situations. Such an approach was quite similar to the law existing in the state of Georgia which was over-

turned by the recent Supreme Court decisions. In this same
line of approach I could also support a law which would
prohibit abortions after ten or twelve weeks in the development of the fetus, but also include ways of helping the
mother who wants to bring the fetus to term. The important
thing to recognize is that the difference between civil law and
personal morality means that one can truly be convinced that
abortion is morally wrong, but still support legislation that
allows for abortion. One must therefore conclude that there
can be no one Roman Catholic approach to the question of
abortion legislation and that a good Roman Catholic legislator could vote for different types of abortion legislation.

The older Roman Catholic approach to the relationship
between civil law and morality in my judgment is no longer
viable in the light of the developments pointed out above.
However, despite these developments, official Roman Catholic statements unfortunately still continue to adopt the older
understanding of the relationship between civil law and morality. An illustration of such an approach is the "Declaration
on Procured Abortion" of the Sacred Congregation for the
Doctrine of the Faith issued on November 18, 1974.[41]

In its consideration of morality and the law, this Declaration in its very first paragraph mentions many of the aspects
that emerged in our discussion under the considerations of
feasibility, but subsequent paragraphs show that the theological approach of this document is that of the older understanding of the relationship between law and morality. In
paragraph 20 the document states: "It is true that civil law
cannot expect to cover the whole field of morality or to
punish all faults. No one expects it to do so. It must often
tolerate what is in fact a lesser evil, in order to avoid a greater
one." Such a consideration starts out with the understanding

---

41. "Declaration on Procured Abortion," Sacred Congregation for the Doctrine
of the Faith (Vatican City: Vatican Polyglot Press, 1974).

that the function of civil law is in terms of applying the natural law. That which is against the natural law ordinarily is also against the civil law although it might be tolerated as a lesser evil in order to avoid a greater one.

The same line of reasoning appears in paragraph 21: "The law is not obliged to punish everything, but it cannot act contrary to a law which is deeper and more majestic than any human law; the natural law engraved in men's hearts by the Creator as a norm which reason clarifies and strives to formulate properly, and which one must always struggle to understand better, but which it is always wrong to contradict. Human law can abstain from punishment, but it cannot make right what would be opposed to the natural law, for this opposition suffices to give the assurance that a law is no longer a law." Insisting that civil law cannot act contrary to the natural law does not accept the understanding of civil law as insuring as far as possible the freedom of the individual. The central framework of the discussion should not be that the civil law does not contradict the natural law, rather it is the question of the civil law protecting and preserving as far as possible the freedom of the individual and interfering only when the public order requires it. The civil law does not sanction actions contrary to the natural law, but rather it safeguards the freedom of the individual in areas where the public order is not involved.

Paragraph 22 of this Declaration goes on to say that a Christian cannot take part in a propaganda campaign in favor of a law allowing abortion or vote for it. Again, on the basis of what has been said above, I would have to disagree with that particular conclusion. However, I definitely agree with the Declaration when it asserts that doctors or nurses should not find themselves obliged to cooperate closely in abortions, but rather should have the right not to do so.

In contrast to the approach taken in the Declaration issued by the Congregation for the Doctrine of the Faith in 1974, a

Declaration of the Permanent Council of the French Bishops on Abortion issued in June of 1973 adopts a somewhat more nuanced methodological approach to the question. The slightly more nuanced approach is indicated in the following statements. "In extending the legal possibilities of abortion, the legislator risks the appearance of encouraging and provoking a lesser estimate of human life."[42] "Even if a law is not destined by itself to pose moral rules, the legislator is not able to deny to the measures which he makes an import or bearing on this order."[43]

Within the context of Roman Catholic thought not only significant theoretical reasons but also important practical concerns make it imperative to follow the second approach to the question of the relationship of law and morality in a pluralistic society. Such an approach indicates that Roman Catholics accept an understanding of the function of civil law which can also be maintained by many others in our society. Many disagreements will continue to exist about the law on abortion, but the tone of the public discussion will be better if both Roman Catholics and others accept the same general understanding of the function of civil law. Likewise, the approach advocated here dispels somewhat the charge that Roman Catholics are trying to force their morality on others. The adoption of the second approach to the question of law and morality by no means denies the fact that one can argue for a law condemning all abortion, but it does argue for a methodological approach which does not see the function of civil law primarily in terms of the application and reinforcement of the natural law. This essay has limited itself to discussing the basis, formulation and application of two dif-

42. "Déclaration du conseil permanent de l'épiscopat français sur l'avortement," *La Documentation Catholique*, LV (1973), p. 677.

43. Ibid. For diverse comments on this declaration, see "Les évêques français expriment un point de vue nuancé sur l'avortement," *Informations Catholiques Internationales*, n. 436 (15 juillet 1973), pp. 10–11.

ferent approaches and opted for the second approach to understanding the relationship between civil law and private morality. Elsewhere I have discussed the contemporary literature on this subject.[44] There remains only one final question to be discussed here.

REACTION TO THE RECENT SUPREME COURT DECISION

The Supreme Court decisions in January 1973 decided that there could be no legislation against abortion in the first trimester, and in the second trimester states could make laws only insofar as this is necessary to protect the health of the mother. Only in the third trimester did the rights of the fetus come into focus.[45] As noted above, I would have preferred a different approach to the law on abortion, even though I did not think a law absolutely prohibiting abortion would be a good one. In the midst of the conflicting opinions in our society, I would have hoped for a more compromise solution in which even greater emphasis might have been given to the rights of the fetus.

The literature of the last two years has indicated many disagreements with the reasoning behind the decision of the Supreme Court.[46] I am not competent to comment on the

44. "Abortion: Law and Morality in Contemporary Catholic Theology," *The Jurist*, XXXII (1973), pp. 162–183. The same essay appears in my *New Perspectives in Moral Theology* (Notre Dame, Indiana: Fides Publishers, 1974), pp. 163–193.

45. Supreme Court of the United States, "Roe *et al.* v. Wade," decided January 22, 1973 (Slip Opinion); "Doe *et al* v. Bolton," decided January 22, 1973 (Slip Opinion).

46. For a summary of the debate on the Supreme Court decisions in particular and the abortion question in general, see Richard A. McCormick, "Notes on Moral Theology: The Abortion Dossier," *Theological Studies*, XXXV (1974), pp. 312–359.

legal and medical difficulties which have been raised against the reasoning of the Court. However, from the viewpoint of history and reason I definitely have problems with the view of the Court. For example, it is said without nuance that ancient religions did not ban abortion or that there has always been strong support for the view that life does not begin until birth.[47] It seems to me that both of these statements are historically inadequate. Likewise, the Court does not properly interpret the delayed animation theory.[48]

Mr. Justice Blackmun in writing the opinion of the Court maintained: "We need not resolve the difficult question of when life begins."[49] In my judgment, the Court has solved the question of when human life begins, at least in terms of the legal protection of such life. The legal protection of life for all practical purposes is the only way in which society can recognize the existence of human life. In addition, Chief Justice Burger in his concurring opinion concludes with the statement: "Plainly, the Court today rejects any claim that the Constitution requires abortion on demand."[50] This seems to try to twist the thrust of the decision which definitely does allow abortion on the woman's request for the first six months of pregnancy, even though in the second trimester some restrictions can be made but only in terms of the health of the mother.

Despite my strong disagreements with the reasoning proposed by the Court and despite the fact that my own approach to abortion law would be different, I can understand why the Court has come to its final conclusion. In our American society the primary purpose of the law is to protect the freedom of individual people, and the benefit of the

47. "Roe," VI. p. 15; IX, p. 44.
48. "Roe," VI, p. 19.
49. "Roe," IX, p. 44.
50. "Roe," Mr. Chief Justice Burger concurring, p. 2.

doubt must be given to that freedom. When one is confronted with an issue in which a very large number of Americans believe they should have freedom, then one can argue on the benefit of the doubt that their rights should prevail. It is very difficult to determine what is the exact sentiment about the feelings of Americans on abortion. The two states which did hold a referendum on such subjects voted against liberalizing abortion laws. Public opinion polls seem to indicate a stand-off on this particular issue, but if the Court were assessing the general feeling of the population as being equally divided on this particular issue, then in the light of the need to give the benefit of the doubt to the freedom of the individual their final conclusion makes sense. Here too I would rather have seen the period for abortions restricted to the first trimester, but the final conclusion of the Court is understandable in terms of the legal tendency to give the benefit of the doubt to the freedom of the individual.

In the last two years following the decision of the Supreme Court, a number of Americans have called for an amendment to the Constitution in the matter of abortion. Senator Helms, Republican of North Carolina, has submitted an amendment stating that every human being subject to the jurisdiction of the United States or of any state shall be deemed from the moment of fertilization to be a person and entitled to the right of life. Senator James Buckley, Conservative of New York, has proposed an amendment specifying that the word person as it applies to due protection in the Constitution applies to all human beings including their unborn offspring at every stage of their biological development, irrespective of age, health, function, or condition of dependency. But the Buckley amendment, unlike the Helm's amendment, allows for abortion in the case of an emergency when a reasonable medical certainty exists that continuation of pregnancy will cause the death of the mother.

It is important to recognize and underline once again that

opposition to abortion is not identified only with the Roman Catholic Church in this country. In fact in the matter of the morality of abortion there are many Protestant ethicians who take a comparatively "conservative" stance; other Americans have also decried the Supreme Court decisions. However, many Roman Catholics, including the Catholic hierarchy of the United States, have advocated a Constitutional amendment to change the decision of the Supreme Court. I personally am opposed to efforts aimed at obtaining a Constitutional amendment. For one thing, it does not seem that a constitutional amendment stands any hope of success. Even though one might argue that a majority of Americans disagree with the Supreme Court decision, I am sure that they will never be able to agree on what the law should be. Some will argue for a very strict law from the very moment of conception, whereas others will allow for some exceptions and perhaps not want to place the beginning of human life at the very moment of conception. It seems to me impossible that a majority of Americans could ever agree on precisely what the abortion law should be. Again, I recognize the right of any American to work for a constitutional amendment in this area, but I personally am opposed to such an approach.

In the light of the present situation, I believe it is imperative for the Roman Catholic Church to recognize as clearly as possible the relationship between civil law and morality. There is a prophetic or teaching aspect to civil law, but civil law cannot be seen primarily in terms of an application of the natural law. Rather, civil law must ensure that "the freedom of man be respected as far as possible, and curtailed only when and insofar as necessary."[51] The proper role of civil law is more limited than in the older Catholic understanding. The Roman Catholic Church cannot and should not always depend on the civil law to back up its own teachings, but,

51. Declaration on Religious Freedom, n. 7.

rather through education, service and other means, should strive to develop an ethos in which its own moral teachings and values can be effectively mediated to its members. Even now I think the efforts of Roman Catholics could be better directed towards this work of education and service rather than absorbed by attempts to amend the Constitution.

5

The Fifth Commandment:

Thou Shalt Not Kill

Contemporary Catholic moral theology has rightly discarded the format of the Ten Commandments as the basis for structuring and developing the Christian life for many reasons. The Commandments are rather generic and have consistently been reinterpreted in the light of changing times. The Commandments do not explicitly view the moral life of the Christian as man's gracious response to the gift of God in Jesus Christ. Even in the Old Testament the Ten Commandments must be seen in the context of the Covenant which is the most important aspect of Old Testament ethics—the loving relationship between God and his people. Thomas Aquinas himself taught that the primary law for the Christian was the internal law—the power of the Holy Spirit dwelling in us—and any written law such as the Beatitudes of the New Testament or the Ten Commandments of the Old Testament is secondary. In addition, the Ten Commandments also emphasize the negative aspects of the Christian life rather than the positive obligation of the moral life of the Christian who is called to be perfect even as the heavenly Father is perfect. Law can no longer be seen as the primary ethical category, but rather greater emphasis is placed on relationality and responsibility without denying the fact that there will always be some need for law in Christian ethics. The Judaeo-Christian tradition in the fifth commandment deals with questions involving human life. Over the years a rather broad and general commandment of "Thou Shalt Not Kill" has been applied to various situations as they arose. This essay will try to develop questions relating to life in a broader context than usually proposed when following the treatment of the fifth commandment given in the manuals of theology.

RESPECT LIFE

Respect for life or the sanctity of life in the Christian perspective comes from the fact that life is a gift from God the creator. The creator has called us all into being; we have not brought ourselves into existence. Life is a precious gift that we have received from the hand of the creator. As human beings we do not have total control over our life or the lives of other humans. Every person exists because of the gracious love of God and is called by God to share in the fullness of his life and love. The theological tradition has expressed this reality by saying that the Christian does not have full dominion over life, even one's own life, but rather has stewardship or imperfect dominion. In this way the value of human life illustrates the Christian understanding of all existence with the primary emphasis on the gift of God but with the need for human beings to respond positively and thus share in the life giving action of God. The fact that life is a gift from God does not mean that human beings are merely passive recipients of the gift of life, but we have the vocation to nourish, protect, defend and improve human life.

Such a Christian understanding of the value of human life as a gracious gift of God is opposed to the value that is often attached to human life by many people including Christians in our contemporary society. Too often we attribute value to human life only in terms of what one makes, does, accomplishes or possesses; but in the Christian perspective the dignity of human life does not rest primarily on one's works or accomplishments. The different theoretical bases for the dignity of human life have enormous practical consequences. Too often it seems that people today want to forget about those who are not contributing to society or who are not successful in terms of acquiring material goods, reputation or power. Christian love can never be selfishly directed just to one's own advantage, for Christian love pays great attention to the needs of the neighbor. In fact, there is always a Christian bias or prejudice in favor of the poor, the weak and the oppressed. The value of human life can never depend primarily on the wealth one accumulates, the position of power that one obtains or even the good works that one does for others. The Christian gospel stands opposed to such an understanding, since it proposes as a criterion of our love for God our love for the poor, the naked, the hungry, the thirsty and the prisoner.

Responsible and creative Christians must incarnate this understanding of the value of Christian life in contemporary society. Our respect for life must bear witness to this basic biblical injunction in today's world. Unfortunately, there are many people in the world today who are hungry either because of epidemics, malnutrition or catastrophes such as drought or floods. There are many people who are living below the poverty line and even close to destitution. Many families are cramped into small, dank and intolerable living quarters, while others live in comparative luxury and worry about how often to change the color of the wall-to-wall carpeting. There are gross inequities existing in our world in which the truly human needs of many are not being met. Unfortunately, most of the developed nations of the world are often using the developing nations and preventing these people from having those things which are necessary for truly human existence.

Within our own country there are many people who live

below the poverty line and do not have the food they need or proper health care or educational facilities. Too often the attitude toward welfare is that people should be able to help themselves, and we have no obligation to help out those people who are lazy or just do not want to work. Implied in this is the concept that human dignity depends on what one does or accomplishes. Compare the amount and the way in which government funds are given to university research and industrial development with the amount of money and the way in which it is given to the basic human needs of people in our society.

Another area of concern embraces those who are not contributing members of our society. Immediately one thinks of the aging and the elderly who are becoming more numerous but who no longer positively contribute in the way of work and often seem isolated and in great need of affection and care. Many people in our society also suffer from different physical and mental disabilities because of which they are often institutionalized. Here too there arises a conspiracy of silence to put these people away in some rural setting and forget about them. The mentally retarded are also in great need of care and affection even though they might not be able to contribute very much to society in the way of wealth. We all know situations in which they have been the occasion of greater understanding of what Christian love really means.

Special mention must be made of those who lack power in a particular society, for these are often the victims of oppression in all its different facets. Think for example, of all the problems of a minority group in any society, especially our own—Black, Indian, Spanish-Americans. Above all think of the lot of the prisoner and how the administration of penal justice does not always respect the dignity of human beings who do not lose that dignity just because they might be imprisoned.

A brief reflection thus brings to mind the many ways in

which we fail to live up to the Christian injunction of respecting life. The sensitive Christian conscience should see in many areas of our life these signs of sin—our failures to live in accord with the Christian understanding of respecting the life of all especially those most in need. To overcome this present situation we must use all the means at our disposal, but the ultimate solution will never be found merely in technology. In the last analysis the sin-filled situation in which we live can only be changed through a continuing and radical conversion or change of heart which is the fundamental moral message of the scriptures. The radical change calls for us to give less emphasis to ourselves and more to the needs of our neighbor.

In the ethos of our consumer society we so easily become involved in fulfilling the false needs that are created that we truly forget the human needs of many others. From a collective viewpoint we Americans as the richest nation in the world must be willing to do with less so that others might have the bare minimum in keeping with their basic human dignity. We cannot continue consuming forty per cent of the world's resources when we form only a comparatively small percentage of the world's population. Christians must make a special effort to say no to false needs and concern themselves with the true needs of others. But again the only way in which this can be brought about is through a radical conversion or change of heart. The manifold questions affecting human life are very complex and involve many political, social and economic realities and relationships. There will never be any simple solutions to these complex questions, but a start must be made. The first step must involve the recognition by all of us of our individual sinfulness and the need to change our hearts so that we truly respect human life and strive to promote and defend human life especially among the weak and the poor.

THOU SHALT NOT KILL

The first section has stressed the positive aspects of what Christian respect for life involves on our part. The second section will consider the negative obligations following from respect for life. In this connection the manuals of moral theology used to consider the questions of suicide, murder, killing an unjust aggressor, capital punishment and abortion. These questions will now be considered in greater detail.

Suicide. The Christian tradition has condemned suicide as wrong because man receives life as a gift from God, and his stewardship does not give him the full dominion to take his own life. Suicide is often an expression of desperation and indicates a lack of hope. Canon law forbids Christian burial to suicides, but this must be interpreted in the light of the actual dispositions of the person. The general pastoral rule is that there is usually great doubt that the person was fully responsible for the suicide so that a Christian burial should not be denied, especially in the light of the needs of the family.

Christians, however, must always take into consideration the biblical text from John 15:13 that greater love than this nobody has than that one lay down one's life for a friend. The Christian tradition does not make an absolute value of human life, even one's own physical life. The tradition has acknowledged that conflict situations can arise when any individual act might have a number of effects, one of which is my own death. The Catholic approach to this question has been based on the distinction between the direct and indirect effect as enunciated in the principle of double effect. Direct suicide occurs when the killing is intended either as a means or an end in itself. Indirect suicide is morally permitted when the following four conditions are fulfilled: 1) the act itself is good or indifferent; 2) the intention is good; 3) the good effect occurs equally as immediate as the evil effect so that the evil effect is not the means by which the good effect is obtained; 4) there is a proportionate reason to justify the indirect taking of life. In extraordinary situations the tradition also acknowledged the fact that God, who is the author of all life, could give a private inspiration to an individual to take one's own life.

Manuals of moral theology point out cases of indirect suicide. In the first book of Maccabees 6:43–47, Eleazar killed the opposing king by courageously fighting his way under the king's elephant and thrusting his sword through the soft underbelly of the elephant with the knowledge that the elephant would collapse on him and kill him. Kamikaze pilots in the Second World War were also judged to be only indirectly killing themselves. However, most authors would not allow the spy or the saboteur to take a pill to kill self lest secrets affecting the lives of many other people be revealed. In this case the killing of self is the means by which the good effect is accomplished. In the other two cases the effects are equally immediate, and the good effect is not produced by the means of the bad effect but might even have come into existence if the bad effect did not occur.

Today a good number of Catholic theologians are questioning the adequacy of the distinction between direct and indirect, since it is primarily based on the physical structure of the act itself and does not give enough importance to the complexity and multiple relationships involved in human actions. I deny the absolute validity of the distinction between direct and indirect as it has been proposed in the tradition. The following chapter will develop my critique of the principle of double effect. On the basis of proportionate reason the spy can take a pill to end his life and thus conceal knowledge which would be detrimental to the lives of many other individuals. In such conflict situations between my life and the lives of others, there could be a proportionate reason to justify the taking of my life. But again one recognizes the value here must be commensurate with the value of human life.

Murder and taking the life of others. Based on the fact that a human being does not have dominion over the life of another, the Catholic tradition has clarified the generic fifth commandment to read that the direct killing of innocent life on one's own authority is always wrong. Catholic theology with its emphasis on human reason maintains that all human beings can come to this same conclusion on the basis of their rational understanding of reality. The tradition has justified the indirect killing of innocent persons if there is a proportionate reason. For example, in everyday life, people drive automobiles even though indirectly some people are killed in automobile accidents.

One type of conflict situation that the tradition acknowledged was the killing of an unjust aggressor. If necessary one may kill an actual unjust aggressor if this is required to save life or spiritual or material goods of great value. Note that here Catholic theologians have been willing to admit that other values, such as spiritual goods (e.g., use of reason, reputation, etc.) or material goods of great value, could be as important as physical life itself.

There are two further considerations in the question of unjust aggression that deserve to be noted. The first concerns whether the killing in this case is direct or indirect. Some theologians maintain that it is indirect because one can never intend the death of another human being, but others say that it is direct and intended because the death of the aggressor is the means by which I defend myself. In my judgment, if one is going to retain the accepted understanding of direct as that which is intended either as an end or as a means, then the killing in this case is direct. Second, it is important to note that the unjust aggression here does not refer to a formal unjust aggressor—that is, one who is subjectively guilty of unjust aggression. The primary moral consideration is not whether the person is subjectively guilty but only whether the person is bringing about an objective conflict situation. In the light of these refinements I would understand murder as the unjustified killing of another. In conflict situations in which one's life or other goods of commensurate value are being threatened, then one could be justified in taking the life of another as a last resort. Here too my approach does not employ the distinction between direct and indirect as the ultimate means of determining and solving conflict situations.

Another question dealing with the taking of human life is capital punishment. Traditionally, Catholic theology, in the light of the state's obligation to protect the common good, has accepted the right of the state to resort to capital punishment in cases of proportionately grave crimes. Today many theologians, myself included, would disagree with the older teaching. Prudentially and historically it does not seem that capital punishment can be justified. One would have to justify capital punishment on the basis of the reasons for which punishment exists.

One of the purposes of punishment is corrective, but capital punishment obviously does nothing to rehabilitate the offender. Second, capital punishment is often defended as a deterrent—only the death penalty will deter people from the most horrendous crimes. But I would argue that the death penalty has not served as a salutary deterrent in the past. A third reason invokes a concept of justice which demands there be vindication for the injustice done. The person who takes another life must forfeit one's own. But this is not the only way of vindicating justice. Why should another life be taken if this is not necessary? The original victim is not brought back to life by the death of the assailant. Often such a concept of vindictive justice seems closer to revenge than a just form of punishment. Since human life is so important a value, I do not think that the state should take human life when it cannot be shown to be absolutely necessary. The arguments as proposed in favor of capital punishment do not in my judgment prove the need for capital punishment, so I strongly oppose it.

Abortion. Roman Catholic teaching has consistently applied its understanding of respect for life to unborn life in the womb. In the whole historical development as well as in the contemporary discussions there are two important questions on which one's teaching on abortion hinges. The first is: when does human life begin? The second is: how does one solve conflict situations involving human life?

The authoritative, hierarchical teaching of the Catholic Church solves the problem of the beginning of human life by saying that in practice one has to act as if human life is present from the first moment of conception, but in theory many Catholics have maintained that human life is not present at the very beginning. Thomas Aquinas, following the traditional teaching proposed by older biological authorities such as Aristotle and Galen, maintained that animation takes place (the soul is infused into the body) or human life begins for males at forty days and for females at eighty days after conception. (I do not know what empirical data they had for their teaching, but I am sure they did share some antifeminine prejudices which entered into such a judgment.) Today some thomistic philosophers still maintain the theory of delayed animation.

As might be expected, there are two possible explanations for Aquinas' teaching. Some maintain that Aquinas based his teaching on the poor biological knowledge which was then accepted as true. The only active element in human reproduction according to their knowledge was the male element. The very word "semen" comes from the agricultural analogy whereby the seed is placed in the ground, dies and then new life shoots up. Until a few centuries ago we knew nothing of the active female element—the ovum—and the union of ovum and sperm. Thomas could not hold that human life begins at conception because at conception there is only the semen which is now present in the uterus of the female. But contemporary knowledge and especially modern genetics prove that from the first moment of conception there is a unique genetic package that is never to be duplicated—except in the case of twins.

The other interpretation gives a more philosophical basis to Thomas' teaching. Thomistic metaphysics accepts the theory of hylomorphism according to which matter and form are the constitutive causes of being. There is a reciprocal causality between matter and form so that the form can be received only into matter that is capable of receiving it. This printed page cannot receive the form of a human soul or even the form of a piano because the matter is not disposed to receive it. So, they argue, in the very beginning the conceptus is not capable of receiving a human form—the soul. Only after some time is the matter disposed to receive such a form. (My difficulty here is that I do not see that there has been a significant development in the matter in the first forty or eighty days after conception so that it is now disposed for a human form whereas before it was not.) It is important to realize that at least in theory there has been this long discussion about the difficult question of the beginning of human life.

Today there are many non-Catholics, and even some Catholics, who cannot accept the Catholic teaching that in practice one must act as if human life is present from the moment of conception. However, it is also important to point out that many other people join the official Catholic teaching in condemning direct abortion. There are three generic approaches about how one determines the beginning of human life—the relational approach, the individualistic-biological approach, and the process approach.

The relational approach maintains that biological or genetic data alone can never determine the beginning of human life. The human being is more than just the biological or genetic. The new life must be recognized as such and accepted by the parents into a loving relationship. I cannot accept the relational criterion in this case. First, nobody seriously proposes that such a relational criterion be employed after birth so that in practice these people do accept a biological criterion such as birth as marking a point after which there is human life. Second, a fully human relationship must be reciprocal, but it is obvious that before sometime after birth the fetus cannot respond in a human manner. Third, in determining the time of death, all contemporary approaches use an individual-biological criterion—heartbeat or brain waves. Fourth, the relational criteria would be rather nebulous and very difficult to apply in practice. When precisely is the relationship present and what are the criteria by which one can determine the presence of this relationship? Although one must recognize the greater importance attached to relationality in contemporary moral thinking, when one is talking about the very minimum required for human life I do not think that a relational criterion is fitting.

The second generic approach employs an individual-biological criterion to determine the beginning of human life. Some choose birth, but it seems that birth tells more about where the child is than what it is. There is just not that much difference between the unborn child one day before birth and the born child one day after birth. Others choose viability, but again this tells more about where the baby can live, and in the light of medical advances viability is a very relative criterion which will occur increasingly earlier in the life of the fetus. Quickening also seems inadequate because it merely records the mother's perception of movement. Some ethicians argue for the presence of brain waves or the early development of the cortex of the brain or the rudimentary formation of the basic systems of circulation, respiration and brain activity. On the basis of such criteria human life begins at about eight or ten weeks after conception. But in my judgment these developments do not really constitute such a qualitative difference between human life and no human life. At this early stage human brain activity is not an actuality but now becomes a possibility; but even before, in terms of evolutionary development, there was also this possibility. In my judgment there is here a question of evolutionary development but not the qualitative difference between human life and no life.

The strong reason for saying that life is present from conception with strengthening support from modern genetics has already been mentioned, but I cannot accept it. I hold that human life begins about the fourteenth day after conception. All descriptions of human beings seem to insist on individuality as a fundamental characteristic, but individuality is not present and achieved before that time. The phenomenon of identical twinning can occur up to fourteen days after conception. Likewise science has discovered the less frequent occurrence of two fertilized ova joining together to form one being before the fourteenth day. Thus there are strong indications that individuality is not present before that time. A confirmatory reason comes from the fact that many fertilized ova are spontaneously aborted without the mother's even being aware of it in those first fourteen days. In practice I maintain that human life is not present until the fourteenth day after conception. At the present time this has only limited practical applicability—after rape or concerning the use of "contraceptive" devices which really prevent fertilization. Some prefer to adopt the third model of process or development. At first many reasons seem to commend such an approach, but in the last analysis this approach must be reduced to one of the other types and must face the question of when in this process of development human life does begin.

The second fundamental question in abortion concerns the solution of conflict situations involving the fetus (and presupposing now it is human life, for if it is not human life then the dilemma is no longer of such great magnitude). In the past Roman Catholic teaching condemned all direct abortion but allowed indirect abortion if a proportionate reason was present. The two most common examples of indirect abortion are the cases of the cancerous uterus and the ectopic pregnancy. As will be developed in the following chapter, I reject the concept of direct and indirect as a solution to conflict situations. As in the question of unjust aggression, if there is an objective conflict so that the fetus is causing harm to the mother the abortion can be justified to save the life of the mother or for some other value commensurate with physical life. Recall that in other conflict situations other values such as spiritual goods or material goods of great value were equated with physical life itself. Thus, for example, if it was in accord with the best medical indications and understanding that the pregnancy would mean that a mother of three would be psychically disabled for a very prolonged number of years (not just a temporary depression), then I could reluctantly justify the abortion.

It should be noted that many Catholic moral theologians writing today disagree with the solution of conflict situations by the application of the concept of direct and indirect as it has been understood in the manuals of theology. To a considerably lesser extent there is also some dissent from the authoritative teaching on the practical acceptance of conception as the beginning of human life. My own teaching constitutes a dissent from the authoritative Church teaching on the two questions of when does human life begin and how does one solve conflict situations, but my dissent is not all that great. Others might even propose a more radical solution.

The teaching on abortion is not a matter of faith, and dissent remains a legitimate option for the Catholic; but also the dissenter must be aware of the dangers involved. In general in our society, I am convinced there is a tendency to deny the humanity of the fetus because it produces nothing. Since one cannot see or hear the fetus, the temptation to abortion is often very strong. The Church should continue to teach in this area and in other areas but always trying to read the signs of the times in the light of the tradition. In teaching on such specific moral problems, as illustrated by the debate about the beginning of human life and solution of conflict situations, the hierarchical Church can never claim that its teaching is so certain that it excludes all possibility of error and the option of dissent.

DEATH AND DYING

Death is a subject which is no longer taboo in our society. A Christian's understanding of death in my judgment recognizes the many complex aspects of the reality. Death is something which is natural for every created thing. The Christian tradition has also seen death as intimately joined with sin and effected by sin, for we are reminded in the scriptures that through sin death came into the world. This aspect of death causes even the Christian to experience it as a break with the past, and death is accompanied by sentiments of fear and trepidation even for the Christian. But death is also seen in the light of the redeeming love of God, for he has transformed death in the resurrection of Jesus. Death transformed by love is the way to life. Death for the Christian does not deny all that went before in life, but rather it breaks with the past in order to transform what went before into the newness of life. The Christian understanding of death must take cognizance of all these aspects of the reality of death, and individual Christians must come to grips in their own existence with the thought and the fact of their dying.

Christian thought about life and death has tried to hold in balance two basic truths—there must be a great respect for life and the need to preserve life; but death is not the greatest evil in the world, and one does not have to avoid death at all costs. A technically precise theological statement of this attitude is that we have an obligation to use ordinary means to preserve life, but we have no obligation to use extraordinary means. The ordinary means of preserving life are best described as those medicines, treatments and operations which offer a reasonable hope of benefit for the patient and which can be obtained and used without excessive pain, expense or other inconvenience. Since the Christian has no obligation to use extraordinary means to preserve life, there is for the Christian the right to die.

The description of ordinary means originally emphasized the question of excessive pain, expense or inconvenience; but in the last few decades with the increasing realization that medicine can keep people alive for a few more hours or days theologians have added the criteria about some reasonable hope of benefit for the person. If a person will only live for a few more hours or days, then one cannot consider the treatment obligatory. The Christian recognizes there is a time when the respirator can be shut off and the intravenous feeding pulled out. There is no obligation to prolong death but only to take ordinary means of preserving life. Naturally there will be differing prudential judgments about what is an ordinary means, but the right to die has been an accepted part of the Catholic tradition.

The Catholic tradition by accepting the distinction between ordinary and extraordinary means has also recognized the importance of the quality of life and denied the absolute value of physical life itself. For example, a person has no moral obligation to move to a different climate and location if this is necessary to add some years to life but will involve proportionately grave inconvenience for the person and family involved. Allowing to die exists not only with the elderly but even with newborn children who, for example, need an operation to sustain life but are very severely malformed.

What about euthanasia or the active and positive interference to bring about death? Traditionally Catholic teaching and the hierarchical teaching authority have opposed euthanasia. Two reasons are frequently given. First, the individual does not have full dominion but only stewardship over one's own life and therefore cannot directly interfere with life. Second, there is a great difference between the act of omitting an extraordinary means and the positive act of bringing about death. To allow one to die is not the same as positively interfering to cause death especially as it concerns the intention and act of the person performing the deed.

These two arguments in my judgment are not absolutely convincing in all cases. Human beings do have some dominion over life and death, for example, by refusing extraordinary means one can intend to die and efficaciously carry out that intention. I grant there is an important difference between the act of omission and the positive act of killing, but in my judgment at the point in which the dying process begins there is no longer that great a difference between the act of commission and the act of omission. I acknowledge problems in determining when the dying process begins (some could argue it begins at birth), so I practically identify the dying process with the time that means can be discontinued as useless but having in mind such means as respirators, intravenous feeding, etc. In practice there will always be a difficulty in determining just when the dying process begins so that one must recognize the potential problem of abuse that can arise and the difficulty in determining laws in this matter. Now and in the future one can expect some others to dissent from past Catholic teaching in this case. Again, despite all the dangers involved, dissent remains a possibility for the Catholic. The matter is so complex that the present teaching as proposed by the authoritative, noninfallible magisterium cannot claim and, to its credit, does not claim to exclude the possibility of error.

Another question concerns the definition of death and the test for death. These questions arise today precisely because the older sign or test for death was often the lack of a heartbeat, but now one recognizes that the heart can artificially continue to beat while the person is really dead. Likewise, the question has arisen in the case of heart transplants, to make sure that the one person is already dead before the heart is transplanted. There is a tendency today to accept brain death as the best criterion or test for determining whether or not death has occurred. However, even with this criterion or test for death, one could still accept the definition of death as the breakdown of the three major systems—heart, lungs and brain—or revise that to the death of the brain alone. From the perspective of moral theology there is no difficulty with accepting these revisions which have lately been put into practice.

CARE OF HEALTH AND MEDICAL ETHICS

The Christian view recognizes the value of human life and the consequent obligation to care for the health of the total person—body and soul. The Christian approach, while acknowledging the importance and value of health, never absolutizes what is itself relative. Risks to health are permitted if there are proportionate reasons to justify them. In this connection questions have arisen about the morality of cigarette smoking and boxing or prizefighting. Can one take the risk to health in these things? In all questions of this type there is need for a prudential judgment, but one must also honestly evaluate the scientific data and not merely accept things because everyone else does them. There is evidence that smoking does constitute a risk to health. There could be other reasons which would justify this risk, such as the mental good of the person or the lack of anxiety, but the danger of self-deception is again ever present.

The use of alcohol and drugs also involves care for one's health and sanity. Here too the traditional approach has avoided the extremes of total condemnation or of blanket acceptance, since the guiding principle is the relationship of drugs and alcohol to the good of the individual person. Alcohol as a part of creation is a good that can be used for either good or ill. A moderate use of alcohol can be a salutary and helpful thing for the good of the whole person. Even the social drinking of alcohol can be a good thing. Likewise drugs can be used to eliminate pain and bring relief from stress and strain, but the danger of abuse is ever present in both drugs and alcohol.

Both alcohol and drugs can readily be used as a neurotic form of escape. Both can create a dependency by which the person loses truly human dignity and freedom becoming a slave or an addict. Abuse of such things can be destructive for the individual, for all those related to the individual and for society itself. Also the availability of drugs and alcohol is one of the problems of an affluent society. Especially in the context of our consumer society, one can easily create a false need for alcohol and drugs. In the case of drugs this does not only refer to hard drugs but also to the tendency of so many Americans to be dependent on many different forms and types of drugs. Obviously the problems of addiction dependency and long-term self-destruction are much greater with the use of hard and habit forming drugs. The use of alcohol and drugs is governed by the Christian virtue of temperance which justifies them in terms of the good of the total person. However, it must also be recognized that an individual for many different reasons might truly feel a personal call to greater abstention in the use of drugs and alcohol.

The care of health is usually associated with medicine. As already mentioned in the first part of this essay the primary moral question in my judgment concerns the need to insure that all people in society and in the world have available to them proper medical care. The focus now will be on proper care for the health of the individual. Here the Christian tradition operated within what might be called the eschatological tension between doing everything possible to overcome sickness and insure health and yet realizing that suffering of some form will always be part of the Christian life, since our life is intimately associated with the Paschal Mystery of Jesus. Sickness and dying often unite the Christian with the death and resurrection of the Lord. Vocations in service of the sick have been continually encouraged in the Christian tradition. Hospitals first came into existence under Christian auspices and continue to be sponsored by Christians. Medical and nursing professions constitute two forms of service to fellow human beings, and the Christian reality sees in them a Christian vocation in the service of mankind.

In general, medical care and treatment for the individual do not usually occasion many ethical problems. The doctor is guided by the good of the patient, and that is the same norm as the ethical criterion. Traditionally, medical ethics was treated under the rubric of mutilation of the body which can be justified for the good of the whole. Catholic theology developed the principle of totality which maintains that a part could always be sacrificed for the good of the whole to which it belongs. Ethical problems could arise only in terms of prudential judgments of what was truly for the good of the individual. The relationship of doctor and patient introduced ethical questions based on that relationship itself with special emphasis on the moral obligation of the doctor to tell the truth to the patient (especially the dying patient) and to obtain the consent of the patient or guardian for operations insofar as this is possible. Especially in cases of newer or experimental procedures used for the good of the individual, the patient has a right to know all the possibilities and risks before making a decision. Special problems arose in Catholic medical ethics when the generative organs were involved. In my judgment our older teaching wrongly maintained that the generative organs could never be sacrificed for the good of the individual or for the good of the marriage itself. Consequently, sterilization and contraception can be justified either for the good of the individual or for the good of the marriage, but these problems are treated elsewhere in greater detail.

New questions came to the fore in medical ethics when the individual was mutilated or treated not for one's own good but for the good of another or the good of the species. Pope Pius XII maintained that the principle of totality could not justify transplants because the organ was taken from one person not for the individual's good but for the good of another. However, on the basis of charity or an extended version of totality, Catholic teaching today justifies organ transplants. An individual may give an organ (usually one of a pair of organs) to another provided that the individual's health and bodily integrity are not seriously or disproportionately jeopardized. The highly publicized heart transplants create different types of problems. The donor must be dead before the heart is taken. The recipient must know precisely and exactly what the chances of success are. Also there is the broader societal question of perhaps devoting an inordinate amount of money and talent to such extraordinary operations while neglecting ordinary medical care for the total population.

Medical experimentation done for the good of the species or the good of another also raises some problems, because again the individual is subject to danger not for personal good but for the good of others. There must be a proper proportion between the good to be achieved and the risk for the individual whose bodily integrity cannot be seriously jeopardized. Above all, the individual must be in a position to freely consent to the experimentation (i.e., have the necessary knowledge and freedom). Some would argue that children and those who cannot consent on their own should never be used in experimentation. I would maintain that children can be used in experimentation if their parents consent and if the risk involved for them is slight. Problems can more readily arise with prisoners and people who are institutionalized, since their ability to consent freely is severely diminished. Society must be vigilant so that the weak and the poor are not taken advantage of in the name of scientific discovery and advancement.

Another contemporary problem in medical ethics concerns the allocation of scarce medical resources. If there are five people who need a certain piece of lifesaving equipment and there are only three pieces of equipment available, who should receive the lifesaving treatment? The first judgment is medical—only those who can truly profit from it. But there still might not be enough equipment for all the people who need it. In this type of situation I uphold the equal dignity of all and acknowledge the great difficulty in most cases of deciding which life is more important. The system of first come first served is probably the most just procedure in ordinary circumstances.

GENETICS AND THE FUTURE OF HUMANITY

In the last few years new questions have arisen with the advent of new knowledge and technology in the area of genetics and the human future. Human beings today have more power and knowledge to make a better future for the whole human race, but we can also never forget our limitations and the sinful abuse to which power can be put.

There are three generic types of questions raised by such advances. First, genetic engineering or gene surgery tries to change the genetic makeup of the individual which causes certain diseases or conditions. Such procedures should be guided by the medical ethics governing all procedures for the good of the individual and based on the proportionate good to be obtained. The second type of question can be described as euphenics, in which the genotype is not treated but rather the phenotype, as in the case of eyeglasses or insulin for diabetes. Here again, since the treatments are employed primarily for the good of the individual concerned, the regular moral principles for medical ethics apply.

The third generic question is called eugenics, or good breeding, based on a recombination of genes to bring about a better human species in the future. Eugenics is either negative (to eliminate bad genes from the human gene pool) or positive (to create a better type of human being). It also provides opportunities for couples to have children who are not now able to have children through the ordinary process of procreation. There are three possible forms that eugenics can take—artificial insemination with sperm that have been stored in sperm banks, in vitro fertilization and subsequent implantation of the fertilized ovum in the womb, and cloning which is the process whereby a genetic twin is produced from just one "parent"—this latter process has been referred to in popular parlance as the xeroxing of people.

Much of the discussion is futuristic at the present time because only artificial insemination with sperm is now possible and feasible, although attempts are being made (possibly even successes) to bring about fertilization in a test tube and then implantation of the fertilized ovum in the womb of a woman. Scientists continue to debate the possibility and feasibility of cloning human beings. At the present time I believe we should say "no" to positive eugenics even if it were possible, because there are too many unanswered questions at the moment. Even from a genetic viewpoint, positive eugenics might rule out the benefits of hybrid vigor as exemplified in the problem of inbreeding through marriages of close relatives. In addition, because something is possible genetically does not mean it should be done humanly. Think of all the psychological problems for the individuals involved if there were 10,000 identical twins of Einstein. What is possible from the genetic viewpoint cannot always be identified with the ultimate human good, but rather all other considerations must also be taken into account. Even more importantly, who would direct the genetic future of the human race and choose the types to be reproduced? If our genetic planners are no better than our foreign policy planners, then there is need for great caution. Here too there is always the danger of thinking that science and technology will be able to solve some very basic human problems which the Christian ultimately believes lie at a level deeper than science or technology can ever touch.

What about such measures being used to provide individual couples with the possibility of having children if they are not able to have any children or to have healthy children through the normal process? In accord with the teaching proposed by Pope Pius XII, some would argue that the natural law demands that conception take place through the act of sexual intercourse by which male semen is deposited in the vas of the female. Although there are important aspects connected with this natural process, I do not believe that procreation must always take place only in this way. In addition, some would maintain that the child must always be the fruit of the love and the bodies of the parents so that the sperm must come from the husband and the ovum from the wife. Here I affirm that this is the ideal way, and there are many important values connected with it, but I cannot make an absolute out of this. I could see in some circumstances for some couples that it would not be a necessity. However, there are

other significant ethical questions which must be resolved in
the case of in vitro fertilization with implantation and cloning. What about mishaps? One cannot merely discard human
beings if the experiment does not work out. Also what about
possible harm to the individual which will only show up later
in life? Before even such experiments are morally justified,
the risk of mishaps or future harm to the individual must be
no greater than such risks in the ordinary process of procreation. Again, society has to be aware of the danger of tram-
meling on the rights of individuals in the name of medical
science and the advancement of the human race as a whole.

PEACE AND WAR

The Christian vision of the world recognizes the great need
and importance of peace for the good of all human beings.
But again the question arises if there are any other values or
reasons which might justify the use of force and war. Christian teaching in the course of history has proposed three
different approaches to this very vexing question.

The first approach can be described as witness pacifism,
and is best illustrated by the pacifism of some of the Protestant sects such as the Mennonites. Pacifism is a requirement
of the Christian gospel, and our lives must always bear
witness to that gospel. Such an approach does not rest on the
assumption that pacifism will always be an effective means of
achieving justice here and now or that it will be accepted by
all human beings. In fact, such sects usually separate themselves from the world because life in the world will sooner or
later involve compromises with the biblical ethic in the form
of violence or some other type of accommodation. In my
opinion, Christian witness pacifism is not the only possible
approach for the Christian. Such an approach absolutizes
peace at the expense of other values such as justice. Some-

times force can be used in the service of justice in this world. Individual Christians, however, can feel a personal vocation to bear witness to this important aspect of the Christian message and embrace pacifism just as others are called to embrace poverty. I do not think that the total Church can adopt such an absolutist approach even though the Christian Church must always strive for peace and justice.

The second approach can aptly be described as the use of nonviolence as an effective means of social change and has been associated with Gandhi, Martin Luther King and the Berrigans. The basic roots of this teaching are three: the gospel calls for nonviolence; nonviolence can be a very effective way to overcome injustice as illustrated in the success of both Martin Luther King and Gandhi; violence always escalates and tends to become counterproductive. Again, there are many important values in such an approach, and one can appreciate the fact that some Christians feel called to adopt this policy; but in the last analysis I cannot accept it. First of all, effective nonviolence cannot be called *the* Christian or gospel approach as opposed to all other approaches. In fact, it must be recognized that nonviolence in this case is proposed as an effective form of resistance. The Sermon on the Mount seems to call for nonresistance, not just for nonviolence. For conceptual clarity the primary distinction exists not between violence and nonviolence but between nonresistance and resistance. Both violence and nonviolence are types of resistance, so that the difference between them, while great, is not as generic or great as one might at first think.

Such an approach, since it claims to be effective, tends to give way to the use of force if force is the only effective way of preventing injustice. This was true historically in the cases of Dietrich Bonhoeffer and Reinhold Niebuhr. Both came to the conclusion that only force and violence would be effective in preventing the injustices wrought by Hitler. Such a theory rightly points out all the problems and dangers connected with violence and killing, but reluctantly the Christian, because of the need of justice, can on occasion justify the use of violence.

The third approach which acknowledges that at times force may be used in the cause of justice has been accepted by the Roman Catholic Church and most other Christian Churches and developed in the theory of just war. The conditions for a just war call for justice in going to war (*ius ad bellum*) and justice in the waging of war (*ius in bello*). Justice in going to war involves the following conditions: a proper intention; declaration of war by legitimate authority; a just cause; war is a last resort when all other means have been exhausted. In the light of the growing escalation of war, the teaching of the recent popes especially Pope Pius XII has restricted the just cause to defense against unjust aggression. Recognizing the dangers and problems connected with violence and killing, this theory insists that war is the *ultima ratio,* and other means for a peaceful settlement must first be exhausted. Here too one must acknowledge the importance of prudence in applying this and the other criteria.

Justice in war calls attention to two principles. The principle of proportionality maintains that war is justified only if the good to be attained outweighs the evil which will accompany it. The Catholic tradition has also insisted on the principle of discrimination, although a few theologians today question the absolute force of this principle. According to the principle of discrimination force can only be employed against the bearers of force. Noncombatants are immune from direct attack, but some noncombatants unfortunately may be killed indirectly if their killing is proportionate to the good to be attained. For example, one can drop a bomb on a military installation even though some noncombatants who are working on the premises in different capacities will also be killed. Their killing is only indirect because the bomb is directly targeted on the military installation and not on a nonmilitary target. However, the saturation bombing of European cities by the Allies during World War II and the dropping of atomic bombs on population centers in Japan constitute severe violations of the principle of discrimination. To their great credit some American Catholic theologians such as Francis Connell, John Ford and Paul Hanly Furfey spoke out during World War II to condemn such bombings.

In the light of the principle of discrimination together with the principle of proportionality, I conclude that the use of large nuclear weapons is always morally wrong. The problem we are facing today is that of possessing and threatening to use weapons which we have no moral right to use. At the very least Christians should strive to do away with our dependence on the deterrent value of possessing such weapons and ultimately aim to destroy the weapons themselves.

There are dangers in accepting the just war theory, starting with the risk of self-deception, since as human beings we are always tempted to justify the wars in which our country is engaged. There is also a great danger of escalation toward nuclear weapons and the fear that violence will get out of hand. Often the possibility of war tempts the strong and powerful nations to make force more important than justice. But on the other hand, the just war as Augustine pointed out is not against the Christian notion of love. In this imperfect and sinful world in which we live one is often confronted with more than one neighbor in need. If a neighbor is being attacked by another, love can urge that one use force to save the neighbor who is being attacked. I accept the theory of just war but emphasize the fact that it is a last resort and involves many possible pitfalls.

Whoever accepts the just war theory must also accept the justified revolution and tyrannicide. The justification and the conditions for the justified revolution parallel those of the just war. The justified revolution avoids two of the problems associated with just war—the chances of escalation to nuclear weapons are not present because revolutionaries usually do not possess such weapons and the danger that the force will be used by the strong and powerful to oppress the weak and powerless is not present because the revolutionaries are themselves the ones who are usually weak and oppressed by others. The justified revolution like the just war can readily go against the principle of discrimination which tries to limit the extent of violence. Violence or force can only be used against the bearers of force. Thus, putting a bomb in the London Tower or hijacking an international airliner filled with innocent passengers are immoral means. The question arises: who are the bearers of force? Does every single person participating in and enjoying the fruits of an unjust society become a bearer of force against the oppressed? In my judgment this might be true in some cases to a certain extent, but not to the extent that I could justify killing people who are not actual bearers of force. Revolutionaries or Freedom Fighters might be justified in using violence against the property of such people who are clearly leaders in the process of oppression.

The Christian with some reluctance recognizes the need that at times violence, killing and force might be needed in the cause of justice. Unfortunately, both in the question of war and in the question of revolution or liberation there is a constant temptation to romanticize and glorify violence. Violence must always be a last resort because it entails killing and suffering and should never be glorified. The whole Christian message calls upon all of us to strive with every possible means to achieve peace and justice in our society.

6

The Principle of Double Effect

The principle of the double effect has been traditionally associated with the teaching of the manuals of Roman Catholic moral theology, but in the last few years many Catholic theologians, myself included, have called into question the concept of double effect as a way of solving conflict situations. Dissatisfaction and discussion of a particular teaching should encourage theologians to examine the teaching in greater depth both in its historical origins and in its contemporary discussions. This essay will attempt to call attention to some aspects involved in the discussion of the meaning of direct and indirect and thus try to advance the contemporary discussion.

The principle of the double effect with its distinction between the direct and the indirect voluntary has been employed by the manuals of theology to solve conflict situations in which an action will entail some evil. The manuals of theology generally propose the following four conditions under which one can be justified in causing evil in conjunction with good: 1) The action itself is good or indifferent. 2) The good effect and not the evil effect is the one sincerely intended by the agent. 3) The good effect is not produced by means of the evil effect. If the evil effect is not at least equally immediate causally with the good effect, then it becomes a means to the good effect and intended as such. 4)

There is a proportionate reason for permitting the foreseen evil effect to occur.

If these conditions are fulfilled, the evil is said to be only indirect and justified on the basis of proportionate reason. The contemporary discussion has focused especially on the third condition—the evil is directly intended and therefore the act is wrong if the evil aspect in the order of physical causality is the means through which the good effect is attained. The discussion of the concept of direct and indirect is intimately connected with the proper description and evaluation of human acts. A systematic discussion of either the human act or the full principle of double effect lies beyond the scope of this study which is interested primarily in evaluating and discussing some of the elements which have surfaced in the contemporary debate.

I. THE TEACHING OF THE MANUALS AND THOMAS AQUINAS

Is the manualistic teaching on the principle of double effect found in Thomas Aquinas? Some of the manuals seem to indicate that the teaching is found in Aquinas' discussion of the right to kill in self-defense in the *Summa Theologiae,* II-II, q. 64, a. 7.[1] Some older theologians such as Lessius, Soto, and Vasquez maintained that Thomas did not in this place enunciate the principle of double effect.[2] In a 1937 dissertation, Vicente Alonso concluded that Thomas did not

---

1. Joseph Mangan maintains that this was the commonly held position before 1937. See Joseph T. Mangan, S.J., "An Historical Analysis of the Principle of Double Effect," *Theological Studies,* X (1949), 45.

2. Leonardus Lessius, S.J., *De Justitia et Jure* (Mediolani, 1613), 1.2, c.9, dub. 8, n. 53; Dominicus de Soto, O.P., *De Justitia et Jure* (Salmanticae, 1556); 1.5, q. 1, a.8; Gabriel Vazquez, S.J., *Opuscula Moralia* (Lugduni, 1620), "De Restitutione," c.2, par. 1, dub. IV.

affirm here the principle of the double effect, and many contemporary Catholic theologians have agreed with this interpretation.[3] J. Ghoos in a long article also tried to prove that the later scholastic theologians of the sixteenth and seventeenth centuries did not develop this principle in the light of Thomas' teaching.[4] Joseph Mangan, however, in *Theological Studies* in 1949, argued that the four conditions of the principle of double effect are found in Aquinas and that later scholastic theologians explicitly developed their theories on the basis of Thomas' teaching.[5]

Mangan in his article offers some rebuttal to Alonso's contention that Thomas employs the Latin word *intendere* to refer only to the end and not to the means. Alonso interprets Aquinas as maintaining that the defender cannot intend the death of the agressor as the end of his action but he can intend the death as a means to his own defense. Mangan argues that Thomas does not allow the defender to intend the death of the aggressor either as an end or as a means.[6] Louis Janssens, however, believes that Mangan has somewhat misinterpreted Thomas on the notion of *intendere*.[7] Mangan also asserts that the third condition for the principle of the double effect; namely, that the good effect must be equally immediate as the evil effect, is also found in Thomas' discussion of self-defense. The only specific evidence produced by Mangan is his translation of Aquinas; namely, "it is therefore wrong for a man to kill another as a means to defend himself."[8]

3. Vicente M. Alonso, *El principio del doble efecto en los comentadores de Santo Tomás de Aquino* (Rome: Gregorian University Press, 1937).

4. J. Ghoos, "L'acte à double effet: Étude de théologie positive," *Ephemerides Theologicae Lovanienses*, XXVII (1951), 30–52.

5. Mangan, *Theological Studies*, X (1949), 41–61.

6. *Ibid.*, pp. 45–49.

7. Louis Janssens, "Ontic Evil and Moral Evil," *Louvain Studies*, IV (1972), 139–140.

8. Mangan, *Theological Studies*, X (1949), 48–50.

It is somewhat difficult to see how such a translation could prove that in the order of physical causality the killing of the aggressor cannot be a means to defend one's life. It is even more difficult to prove that Thomas is talking about the third condition, in the light of Thomas' original wording: *illicitum est quod homo intendat occidere hominem ut seipsum defendat.* Thus, in my judgment Mangan does not prove that the accepted notion of double effect, especially with its third condition, is found in Aquinas.

The purpose of the following discussion is not to delve more deeply into the question of the historical origins of the principle of double effect but to illustrate the problems created for a proper understanding of Aquinas because of the tendency of theologians to interpret him in such a way as to bolster a particular position they seek to defend. There is a constant danger of interpreting texts of Thomas or other authoritative figures so as to support one's own position on a particular point. Such interpretations are not necessarily wrong, but the investigator must be alert to the danger that factors other than an objective reading of the texts and historical contexts might be influencing the interpretation. Three concrete illustrations on the relationship of II–II, q. 64, a. 7 to the principle of double effect will make the point.

T. Lincoln Bouscaren in *Ethics of Ectopic Operations,* the revised book form of his famous doctoral dissertation, argues for the liceity of the removal of an ectopic pregnancy. In such a case the removal of the fetus is indirect because one removes a tube which is pathological. The tube, either because it has ruptured or because it will rupture in the future, is the source of the problem for the mother. The formal object of the intention and the immediate material object of the action is the removal of the pathological tube which happens to contain a fetus. The removal of the fetus is neither directly intended nor directly done.[9]

9. T. Lincoln Bouscaren, S.J., *Ethics of Ectopic Operations,* (2nd rev. ed.; Milwaukee: Bruce Publishing Co., 1944), pp. 147–155.

Bouscaren begins by citing the historical development of the question of craniotomy with special emphasis on the responses of the Holy Office at the end of the nineteenth century condemning the opinion that craniotomy or direct abortion of the fetus is ever justified.[10] The book then develops the fundamental principles involved in the question of abortion in conflict situations, highlighting Aquinas' teaching as proposed in II–II, q. 64, a. 7. Bouscaren here interprets Thomas as proposing the four conditions for the principle of double effect and asserts that such an interpretation is not only obvious and necessary but also the commonly accepted interpretation of Catholic theologians.[11]

One false solution proposed for the case of ectopic pregnancy was that the fetus in this case could be an unjust aggressor and be directly expelled. Bouscaren invoked an 1898 ruling of the Holy Office against such an argument.[12] "Yet, considering merely the intrinsic reasons pro and con, one must admit that, as long as that principle is granted which allows the direct killing of a materially unjust aggressor on private authority, it will be very difficult to take the ectopic fetus outside the operation of that principle."[13] Bouscaren thus openly expresses his anxieties. He definitely wants to prohibit any direct abortion, but he sees difficulty in constructing a convincing intrinsic argument if one accepts that a materially unjust aggressor may be directly killed. His interpretation, that even in II–II, q. 64, a. 7, Aquinas maintains that the killing cannot be direct in the sense that is understood today, thus supplies him with the convincing rational refutation of those who would allow the direct abortion of an ectopic fetus.

Whereas Bouscaren interprets Aquinas in his passage on

10. *Ibid.*, pp. 3–16.
11. *Ibid.*, pp. 31–34. Note that Bouscaren originally wrote this before Alonso's interpretation was published.
12. *Ibid.*, pp. 48–52.
13. *Ibid.*, p. 50.

killing in self-defense as proposing the four conditions of the double effect and maintaining that even the killing of a materially unjust aggressor cannot be directly intended or directly done, John C. Ford argues that Aquinas in the celebrated passage under consideration does not propose a modern understanding of the double effect and does allow direct killing of the unjust aggressor.

Father Ford's consideration of this question comes in the context of a courageous article written in 1944 which condemned obliteration bombing which the Allies were then doing in the course of World War II. According to the principle of the double effect and its application to the waging of war, one can never directly attack noncombatants. Ford argues strenuously against any attempt to say that the bomber can let his bombs drop on the city but withdraw his intention so that he is not intending to hit or kill the noncombatants existing in the city. The bomber, according to the principle of the double effect, can neither directly intend nor directly do the killing of noncombatants.[14]

Ford realizes that some could argue against his opinion by appealing to the teaching of Thomas Aquinas that in killing an unjust aggressor you permit his death to save your own life. Ford denies a parallel between the two cases because Thomas Aquinas in discussing the killing of an unjust aggressor does not elaborate the principles of the double effect as they are known and formulated in contemporary theology. Ford's thesis rests on the presupposition that Thomas maintained the defender directly intends and directly kills the unjust aggressor as a means of self-defense but not as an end. In this case the killing of the aggressor is the means by which the defender saves himself, which would be against the conditions of the double effect. Ford does not want to admit that

---

14. John C. Ford, S.J., "The Morality of Obliteration Bombing," *Theological Studies*, V (1944), 261–309.

Thomas says the aggressor is killed only indirectly, because then other people could argue that in the case of dropping bombs indiscriminately on cities the killing of noncombatants is indirect if one merely removes his intention from killing noncombatants.[15]

A third opinion about Thomas' teaching in II–II, q. 64, a. 7 has been proposed by Paul Ramsey. The Protestant theologian sees in Thomas' consideration of killing an unjust aggressor an early formulation of the principle of the double effect. Later development of the principle in at least one school of Catholic theology added the stipulation that, in addition to the good as the only proper object of one's formal intention, the good itself had to be the direct material object of the physical act so that the good could not be produced through the bad effect as a means. Once this later stipulation was added to the principle of double effect (neither directly done nor directly willed), then it seemed better not to apply the principle of double effect to the case of killing the unjust aggressor but only to the case of killing the innocent.[16]

Ramsey proposes a most intriguing reason for his position—a reason which is a central theme developed in his theory on war. The Protestant theologian shows a great familiarity with Catholic teaching on double effect and the specific instance of not directly killing noncombatants. However, he wants to assert that the origin of this principle is not derived from natural law or justice as Roman Catholic theology claims but from Christian love and charity. Ramsey sees love as the primary and controlling concept in Christian ethics. In a development in his own thinking in the late 1950's and early 1960's, he acknowledged there also can be a place for natural justice in Christian ethics, but that love

15. *Ibid.*, pp. 289–290.
16. Paul Ramsey, *War and the Christian Conscience* (Durham, North Carolina: Duke University Press, 1961), pp. 34–59.

always aims to transform justice.[17] In the matter of war
Ramsey holds that for Christian ethics, it is love that both
justifies the Christian's participation in war and also places
limits on what can be done in war. The principle that noncombatants cannot be directly killed arose first from Christian love and not from natural justice.[18]

There has been a development in theology in the matter of
killing an unjust aggressor which indicates a shift from a
theological ethic based on love to one based on natural
justice. Augustine both justified and limited war on the basis
of Christian love for the neighbor in need. Augustine, however, condemns the Christian who avails oneself of the civil
law which allows one to kill an aggressor in order to defend
oneself. No disciple of Christ can love life or property more
than he loves God and his neighbor. Love does not allow the
Christian to take a neighbor's life in order to save one's own.
The primary concern of Christian love remains the neighbor
and the neighbor's needs.[19]

The teaching espoused by many Roman Catholics today
approaches the question of killing an unjust aggressor from
the viewpoint of natural law justice and not from Christian
charity. The unjust aggressor by injustice has lost the right to
life and thus the defender may directly kill the attacker both
in the intentional and in the physical orders. However, from
the viewpoint of Christian love the unjust aggressor does not
lose the right to life because Christian love surrounds the
weak, the poor, and the unjust with immunity. Love does not
allow us to save ourselves by killing our neighbor even if the
neighbor has been unjust.[20]

17. Paul Ramsey, *Nine Modern Moralists* (Englewood Cliffs, New Jersey: Prentice-Hall, 1962), especially the Introduction.
18. *War and the Christian Conscience*, pp. xv–xxiv; 3–59; Paul Ramsey, *The
Just War* (New York: Charles Scribner's Sons, 1968), pp. 141–278.
19. *War and the Christian Conscience*, pp. 15–39.
20. *Ibid.*, pp. 46–59, especially p. 54.

Ramsey interprets Thomas as a midway point in the development toward the generally accepted contemporary Catholic teaching. Thomas maintains that one cannot intend the death of the unjust aggressor either as an end or as a means, but he does not mention the question of directness in the physical order which was only developed later. According to Thomas, one can kill an unjust aggressor in self-defense but one can never intend to kill the aggressor either as an end or as a means. The proper interpretation of this thomistic text for Ramsey does not depend ultimately on a thorough study of the words used by Thomas but must be seen in the light of the historical development about the possibility of a Christian killing an unjust aggressor in self-defense.[21]

Augustine rejected such a killing in self-defense because the Christian would then love one's own life and property more than God and neighbor. The canonists before Aquinas were already introducing natural law arguments and Aquinas himself gave them a much greater role than Augustine. Unlike Augustine, Thomas does allow killing in self-defense, but like Augustine he continues to see some difficulty with this killing and thus insists that the defender can never intend to kill the attacker either as an end or as a means. "Profoundly at work in his line of reasoning is what justice transformed by love requires to be extended even to him who wrongfully attacks. This is what produced the original statement of the

---

21. *Ibid.*, pp. 56ff. In proposing that the defender may not intend the death of the aggressor either as a means or as an end, Ramsey is disagreeing with the interpretation proposed by Alonso. Although Ramsey claims that his interpretation is not based on the meaning of the words used in the text, he earlier explicitly stated that Thomas' meaning is plain from his words that "it is, therefore, wrong for a man to intend to kill another as a means to defend himself" (p. 51). However, in this case Ramsey is using Mangan's translation of Aquinas which, as already mentioned, is not accurate. Interestingly, when Ramsey first quotes the entire passage from Aquinas he does not employ this translation but rather translates the passage as "it is not lawful for a man to intend killing a man in self-defense" (p. 40).

so-called rule of double effect. This principle was born precisely out of an attempt to put into practice a not so equal, Christian regard for the unjust man."[22]

Ramsey proposes a fascinating explanation of Thomas' teaching on killing an aggressor in self-defense. In my estimation, however, Ramsey's ingenious interpretation is not accurate. Footnote twenty-one shows his interpretation is based at least partially on an inaccurate translation. Likewise, Thomas could very well arrive at this teaching solely on the basis of natural law or natural justice reasoning without appealing to Christian love. Ramsey also mistakenly thinks that the attacker's guilt means that the aggressor loses the right to life in the generally accepted interpretation of the double effect by Catholics, but this is not the case because a materially unjust aggressor can also be killed. I agree with Ramsey that Thomas in this passage does not employ the four conditions for the double effect as they are found in manuals of Catholic moral theology. The example of Ramsey, as well as the illustrations of Bouscaren and Ford, has been mentioned merely to indicate the danger of "inegesis" in any interpretation of the passage in Thomas on killing in self-defense. Ramsey's more recent writings on the principle of the double effect will be discussed in Chapter 8.

II. ORIGIN OF CONFLICT SITUATIONS

The principle of double effect arose in Catholic theology as one way to handle conflict situations. Our actions at times will involve some evil so that ethicians attempt to find a way to determine how and if actions can be justified when some evil is produced. This present section of the paper will try to

22. *War and the Christian Conscience*, pp. 43, 44.

examine some of the explanations proposed for the origin of the fact that our actions will very often involve some evil.

Peter Knauer, who was one of the first to question the manualistic teaching on double effect, proposes a newer theory based on the distinction between physical and moral evil. Knauer's new principle is: moral evil consists in the permission or causing of physical evil without a commensurate, or proportionate, justifying reason. In this way Knauer attempts to overcome the physicalism attached to Catholic moral teaching in general and especially to the third condition of the principle of double effect that the evil effect cannot be the immediate material object of the physical act.[23]

Louis Janssens has developed the concept of ontic evil as distinguished from moral evil to show the origin of the existence of some evil aspects in all our actions. Ontic evil is always present in our concrete actions for it essentially arises from the consequences of our own limitations. Each concrete act implicates evil because we are temporal and spatial human beings, live together with others in the same material world, and are involved and act in a common sinful situation.[24] Other Catholic theologians such as Schüller and Fuchs call upon the same basic distinction and indicate that very often our actions will involve nonmoral (Schüller) or premoral (Fuchs) evil.[25]

23. Peter Knauer, S.J., "La détermination du bien et du mal moral par le principe du double effet," *Nouvelle Revue Théologique*, LXXXVII (1965), 356–376; Knauer, "Das rechtverstandene Prinzip von der Doppelwirkung als Grundnorm jeder Gewissensentscheidung," *Theologie und Glaube*, LVII (1967), 107–133. This article which is a revised version of the original has been translated into English as "The Hermeneutic Function of the Principle of the Double Effect," *Natural Law Forum*, XII (1967), 132–162.

24. Janssens, *Louvain Studies*, IV (1972), 134.

25. Bruno Schüller, S.J., "Zur Problematik allgemein verbindlicher ethischer Grundsätze," *Theologie und Philosophie*, XLV (1970), 1–23; Schüller, "Typen ethischer Argumentation in der katholischen Moraltheologie," *Theologie und*

I agree with Janssens, Schüller and Fuchs in avoiding the term physical evil as the type of evil distinguished from moral evil. One of the problems with Roman Catholic natural law theory in the past has been the tendency to equate the moral act with the physical structure of the act. By retaining the word physical as that evil distinguished from moral evil, one employs a word which can be associated with just one aspect of premoral or ontic evil. There is thus a danger of attributing too much importance to the physical aspect of reality. The moral judgment is the ultimate human judgment which must take into account all particular aspects of a given question. Nothing is perfect from every human perspective so that the physical aspect, like the psychological, the sociological, the pedagogical, and the aesthetic, can never be identified with the ultimate moral judgment, even though at times the moral judgment will be in accord with one or more of these particular aspects including the physical.

The inaccuracy in describing the evil involved as physical evil is illustrated in Knauer's treatment of contraception.[26] Although I totally agree with his conclusion that artificial contraception often can be and is a good, still I have difficulty with his reasoning. One can readily agree with the contention that the problem in past Catholic teaching arises from identifying the moral with the physical aspects of the act. Knauer admits that it is a physical evil for a marital act to lose its procreative power, but this only becomes a moral wrong if it is done without a commensurate reason. Such an analysis, in my judgment, seems to give too much attention to the physical, for there are many other aspects of the marital act that must be considered. To have more children

Philosophie, XLV (1970), 526–550. Joseph Fuchs, "The Absoluteness of Moral Terms," *Gregorianum,* LII (1971), 415–458.

26. Knauer, *The Natural Law Forum,* XII (1967), 158. Also Knauer, "Uberlegungen zur moraltheologischen Prinzipienlehre der Enzyklika 'Humanae Vitae,' " *Theologie und Philosophie,* XLV (1970), 60–74.

than one can properly educate in the true sense of the term is
a premoral evil. For a couple to be unnecessarily deprived of
sexual relationships for a long period of time can properly be
called a premoral evil. In other words there are many values
and aspects that must be considered in addition to the
physical. By speaking only about physical evil, Knauer seems
to give a greater normative importance to the physical than it
deserves, for it is only one particular aspect of the total
picture. Even the term ontic evil, although more accurate
than physical, has certain metaphysical presuppositions
which would not be acceptable to all. Thus the term premoral evil as distinguished from moral evil seems to me to be
more accurate.

In Janssens' very perceptive analysis, ontic evil essentially
arises as a natural consequence of our human limitations.
Although Janssens makes this statement and spends most of
his time discussing the reality of human limitation as a source
of conflict situations, he does add one brief paragraph about
the sinfulness of the situation as another contributing factor.[27] In my judgment any accurate assessment of the reason
for conflict situations must acknowledge the two generic
sources of such situations—human limitation and sinfulness.
Roman Catholic theology in its general structure has not
given enough importance to the reality of sinfulness—which is
one reason why it has had difficulty in adequately approach-
ing the problem of conflict situations and also some of the
questions proposed in the debate about situation ethics.

Sinfulness for the Christian always remains present in our
human existence. I am not understanding sinfulness in this
case as the individual sinful acts of a person or even the
sinfulness of the person placing the act but rather the cosmic
and interpersonal aspects of sinfulness which become incarnate in the world in which we live. Sometimes the presence

---

27. Janssens, *Louvain Studies,* IV (1972), 138.

of sin forces us to act in a way which would not occur if there were no sin incarnated in the structures of human existence.

To deal with some conflict situations I have proposed a theory of compromise which is based on the recognition of the reality of sin in all its ramifications. Sin is present in life and society, and the Christian is called upon to overcome sin; but sin will not be fully overcome until the end of time. One could interpret the traditional Catholic teaching that something could be wrong in the objective order but not subjectively sinful as a recognition of the fact that human limitation and even human sinfulness can somehow or other affect the subjective realm but not the objective realm. The theory of compromise recognizes that sin affects the objective order as well as the subjective order. However, compromise also recognizes that the Christian is called to attempt to overcome the reality of sin as well as acknowledging that sin will never be completely overcome this side of the eschaton. Meanwhile, the presence of sin occasionally forces us to do things which under ordinary circumstances we would not do. The word compromise tries to indicate the tension involved in recognizing even in the objective order the fact that sin is present and the Christian tries to overcome it, but at times the Christian will not be able to overcome sin completely.

With its recognition of the presence of sin such an approach does have affinity with some Protestant approaches to conflict situations, but there are important differences. The theory of compromise gives more importance to the reality of sin bringing about the conflict situations than the manualistic moral theology did, but it also has a less radical view of sin than some Protestant approaches. Sin does not do away with all ethical distinctions and differences based on creation and redemption. In the darkness of night all cats are not gray. From one aspect, in the objective order the act is good because in the presence of sin there is nothing else that can be done. However, from another aspect one recognizes that the act should not be done if there were no sinful situation present.[28]

Some might raise the objection that one cannot say that the objective rightness of an act might depend on the presence of sin. However, I believe that this contention has already been made by Aquinas himself. Recall the difference in the teaching on private property proposed by Thomas Aquinas and by the recent popes. Whereas the popes of the nineteenth and twentieth centuries base their teaching on the dignity of the person and the need to protect that dignity,[29] Aquinas based his teaching on the fall of man or human sinfulness. Private property for Thomas is primarily justified because of the fall of man.[30] This does not mean that the presence of sin can justify anything or that there are no limits on the theory of compromise, but it does indicate that even in Aquinas there was this recognition of the presence of sin which might justify certain actions.

Keeping in mind my understanding of the two origins of conflict situations and the need for a theory of compromise based on the presence of human sinfulness, one can compare this approach to a particular problem with the approach taken by Knauer. In a final footnote in an English translation to one of his articles he endeavors to answer a question proposed by the editor about a woman who commits adultery in order that her children may be removed from a

28. For a more complete development of the theory of compromise, its application to different cases including homosexuality and its differences from some Protestant approaches, see my *A New Look at Christian Morality* (Notre Dame, Indiana: Fides Publishers, 1968), pp. 169–173; *Catholic Moral Theology in Dialogue* (Notre Dame, Indiana: Fides Publishers, 1972), pp. 184–219.

29. E.g., Pope Leo XIII, *Rerum Novarum,* n. 5–16, *Acta Sanctae Sedis,* XXIII (1890–91), 642–648; Pope Pius XI, *Quadragesimo Anno,* n. 44–52, *Acta Apostolicae Sedis,* XXIII (1931), 191–194; Pope John XXIII, *Mater et Magistra,* n. 104–121, *Acta Apostolicae Sedis,* LIII (1961), 426–431.

30. *Summa Theologiae,* II–II, q. 66, a.2.

concentration camp.[31] This case is similar to the now famous case of Mrs. Bergmeier proposed originally by Joseph Fletcher. Mrs. Bergmeier had sexual relations with a willing guard to become pregnant, since women who were pregnant were released from the concentration camp and allowed to return home.[32] Knauer denies the justification of such actions because in the end life or freedom have no value if one is forced in principle to give up all human rights and be exposed to every extortion.[33]

I disagree with Knauer's practical solution and see here the elements of a solution based on a theory of compromise. Truly this is a sinful situation brought about by the evils of war and concentration camps so that the woman is forced to use some means to be reconciled with her family or to have her children freed which obviously she would not use under ordinary circumstances. In my judgment it is unreal to deny that at times the presence of sin exercises what might be called a form of extortion and forces us to do things which under ordinary circumstances we would not want to do. Knauer's negative solution to this case fits in with his failure to recognize the presence of sin as one of the sources of conflict situations in human existence.

From my perspective it is important to remember that there are two ultimate sources of the origin of conflict situations—human limitation and human sinfulness. The theory of compromise corresponds to the origin of conflict situations based on the presence of sin in the world. For this reason, compromise can never be an adequate explanation of all the conflict situations which arise. One must also develop philosophical approaches which come to grips with the problems of finitude.

31. Knauer, *The Natural Law Forum,* XII (1967), 162, n. 24.
32. Joseph Fletcher, *Situation Ethics: The New Morality* (Philadelphia: Westminster Press, 1966), pp. 164, 165.
33. Knauer, *Natural Law Forum,* XII (1967), 162, n. 24.

In the past Catholic theology has not given enough importance to the reality of human sinfulness as causing conflict situations, but one contemporary author does give so much importance to this aspect that he apparently does not attribute enough importance to the aspect of human limitation as a source of conflict situations. Nicholas Crotty objects to the solution of conflict situations based on a distinction between physical and moral evil, for these situations involve a true lack of moral values. He emphasizes that sinfulness is at the root of conflict situations although he mentions in passing that some conflict situations may seem more attributable to the human condition as such and human creatureliness. Crotty maintains that in conflict situations our choices always involve moral evil.[34]

I would rather reserve the word moral evil for the ultimate description of the act with its emphasis on the intention of the person who is placing the act. The evil attributable to our situation as finite and limited creatures is truly a premoral or nonmoral evil. The evil resulting from sin is connected with moral evil, and the presence of sin in the situation is due to moral evil; but it is significantly different from the moral evil, denoting the agent's act with its emphasis on intentionality. Thus I do agree with Crotty in asserting that we are dealing with more than just physical evil brought about by human finitude, but unfortunately he does not give enough importance to human limitation.

A third source of conflict situations stems from the fact that the fullness of the eschaton is not yet here. As explained in Chapter 3 this source of tension and even conflict applies especially to areas of biblical and Christian morality such as divorce and points to the fullness of the eschaton which is never totally present in this world. These three sources of the

---

34. Nicholas Crotty, "Conscience and Conflict," *Theological Studies,* XXXII (1971), 208–232.

origin of conflict situations may even overlap in explaining a particular conflict, but a Christian ethical theory which neglects any one of these sources cannot approach the problem of conflict situations.

III. DANGERS OF ALL INCLUSIVE EXPLANATIONS

This section will discuss many different questions which have arisen in the debate about the principle of the double effect. The unifying thread in the following considerations stems from a common defect of an attempted all inclusive approach or an oversimplification which does not explain all the diverse questions that need to be properly explained. The danger of oversimplification or too inclusive an approach remains a constant source of difficulty in many academic questions. The Catholic theologian by his own tradition tends to strive for a synthetic approach insofar as this is possible, but at times one cannot achieve such a synthesis.

Difficulties with the present applications of the principle. Both the historical origin of the principle of the double effect as well as the diverse number of content questions it tries to solve indicate there can be a problem of too inclusive an approach in this particular matter. Historically, it is admitted that the principle was gradually applied to cover a number of different questions and did not arise in a systematic way. The principle of double effect has been applied to questions of conflict situations involving human life—killing, self-defense, abortion, war, euthanasia, suicide, as well as for situations of contraception, sterilization, cooperation in actions of others, and scandal. These situations are so diverse and involve so many different elements that one wonders if it is possible to have a coherent, all inclusive explanation covering all of them.

The previous section has already mentioned my dissatisfaction with the teaching on contraception and sterilization. I do not think there is any moral difference between direct and indirect sterilization, and I believe that both of them can be permitted for the same proportionate reason which does not have to be of great gravity. The concept of direct based on the physical causality of the act in this particular case does not seem to make any moral difference whatsoever. My ultimate reason for asserting this is the understanding that human beings have more stewardship over generative organs than the traditional Catholic teaching would admit.[35]

Likewise, in the case of cooperation I deny the moral significance involved in the concept of direct cooperation based on the physical structure of the act itself. There exists a variety of terminology among the authors considering the question of cooperation, but in this case the exposition of Merkelbach will be followed. Merkelbach explicitly applies the principle of the double effect to the case of cooperation and explains the principles involved. Formal cooperation in which one intends the sin of the principal agent is always wrong because of the sinful intention. Immediate material cooperation in which one cooperates in the sinful act itself is always wrong because the act itself is not indifferent (one of the conditions of the double effect) but always wrong. Mediate material cooperation is ordinarily illicit but is *per accidens* licit if there is a proportionate reason. In this third case the act of cooperation is indifferent in itself and the evil effect (the sin of the other) can be permitted if there is a proportionate reason.[36]

---

35. For a further explanation, see my article, "Sterilization: Roman Catholic Theory and Practice," *The Linacre Quarterly,* XL (1973), 97–108.
36. Benedictus H. Merkelbach, O.P., *Summa Theologiae Moralis,* Vol. I: *De Principiis* (10th ed.; Bruge, Belgium: Desclée de Brouwer, 1959), pp. 400–405, n. 487–492.

I disagree with the fundamental basis for saying that immediate material cooperation is wrong because my action is intrinsically evil and not indifferent. One does not immediately materially cooperate with an act which is intrinsically wrong but rather with a person who has a right to act in accord with one's conscience provided that other innocent persons or the public order are not hurt. The older understanding of the concept of cooperation needs to be changed in the light of the present teaching on religious liberty,[37] but this entire question will be discussed in depth in the next chapter.

Even in the area of conflict situations involving life and killing, many Catholic theologians acknowledge that the principle of double effect does not adequately handle all the problems involved. The precise point in question concerns the fact that an action is always wrong if in the physical causality of the act the good effect does not occur equally immediately or before the evil effect. According to the third condition of the principle, if the evil effect in the order of physical causality occurs first then the good is obtained through an evil means and the act is direct. In the question of unjust aggression many Catholic theologians allowed such a direct killing of the aggressor in order to defend life or other values of great import if there were no other means of defense available. The moral decision in such cases does not rest on the physical structure of the act but solely on the basis of proportionate reason. Unjust aggression does not depend upon the formal or subjective guilt of the aggressor but rather on the fact of aggression itself as indicated by the generally accepted teaching that one can also kill a materially

37. Declaration on Religious Freedom, n. 7. See also the footnote explanation given by John Courtney Murray, S.J., in *The Documents of Vatican II*, ed. Walter M. Abbott, S.J. (New York: Guild Press, 1966), p. 686.

unjust aggressor in self-defense. The principle of double effect does not apply in this case.[38]

In the late nineteenth century the Holy Office would not allow the concept of unjust aggressor to be applied to the fetus so that direct abortion was never allowed, although physically direct killing was permitted for a proportionate reason in the case of the unjust aggressor outside the womb.[39] Thus there are different approaches within the traditional Roman Catholic theology to questions of killing outside the womb and inside the womb.

All these indications point up the difficulty of accepting in a univocal and universal way the concept of direct and indirect as it has been used to solve so many different conflict situations in Roman Catholic theology. One must carefully distinguish what particular conflict situations are being discussed. However, in many of the present discussions about double effect and the solution of conflict situations there seems to be the same difficulty; namely, a too inclusive attempt to explain too many different types of cases which cannot really be grouped together. This essay will now try to point out some of the dangers of overgeneralization in the recent discussion about the double effect.

Knauer and Janssens. Knauer and Janssens, for example, both correctly recognize the danger of physicalism in Catholic moral theology and thus deny the third condition of the principle of the double effect which insists that the good effect must follow equally immediately as the evil effect in terms of the physical causality of the act. In their discussion

38. This is the more common teaching among Catholic theologians according to Marcellinus Zalba, *Theologiae Moralis Summa,* Vol. II: *Tractatus de Mandatis Dei et Ecclesiae* (Madrid: Biblioteca de Autores Cristianos, 1953), pp. 275–279.

39. For these different decrees and theological comment about them, see Bouscaren, pp. 21–24.

both authors take up questions which have caused some discussion within the parameters of traditional Catholic moral theology. Knauer applies to these questions his basic principle that a physical evil becomes a moral evil only if there is no commensurate reason for permitting or causing the evil. The purely physical series of events is irrelevant to the moral qualifications of good or evil. Thus a mutilation is not direct unless there is no proportionate reason. Killing an unjust aggressor and capital punishment are not direct killings if they can be justified by a proportionate reason. Taking something that does not belong to one is morally wrong only if there is no proportionate reason. For the poor man in extreme need taking something is not wrong, since his extreme need constitutes such a commensurate reason. Likewise, a false answer may be given to an indiscreet question if it is necessary to protect an important secret. A moral judgment is rationally possible only when in a concrete act it is established whether the reason for the act is commensurate or not.[40] Yes, murder is always wrong but this description contains the judgment of commensurate reason.[41]

Louis Janssens, invoking the name and the teaching of Thomas Aquinas, in a somewhat similar vein rejects the older teaching on double effect with the special emphasis on the third condition stressing the physical causality of the act. Aquinas proposes the general theory that an act is morally good when the exterior act (the material element or the means) has a due proportion (*debita poportio*) according to the measure of reason to the morally good end. The means is never looked at as just a physical act in itself but due proportion means that there must be no interior contradic-

40. Knauer, *Natural Law Forum,* XII (1967), 150–154.
41. *Ibid.,* p. 155.

tion between the means and the end in the light of the total act.[42]

Janssens considers many of the same cases as Knauer (artificial contraception, stealing, killing) and he even argues that Thomas Aquinas was not consistent in his understanding of lying, for he did not admit a proper distinction between the ontic evil of false speech (*falsiloquium*) and the moral evil of lying which occurs when there is no proportionate reason.[43] Note that both Knauer and Janssens, in the call for commensurate reason or due proportion, see the weighing of values between the external act and the end intended. Thus they do not explicitly invoke a broad calculus of all the values involved in a situation in a purely utilitarian fashion.

In practice I agree with the solutions given by Knauer and Janssens to all the above cases, but interestingly both authors concentrate on the questions that have caused problems within the ambit of traditional Roman Catholic moral theology. In the broader discussion of ethics in Protestant religious and philosophical discussions today, other topics have been considered which are not explicitly mentioned by Knauer and Janssens. These include such questions as adultery, fornication and other aspects of sexuality, euthanasia and the killing of noncombatants or other innocent persons. It is rather difficult to assess how these two authors would deal with such problems, but their general theory could readily arrive at solutions different from those traditionally accepted. Yet there are also other indications that these authors would still maintain the older teaching in these areas. In my judgment, John T. Noonan, Jr., the editor of *The Natural Law Forum,* proposed his question about adultery to Peter

42. Janssens, *Louvain Studies,* IV (1972), 116–133; 139–153.
43. *Ibid.,* pp. 140–151.

Knauer precisely to see how Knauer would respond to such a question in the light of the more general theory that was proposed in his article and exemplified in solving the cases that had heretofore caused difficulties in Roman Catholicism.[44] Logically, one could very well argue that adultery in this case is justified because there is a proportionate reason. The purpose of the act and its end is to either insure the proper upbringing of the children by reuniting the whole family or to improve the marital relationship by reuniting the wife with her husband and children. However, Knauer maintains the act is wrong in this case.

At the very minimum, it seems that the theory and some of the statements made by both Janssens and Knauer need nuancing or modification in the light of a negative response to the questions mentioned above. Janssens maintains as a principle that it is impossible to pronounce a moral judgment on an external action which contains ontic evil if this action is viewed only as a factual and actual event without any consideration of the end of the interior act of the will.[45] Knauer also indicates that an act cannot be judged only according to its external appearance without a consideration of commensurate reason.[46]

Knauer and Janssens rightly reject the identification of the physical order with the moral order, but in my judgment they fail to recognize or at least to explicitly point out that there are times when the physical aspect of the act does make a difference in the moral evaluation of the act. There is a difference, in my judgment, between permitting one to die by withdrawing extraordinary means and positively interfering to bring about death. The end of the action is the same

44. Knauer, *Natural Law Forum,* XII (1967), 162, n. 24.
45. Janssens, *Louvain Studies,* IV (1972) 148.
46. Knauer, *Natural Law Forum,* XII (1967), p. 138 and *passim; Nouvelle Revue Théologique,* LXXXVII (1965), 360, 361.

in both cases but the means are different. Likewise, there is a difference between the direct and the indirect killing of noncombatants even though the same number of people might die in both cases. One can even hold the above distinctions as morally meaningful and still admit that in some circumstances one can interfere to bring about death or even directly kill noncombatants. At the very minimum in these questions and in the questions of sexuality it seems that the authors must give more explicit attention to the reality of the physical aspect than their previously enunciated positions have done.

Debate about utilitarianism. The generic danger of an overly inclusive or overly simplified approach to these questions under consideration also surfaces in the failure of some of the recent writings to consider other philosophical approaches to the same questions. Specifically, much recent Catholic writing has not given enough recognition to the insights gained in the debate about utilitarianism in English philosophical discussions. This debate has raised significant difficulties with a simple act utilitarianism which justifies an action in terms of the calculus of whatever will produce the greater good.[47]

For the particular purposes of this essay there are three pertinent defects in some act utilitarian analyses that should be of concern to the present debate about double effect. Since utilitarianism is interested in the consequences of our actions and determines the good act on the basis of a consequentialist analysis, perhaps not enough importance will be given to the subjective aspect of the human act and the

47. See, for example, *Studies in Utilitarianism,* ed. Thomas K. Hearn, Jr., (New York: Appleton-Century-Crofts, 1971). For a review of some aspects of the debates over utilitarianism and their relationship to contemporary debates within Roman Catholicism, see John R. Connery, S.J., "Morality of Consequences: A Critical Appraisal," *Theological Studies,* XXXIV (1973), 396–414.

person placing the act. There is danger of forgetting the distinction between doing and happening. Morality is not based only on what happens or what results, but the doing or the relationship of the act to the subject is important and sometimes the physical structure of the act has something to say about this. For example, the only moral factor is not just the number who are killed but also the way in which they are killed or the way in which the subject relates to that killing.[48] Many types of utilitarianism might recognize this distinction but there remains the danger that such a calculus might operate only in terms of what happens and not what is done.

Perhaps the most common complaint against utilitarianism concerns the inability to give enough importance to considerations of justice or fairness. The reason for this difficulty comes from the tendency of some utilitarian approaches to swallow up the individual in the light of overall utility. A calculus based on the greatest good of the greatest number means that the rights of certain individuals might give way to good results for corporate utility.[49] Thus many authors see the need to supplement or even correct utilitarianism by stressing claims of justice or faithfulness or human dignity to safeguard the individual and his rights in the face of a broader utilitarian calculus.[50]

H. J. McCloskey first raised a case which has caused some comment in the literature and refers to the justice feature of our actions. Suppose that a sheriff were faced with the choice

48. Thomas Nagle, "War and Massacre," *Philosophy and Public Affairs,* I (1972), 124, 125.

49. John Rawls, *A Theory of Justice* (Cambridge, Mass.: Belknap Press of Harvard University, 1971); David Lyons, *Forms and Limits of Utilitarianism* (Oxford: Oxford University Press, 1965); William K. Frankena, *Ethics* (Englewood Cliffs, New Jersey: Prentice-Hall, 1963), pp. 38–42.

50. For the need of a similar corrective in an approach to technology assessment and genetics, see LeRoy Walters, "Technology Assessment and Genetics," *Theological Studies,* XXXIII (1972), 682.

either of framing a black for a rape (knowing that the black was not guilty) and thus preventing serious anti-black riots which would lead to the loss of much life and increased hatred, or of hunting for the guilty person and thereby allowing the anti-black riots to occur while doing the best he could to combat them. By framing the one innocent person it seems that much greater good could be accomplished because many more lives would be saved, but justice considerations certainly do not allow such an approach.[51] This paradigm could be expressed in many different ways and with many different numbers. Can one innocent person be directly killed or framed to save the lives of 10 or 20 or 200 or 2000?

Throughout this section there has been the need to make nuanced statements about a utilitarian calculus because some could say a utilitarian calculus must also take into account considerations of justice and therefore could also arrive at the conclusion that there is no proportionate reason that could ever justify the direct killing of an innocent person to save any number of other people.[52] However, in this case one then faces the argument of whether the act is wrong because it has bad consequences or it has bad consequences because it is wrong. Even if some would hold that the justice feature can be overridden by the very important goods to be attained, at least justice and fairness must be considered.

A third difficulty proposed against act utilitarianism concerns its individualism and failure to give enough importance to community and social aspects of reality. Rule utilitarianism as a modification of act utilitarianism tries to respond to this criticism by insisting that certain rules are justified by a

51. H. J. McCloskey, "An Examination of Restricted Utilitarianism," in *Studies in Utilitarianism*, p. 234.

52. For such an approach, see Richard A. McCormick, S.J., *Ambiguity in Moral Choice* (The 1973 Pere Marquette Theology Lecture, Marquette University, Milwaukee), pp. 86–93.

utilitarian calculus even though one individual might achieve
a greater good by violating the rule in a particular case. [53]
This communal aspect of the question and the effect of the
act on society do not often appear in Catholic discussions
today. Moral theologians cannot consider only the individual-
istic aspect of the question but must discuss the relationship
of these actions to society even though such a consideration
might not result in an absolute norm.

The above three considerations have surfaced in the discussion about human acts in recent English and American philosophical literature. The Catholic moral theologian who is
rightly questioning the older teaching on double effect must
learn from these and other debates which have been taking
place. There must be a continual and ongoing dialogue with
all other approaches to the question of the proper understanding of the moral evaluation of human acts. The discussions raised by utilitarianism indicate the dangers involved in
an overly simplistic approach which does not give enough
importance to the rights of the individual.

Germain Grisez. An opposite error is to so accentuate the
individual that one does not give enough importance to the
multiple ways in which the individual is related to others and
to society. I strongly reject the utilitarian attempt to down-
grade the individual human being in the name of better
overall consequences for society as a whole, but one cannot
so stress the individual that one's relationships with others
are forgotten. Such an emphasis, in my judgment, is present
in the creative revision of double effect proposed by Germain
Grisez. Grisez is dissatisfied with the third condition of the
double effect and its physicalism, but at the same time he
also is opposed to any form of utilitarianism as well as the

53. J. B. Schneewind, "Introduction," in *Mill's Ethical Writings,* ed. J. B.
Schneewind (New York: Collier Books, 1965), especially pp. 32–37; John Rawls,
"Two Concepts of Rules," *Philosophical Review,* LXIV (1955), 3–32.

newer theories proposed by Van der Marck, Van der Poel, and Knauer.[54]

Grisez understands the principle of the double effect in the light of his more general ethical theory. Grisez proposes that there are certain basic human goods which human beings can never directly go against. Earlier he upheld the condemnation of contraception because here one goes directly against the basic human good of procreation in order to achieve some other good.[55] In the development of his ethical theory and the discussion on abortion, Grisez mentions eight fundamental human goods. The end cannot justify the means when the means in question involves turning against a good equally basic, equally an end, equally a principle of rational action as the good consequence sought to be achieved. In the context of abortion Grisez talks only about the basic good of life which he claims all people would have to consider as one of the basic human goods which one can never directly go against.[56]

Grisez rejects the manualistic interpretation of direct on the basis of the physical causality of the act and proposes a new understanding which sees the particular action as a means, and direct only if it is not part of the indivisible process set off by the action of the agent. "From the point of view of human moral activity, the initiation of an indivisible process through one's own causality renders all that is involved in that process equally immediate."[57] In such a case the moral agent causes simultaneously, from a moral viewpoint, everything that follows from the one action he has

54. Germain Grisez, *Abortion: The Myths, the Realities, and the Arguments* (New York: Corpus Books, 1970), pp. 287–307; 328–334.

55. Germain G. Grisez, *Contraception and the Natural Law* (Milwaukee: Bruce Publishing Co., 1964), 68–72.

56. Grisez, *Abortion: The Myths, the Realities and the Arguments,* pp. 311–321.

57. *Ibid.,* p. 333.

initiated. Even if the good effect comes about through the mediation of the evil effect, the action is not direct if the good effect results from the initiating action of the person and does not demand a subsequent action by the person or someone else.

In the light of his principle that one can never directly go against the basic human good of life, Grisez examines the various questions which have been discussed most frequently in the recent literature. Killing in self-defense is not a direct killing, for here the various aspects of the external act (protecting self and killing the aggressor) are indivisible. Likewise, in war acts directed against the bearers of unjust force involve only indirect killing because in one indivisible act the unjust force is stopped and the killing occurs. Acts of torture, terror and reprisal can never be justified because they intentionally attack persons in order to achieve good effects only through distinct and ulterior human acts. Grisez logically opposes capital punishment as it presently exists in countries like the United States because the good of preventing further crime is achieved in subsequent human acts and not in the execution itself. Thus capital punishment involves a direct killing.[58]

An abortion is indirect if the very same act, indivisible as to its behavioral process, has both the good effect of protecting human life and the bad effect of destroying it. If the good effect is obtained in and through the same indivisible process which is initiated by the abortifacient procedure, then the abortion is not direct. But one can never sacrifice the life of the fetus for a value other than life.[59] Grisez calls the abortion indirect if the life of the mother is saved by the action of the abortion itself; but if a further human act is required to save the life of the mother, then the abortion is direct and not moral.

58. *Ibid.*, pp. 334–340.
59. *Ibid.*, pp. 340–346.

What about Grisez's solution? In principle if a good effect other than the life of the mother (e.g., physical or mental health) is attained in and through the indivisible abortifacient process, the abortion is not directly intended, but such an abortion is wrong because only the life of the mother can be a proportionate reason. However, in the case of self-defense against unjust aggression traditional Catholic theology justifies killing to protect values other than life.[60] It seems to me that Grisez must logically hold that killing an unjust aggressor is moral only in defense of life. I, myself, would allow the reluctant killing of the aggressor in cases involving other commensurate values, and likewise I would allow abortion for the sake of important values somewhat commensurate with life itself (e.g., grave danger of severe mental illness with lasting permanent effects for the mother).

The criterion of one indivisible act is better than the older criterion but is still, in my judgment, insufficient and inadequate. Just because a second act is required to bring about the good effect does not mean that the abortion is thereby direct and not justified. Paul Ramsey with his immense medical knowledge points out the inconsistency in such an approach which would justify abortion in some conflict situations but not in others. In the case of abortion to save the life of the mother suffering from misplaced acute appendicitis or in a special case of aneurysm of the aorta, it is necessary to abort the fetus and then to intervene with another human act to save the life of the mother. In accord with Grisez' thesis such an action would be a direct abortion and immoral.[61]

I disagree with Grisez both in practice and in theory. Practically, I would allow abortion in those cases when

---

60. Zalba, pp. 275–279.
61. Paul Ramsey, "Abortion: A Review Article," *The Thomist,* XXXVII (1973), 218.

another act is necessary to achieve a proportinate good effect. Theoretically, while Grisez has moved away from the physical causality of the act as determinative, he has still accepted the criterion of one physical human act with no other intervening act. I believe this criterion is in keeping with his own ethical theory and its insistence on the individual human person without enough emphasis given to the multiple relationships in which the individual exists.

Grisez' theory starts with the individual face to face with certain basic human goods that one can never directly go against. I would tend to see the individual in a relationship with other human beings and in an intricate relationship with the multiple goods. My optique, while avoiding some of the problems of subordinating the individual to the societal good mentioned in the discussion of utilitarianism, gives more importance to a relational understanding than does Grisez. In such a relational approach it is easier to admit the fact that conflict situations can arise and one can directly go against some basic human goods in order to save other proportionate goods.

In the solution of conflict situations calling for a proper description of the human act, my approach would not see the human act defined only in terms of the indivisible physical process of the act initiated by the individual actor. Rather, the full human act must also be seen in terms of its relationship with other human beings and their responses to that act. This general consideration serves as the basis for my solution of conflict situations in abortion based on judging the proportionate values involved and not in any way determined by the physical structure of the one individual act. Grisez' approach to this whole question of conflict situations both in its theoretical denial of any possibility of a direct killing and in its criterion of the one indivisible act coheres with his basic philosophical approach. My practical differences with him also point to a different understanding which gives more stress to the relational aspect of man than does Grisez but tries to avoid some of the problems created by any attempt at subordination of the individual to the good of society.

Richard McCormick. Richard McCormick has tentatively proposed a new approach to the question of double effect which avoids some of the dangers already mentioned, but his approach still occasionally suffers from a too inclusive and global understanding of direct and indirect. McCormick argues that the physical structure or causality of the act can never be determinative in deciding the morality of a particular action. Moral judgments are always based on proportionate reasoning. But many of the newer approaches which mention only proportionate reason as a substitute for the old principle of double effect forget that there is still an important distinction between an intending and permitting will. The relationship of the evil done to the will of the action, what McCormick calls the psychological intention, determines whether the will is intending or permitting.[62]

That which stands in relationship of means to an end is necessarily the object of an intending will even if not willed for itself, while that which is merely an effect or aspect need not be the object of an intending will. There is a difference between direct and indirect involving the difference between an intending and a permitting will and also based on the physical aspect of the act. The action is direct if the evil effect is the means by which the good is brought about and evil as means is different from the evil as effect. However, the

---

62. McCormick, *Ambiguity in Moral Choice,* pp. 58–93. McCormick's earlier discussions of these questions including the development in his own thought can be found in the surveys of Moral Theology appearing once a year in *Theological Studies.*

test for whether or not the evil is a means, the act direct and the will intending is best proposed by Grisez; namely, the divisibility of the human act.[63]

Both the intending and the permitting will are to be judged teleologically: that is, by the presence or absence of a proportionate reason. The fact that an act is direct is never in itself a sufficient reason for saying that it is always wrong. It can only be wrong if it is not justified by a proportionate reason which McCormick understands in accord with Knauer's approach. He illustrates his meaning by talking about the principle of discrimination in warfare which protects the innocent from direct attack. McCormick proposes this as a practically exceptionless principle based on teleological, not deontological, reasons. Taking all things into account it seems that the evil consequences of such an action would outweigh the good to be achieved by such an action. If the killing is indirect, obviously a much lesser reason would be able to justify it in certain circumstances.[64] The terms direct and indirect refer to two different realities and indicate two different types of willing which can never be totally determinative of morality but at times may call for different proportionate reasons.

McCormick's approach in my estimation is in the right direction, but it needs further nuancing and correction in terms of the general problem of a too inclusive approach. In this connection, I disagree with some of the examples cited by him, the criterion proposed for the distinction between direct and indirect, and the fact that the difference between direct and indirect constitutes the difference between an intending and a permitting will.

63. *Ibid.*, pp. 57–68 and especially 72–76. Note that McCormick is willing to accept Grisez's criterion, but also speaks about accepting it only provisionally after indicating some possible difficulties with it (p. 73).

64. *Ibid.*, pp. 83–96.

To illustrate the difference between an intending and a permitting will based on the relation of the will to the act, McCormick proposes the case of direct and indirect sterilization. McCormick merely uses his example to point out the difference between direct and indirect and for the moment he assigns no moral differences to this distinction.[65] I see no meaningful difference at all between direct and indirect sterilization, and it does not constitute in my judgment the difference between an intending and a permitting will. The stewardship which human beings have over the body and sexual functions gives one the right to interfere with the generative system if there is some proportionate reason for so doing.

Also I disagree with McCormick in understanding the meaning of direct and indirect (even though it is only a limited and not an ultimate consideration) in the light of Grisez's approach. Earlier I have expressed both theoretical and practical difficulties with such a criterion. It seems that the emphasis in Grisez's approach on the individual is ultimately incompatible with McCormick's own insistence on proportionate reason which definitely presupposes a more relational understanding of the human ethical model.

McCormick in the course of his presentation acknowledges that the question of direct or indirect does not always make a moral difference. I think one can build on McCormick's general thrust but make some clarifications. He seems too ready to identify the psychological intention or the intending will with the physical causality of the act understood in Grisez's sense. It might be helpful here to follow the older formulation of the conditions of double effect and accept as a separate condition that the evil aspect or effect cannot be psychologically intended. This would then make the psychological intention a separate category. But the real crux of the question then is the relationship of the physical causality or

65. *Ibid.,* pp. 73, 74.

structure of the act itself to the will. Does this involve significant moral differences? Against some authors, I would assert that sometimes the physical structure of the act does make a difference; but against the traditional approach I would assert that very often the physical structure of the act does not make a significant moral difference. Such an approach follows McCormick's basic thesis, but does not accept Grisez's criterion of direct and indirect.

When does the physical structure of the act make a difference? There is need for continued discussion on this matter. Two important areas where the physical causality of the act does make an important difference are the question of killing innocent persons, which is well illustrated by the principle of discrimination in warfare and the question of euthanasia, although in the latter this difference does not involve an absolute prohibition.[66] These questions were discussed briefly in Chapter 5.

There is one final criticism of McCormick's position. He admits there are norms that are teleologically established and are "virtually exceptionless." McCormick suggests that virtually exceptionless norms are based on the presumption of common and universal danger.[67] There is some validity on occasion in such a principle, but it should not be generally used for all occasions. McCormick notes its derivation from positive law, but positive law and moral truth are two different realities. Such a moral principle too easily enshrines the status quo. At the very least it is difficult to prove, and in the moral sphere the presumption should not always be in favor of the societal status quo. In a sense this approach has many

66. Elsewhere, I have argued that once the dying process begins I no longer see an overriding moral difference between the positive act of interfering to bring about death and the act of omitting (or even positively removing) extraordinary means with the same purpose in view. See, *Politics, Medicine and Christian Ethics: A Dialogue with Paul Ramsey* (Philadelphia: Fortress Press, 1973), pp. 152–163.
67. McCormick, pp. 91–92.

of the nuances and difficulties associated with the wedge argument since it is based on the presumed effects on society. If some type of action is deemed right in itself, human reason should be able to distinguish that type of action from all other similar types and thus prevent harm to society which might result if these other kinds of actions were then adopted.

There are many other questions which can and should be raised in terms of the present discussion. For example, ethicists need to consider the meaning and importance of temporal immediacy which perhaps was raised in a certain sense by Grisez. However, the purpose of this essay has not been to solve all the problems connected with the principle of double effect. This third and longest section has merely tried to indicate a number of problems and difficulties, all of which revolve around the common problem of striving to give too all-embracing or all-inclusive responses to the questions raised by the many conflict situations in human existence.

7

Cooperation in a Pluralistic Society

Questions of cooperation arise when a person—either an individual person or a moral person—works together with another in producing a particular action. Ethical problems result when the person is asked to cooperate in an act which one believes to be wrong. Such problems will frequently occur in a pluralistic society where there are conflicting ethical beliefs.

Cooperation has been an important topic in Catholic moral theology especially in the twentieth century. To illustrate this point one can readily find in the literature of moral theology many references to questions involving cooperation. Journals published for priests in all languages generally contained a section in which a moral theologian responded to ethical problems and questions, and problems of cooperation were frequently discussed. For example, John McCarthy in the 1950's published two volumes belonging to the genre of responses to cases of conscience.[1] These responses had originally been published by him for the guidance of priests and confessors in the *Irish Ecclesiastical Record* in the fifteen year period before their publication in book form.

---

1. John Canon McCarthy, *Problems in Theology*, Vol. I: *The Sacraments* (Westminster, Md.: Newman Press, 1956); Vol. II: *The Commandments* (Westminster, Md.: Newman Press, 1960).

On at least ten different occasions in these volumes McCarthy responds to questions involving problems of cooperation in various areas—cooperating in giving a Protestant minister bread and wine for a communion service; financial support for the building of Protestant churches; cooperating in the Oxford Group movement; abortion; cooperation of a landlady in the acts of tenants; cooperation of a worker with an employer who asks the worker to cheat; restitution coming from cooperation; a spouse cooperating with the use of artifical contraception; a lawyer and client; a doctor and patient.[2]

Medical ethics obviously furnishes many questions of cooperation. The Catholic textbooks in medical ethics invariably outline the accepted teaching within the Catholic Church on cooperation, often in the context of general principles which will then be applied to the specific questions of medical ethics. Edwin Healy, for example, devotes more than ten pages to the discussion of cooperation and treats such practical cases as illicit operations, abortion, contraception, sterilization, medical partnership, summoning a non-Catholic clergyman for a dying patient, calling attention to mistakes in surgery.[3] Questions of this type are obviously still arising at the present time.

In the more recent periodical literature on the American scene there is great emphasis today on the role of Catholic hospitals. Catholic hospitals adhere to the Ethical and Religious Directives for Catholic Health Facilities proposed by the American bishops in their present form in 1971.[4] Many people in society in general and some within the Roman

2. McCarthy, I, 416–419, 423; II, 45–55; 112; 148–149; 241–245; 333–336; 377; 401; 418–419.
3. Edwin F. Healy, *Medical Ethics* (Chicago: Loyola University Press, 1956), pp. 101–112.
4. *Ethical and Religious Directives for Catholic Health Facilities* (Washington: Department of Health Affairs, United States Catholic Conference, 1971).

Catholic Church do not agree with all the teachings contained in these directives.[5] Legal cases have been brought against Catholic hospitals to perform sterilizations. Some fear that Catholic hospitals may be faced with court orders to perform other types of now forbidden operations, including abortions. While there is a feeling among a few that Catholic hospitals will not be able to continue to exist in this country in the future if they adhere to their ethical code, others maintain there is a legal and constitutional right for Catholic hospitals to continue to exist and to act in accord with their stated religious code of ethics.[6]

Problems involving the Catholic hospital are very complex, since they involve matters of federal funding and the rights of non-Catholics. Much of the discussion has been in terms of the legal aspects of the question, but it is important to recognize the moral and ethical aspects. This essay cannot attempt to solve definitively these very complicated issues, but it will try to clarify the understanding of cooperation and thus provide indications for solutions to these questions.

THE TEACHING OF THE MANUALS ON COOPERATION

The teaching of the manuals of moral theology and of medical ethics on cooperation follows the same pattern and

---

5. For a negative critique of these directives, see "Catholic Hospital Ethics: The Report of the Commission on Ethical and Religious Directives for Catholic Hospitals Commissioned by the Board of Directors of the Catholic Theological Society of America," *Proceedings of the Catholic Theological Society of America,* XXVII (1972), 241–269; also published in *Linacre Quarterly,* XXXIX (November 1972), 2–24. For a negative critique of this report, see Donald J. Keefe, "A Review and Critique of the CTSA Report," *Hospital Progress,* LIV (February 1973), 57–69.

6. For the most recent review of the situation and defense of the rights of the Catholic hospital, see Eugene J. Schulte, "Challenge to Individual and Corporate

comes to the same general conclusions, although there is occasionally different terminology. Cooperation is often defined as the concurrence with another person in an act which is morally wrong. Cooperation may be either positive or negative, but the more important distinction exists between formal and material cooperation. Formal cooperation, by which the cooperator consents to the sin or the bad will of the principal actor either explicitly by intending the sin or implicitly by immediate cooperation in an action which is intrinsically wrong, is always wrong.[7] Some authors, e.g., Merkelbach, describe the second type of formal cooperation as immediate material cooperation because the cooperator does not explicitly join one's will with the evil will of the principal actor, but such cooperation is nonetheless always wrong.[8] Material cooperation, since it helps one perform an evil action but does not involve concurrence with the bad will or immediate concurrence in an intrinsically evil act, is wrong but can be justified if proportionate reasons exist with more serious reasons required when the cooperation is more closely related to the act of the principal agent.

Catholic ethicists developed a casuistry to indicate how prudence should decide different cases of material cooperation.[9] Remote and nonnecessary cooperation can be justified by a slight reason; for example, an orderly can work for a

Rights," *Hospital Progress,* LV (February 1974), 52–56; William Andrew Regan, "An Analysis of the First Amendment Rights of Catholic Health Facilities," *Hospital Progress,* LV (February 1974), 66–68.

7. Marcellinus Zalba, *Theologiae Moralis Summa,* Vol. I: *Theologia Moralis Fundamentalis* (Madrid: Biblioteca de Autores Cristianos, 1952), 918; I. Aertnys, C. Damen, J. Visser, *Theologia Moralis,* 17th ed. (Rome: Marietti, 1956), I, 377, 378.

8. Benedictus Merkelbach, *Summa Theologiae Moralis,* Vol. I: *De Principiis,* 10th ed. (Bruge, Belgium: Desclée de Brouwer, 1959), 401, 402.

9. These distinctions involve a distillation of the material as discussed by the authors mentioned thus far. For an enunciation and application of the principles to questions of medical ethics, see Healy, pp. 104–112.

hospital in which abortions are performed merely because of the salary he receives. Remote necessary or proximate non-necessary cooperation can be justified for a grave reason, whereas proximate necessary cooperation can be justified only for a notably grave reason. Thus doctors may serve as first assistants at an illicit operation if they fear that otherwise they might lose their positions provided that they not do the actual illicit operation itself. Catholic nurses, whose cooperation is somewhat less proximate, may assist at illicit operations in a state institution even though they could find employment elsewhere, because they can do much good in these institutions and thus compensate for the occasional and unavoidably material cooperation in evil.[10] Proximate necessary cooperation in an act which harms a third person can be justified only to avoid a similar or slightly less evil to one's self. Thus a pharmacist may give poison to a man who is going to kill his wife if the man threatens the pharmacist with a gun if he refuses to cooperate. Cooperation which is proximately necessary for a grave public evil cannot be justified by any private advantage.

The general teaching on cooperation as well as the rules of prudence are proposed in just about the same way by all the authors of textbooks. The manuals of moral theology which generally follow the pattern of the ten commandments in their structure (especially those of the Jesuit and Redemptorist schools) treat cooperation as one of the sins against charity. Cooperation is thus closely associated with scandal, another sin against charity, which is defined as any deed or word which is sinful or seemingly sinful and affords another the occasion of spiritual ruin.[11] Benedict Merkelbach and

10. Gerald Kelly, *Medico-Moral Problems* (St. Louis: The Catholic Hospital Association, 1958), p. 334.

11. G. J. Waffelaert, *Sur la coopération et sur l'espèce morale du scandale* (Bruges: Vandenberghe-Denaux, 1883).

other authors following the Dominican tradition consider cooperation under external causes of sin, whereas scandal is discussed under the virtue of charity.[12] However, these are comparatively minor questions of structure and do not affect the general agreement found among all authors.

HISTORY OF THE CONCEPT

Although there is general agreement on the meaning and rules affecting cooperation, this teaching as it exists in the manuals does not go back to the explicit teaching of Thomas Aquinas. Aquinas does not make the distinction between material and formal cooperation with the respective definitions as found in the manuals. In one place in the *Summa Theologiae,* Thomas discusses cooperation in the context of restitution. Here Aquinas accepts the traditionally enumerated ways in which one can cooperate in the act of another. The Angelic Doctor maintains that in five cases the one who helps in the act of another is held to restitution although the primary obligation of restitution rests with the primary cause of the act (II–II, q.62, a.2). In another context Aquinas accepts the fact that the artisan commits a sin in making things such as idols which cannot be used by others without sin (II–II, q.169, a.2, ad.4).

Thomas Sanchez, one of the most important figures in the history of moral theology who died at the beginning of the seventeenth century, considers cooperation as a particular case of scandal but does raise questions about cooperating with acts that are indifferent and with acts that are intrinsically wrong. Although Sanchez talks about intrinsically wrong actions, there is ambiguity about whether his terminology refers to acts understood in their essence or acts which

12. Merkelbach, I, 401–*402.*

are intrinsically wrong in the concrete circumstances. It was
up to later theologians to differentiate theoretically in a more
accurate manner between cooperation and scandal and also
to introduce the accepted terminology of material and formal
cooperation.[13]

The seventeenth and eighteenth centuries in Catholic moral
theology witnessed a struggle between laxists and rigorists
which was marked by papal intervention condemning extremes on both sides.[14] In 1679, sixty-five propositions were
condemned by the Holy Office many of which had originally
been proposed for condemnation at the University of Louvain.[15] One condemned proposition stated that a servant
who knowingly helped his master to climb through a window
to ravish a virgin does not sin mortally if he does it through
fear of great harm or loss.[16] Subsequently, theologians de-
bated about the exact meaning of this condemnation and the
reason for it. Is this act condemned because it is intrinsically
wrong in all circumstances or is it condemned because there
is not a sufficient reason to justify it in this case? Before St.
Alphonsus the vast majority of theologians held the former
opinion, but some few did maintain the latter.[17] St. Alphonsus Liguori, the outstanding moral theologian of the eighteenth century, who was later declared a doctor of the
Church and patron of moral theologians and confessors, in
the first edition of his moral theology, which was basically a

13. Thomas Sanchez, *Opus Morale in Praecepta Decalogi* (Lugduni: 1641),
lib.1, cap. VI,VII; Roger Roy, "La coopération selon Saint Alphonse de Liguori,"
Studia Moralia, VI (1968), 390–398.

14. Bernard Häring, *The Law of Christ* (Westminster, Md.: Newman Press,
1961), I, 20–22.

15. H. Denzinger, A. Schönmetzer, *Enchiridion Symbolorum Definitionum et
Declarationum de Rebus Fidei et Morum,* 32nd ed. (Barcelona: Herder, 1963), p.
457.

16. Denzinger, p. 464, n. 2151.

17. Roy, *Studia Moralia,* VI (1968), 415–421.

commentary on the text of Herman Busembaum, proposed the opinion that such acts were intrinsically wrong.[18]

In subsequent editions of his moral theology, however, Alphonsus adopted the second opinion. Such a development set the stage for a discussion of the meaning of an intrinsically wrong act and for pointing out the differences between material and formal cooperation. Alphonsus argues that the acts of the servant are not intrinsically wrong so the cooperation is only material. But the crime of ravaging a virgin is so monstrous that only a reason of extreme necessity such as a fear of death could excuse and justify the cooperation. In his theoretical exposition Alphonsus distinguishes between formal and material cooperation, describing the formal as concurring with the bad will of the other which is always wrong. Material cooperation, on the other hand, concurs only to the bad action of the other. Formal cooperation always involves an influence on the will of the principal agent, but this can take place in a twofold manner—by intending the evil or by cooperating immediately in an act which is intrinsically wrong and thus influencing the will of the other. In material cooperation the act itself done by the cooperator cannot be intrinsically wrong but must be good or indifferent.[19]

Alphonsus thus presents the framework within which cooperation has been discussed in Roman Catholic theology to the present time. The only theoretical point of difference in the contemporary discussions, as pointed out above, concerns whether or not immediate cooperation in an intrinsically wrong act is formal cooperation or immediate material cooperation. In practice, however, there is no difference because no author would justify cooperation in such a case despite

18. Alphonsus de Ligorio, *Medulla Theologiae Moralis R. P. Hermanni Busembaum Societatis Jesu Theologi, cum Adnotationibus* (Neapoli, 1748), 1.2, t.3, c.2, d.5, a.3.

19. Alphonsus Maria de Ligorio, *Theologia Moralis,* ed. Leonardus Gaudé (Romae, 1905), 1.2, t.3, c.2, d.5, a.3, nn.61ff.

the difference in theoretical understandings. It is precisely this question of cooperation with an act which is intrinsically wrong which has been frequently emphasized in the Roman Catholic teachings on cooperation with non-Catholic worship services, the publishing of immoral books, cooperation in onanism or cooperation in medical operations which are judged to be intrinsically wrong.

In my judgment there is an element missing in the accepted understanding of cooperation, and the inclusion of this element calls for theoretical and practical changes in this teaching. The missing aspect refers to the subjectivity and rights of conscience of the person who is acting. The older definitions assume that one concurs with either the bad will or the bad act of the principal actor. But the important thing is to realize that one is cooperating with a person and not just with an act or a will. Thus one must consider the rights of the person in this case and not merely the factor of a bad will or a bad act, although these do remain important considerations but not the only ones. A comparison with the newer teaching on religious liberty in the Roman Catholic Church should indicate why one must begin to see cooperation also in terms of the person and not just in terms of the will or the act. Chapter 4 has developed at great length the meaning of religious liberty, its bases and the limitations on the right to religious liberty.

A REVISED UNDERSTANDING OF COOPERATION

The teaching on religious liberty has both similarities and dissimilarities with the question of cooperation. First it is important to point out the dissimilarities. Cooperation refers to the fact that the individual positively concurs in the act of the principal agent. In the case of religious liberty there is no concurrence with the act of the other person but rather there is the recognition that society has to allow the person to perform those acts based on one's religious beliefs. Also religious liberty concerns the relationship of the government to the individual and not the relationship of one individual to another. In addition, religious liberty is not exactly the same as all other kinds of liberty. Since religious freedom refers to matters of such great importance, it can be somewhat differentiated from other types of freedom.

The argument for a changed understanding of cooperation does not rest on an exact parallel with the question of religious liberty. However, the analogy with religious liberty is used to indicate that in both cases the dignity of the human person and the rights of the human person to act with responsible freedom must be taken into account. The older approach denying religious liberty emphasized the concept of objective truth rather than the dignity of the person.[20] Roman Catholic moral theology in general has rightly been criticized for the fact that its moral teaching in the last few centuries has given so much emphasis to the objective and even the physical that it has not given enough importance to subjectivity and freedom. The newer approach to religious liberty recognizes this fact and indicates a dimension that had not heretofore been considered. In the case of cooperation it seems that one must also consider the right of the individual person to act in accord with one's own decision of conscience.

The older approach to cooperation understood the action of the cooperator as concurring with the will or the act of the other person. If the will was bad or if the act was bad, then there was either formal or material cooperation. But is it adequate to describe the action merely as cooperating with a

20. For an exposition and refutation of this position, see John Courtney Murray, *The Problem of Religious Freedom* (Westminster, Md.: Newman Press, 1965), pp. 7–17; also Eric D'Arcy, *Conscience and Its Right to Freedom* (New York: Sheed and Ward, 1961).

bad will or a bad action? This could be a partial explanation, but a more adequate description understands cooperation as concurring not primarily with a will or with an act but with a person. The person, however, may have a bad will (e.g., a criminal planning a robbery) or may do a bad act (needlessly hurt an innocent person). The point is that the full understanding of cooperation must take account of the dignity of the other person and that person's right to act in accord with one's own responsible freedom. Nevertheless, one cannot ignore the elements of a bad will or a bad act which have been part of the consideration in the past.

There is another factor which should also change somewhat the traditional teaching on cooperation. As mentioned, one of the most important parts of the Roman Catholic teaching has been the fact that one cannot cooperate with an action which is intrinsically wrong. However, there is much dispute today even within Roman Catholic theology about the whole question of what, if anything, is intrinsically wrong.[21]

At the very minimum, we are often dealing in a pluralistic society with cases in which the individual person does not believe that his or her action is in any way wrong, although I might believe it is wrong. In these cases even in accord with the older understanding it is impossible to speak about the bad will of the primary agent. The older Catholic theology recognized that there could be invincible ignorance in these cases. There can be no formal cooperation when the individual involved does not have a bad will. There are two other aspects that must be mentioned. First, there is the right of the cooperator to act in accord with conscience and not to be forced to do something she or he believes is wrong. Second, there is the right of the principle agent but also the limits on

21. For a summary of some recent thinking on this question, see Richard A. McCormick, "Notes on Moral Theology" which appear once a year in *Theological Studies.*

the rights of the principal agent which, in my judgment, are similar to the limits placed on religious freedom and governed by the criterion of public order with its threefold content of an order of justice, an order of peace, and an order of common morality.

THE DOCTOR

How does this understanding of cooperation work in practice? Take as an example the doctor who believes in conscience that sterilization is wrong when done for contraceptive purposes but has a patient who believes it is morally and medically good.[22] Here is a conflict of rights—the rights of both to follow their own consciences. In normal circumstances one can readily uphold the right of both persons to act in accord with their own consciences. The doctor in conscience can refuse to do what is personally believed to be wrong, and the patient can find another doctor to perform the operation. Obviously, society profits very much if we respect the freedom of individuals in these matters. Moral integrity certainly calls for people to act in accord with their consciences, and the neutral outsider can applaud the actions of both.

Could the doctor come to a different conclusion? In the past the traditional approach of Roman Catholic theology would not allow the doctor to come to another answer because the act is intrinsically wrong. However, the doctor can do such an operation without cooperating with the bad will of the patient because the patient has no bad will in this

22. I believe that one can be a good Roman Catholic and still hold that contraceptive sterilization is often morally right. However, in this case I am presupposing that the individual doctor in conscience believes that such sterilization is wrong.

case. The doctor, although personally believing that the action is wrong, could reason that the patient has the right to obtain the needed medical care that one needs and wants. In this society we daily live with people who do things we believe are wrong. Without unduly sacrificing personal conscience, the doctor could argue that in this case one is providing the service for which this individual person has a right even though the physician disagrees with the operation from a moral perspective. The doctor by this action is not saying that this particular operation is right but is saying that the person has the right to this particular operation even if the physician is opposed to it on moral grounds.

Does not such a solution open the door to justifying any type of cooperation? No. There are limits on the cooperation as proposed in the criterion of public order. One should not cooperate with another if this harms the public order—the rights of other innocent persons, the peace and common morality of society. Thus one could not immediately cooperate in lying or stealing which are opposed to justice and to the common morality necessary for public order.

The above argumentation in no way implies that the doctor is just a conduit or robot who has no freedom in this matter. There is no doubt that in this case the doctor is an immediate cooperator, and the physician could refuse such cooperation because of personal conscience claims. But, by accepting the fact of a pluralistic society and the rights of the other person, the doctor could in good conscience perform the sterilization for someone who believes it is medically and morally indicated.

Could the doctor perform an abortion in similar circumstances? The patient believes there is nothing wrong with such an abortion in the particular case, but the doctor believes it is the immoral killing of an innocent human being. There remains a great difference between this and the case of sterilization, for here harm is done to a third, innocent party.

If the doctor truly believes abortion to be the killing of innocent persons, I do not see how the physician could ever perform such an operation except in the most extreme cases. One cannot immediately cooperate with another person to act in accord with this person's conscientious decision if such an action is going to cause disproportionate harm to another person or to the public order. Thus, in this question, the limits of cooperation, which are somewhat similar to the limits proposed in the case of religious liberty, become determinative. In this case it is not simply the right of the doctor and the right of the patient but also the right of the innocent third party (at least according to the doctor's belief) that must be taken into consideration. Note the difference between cooperation with its greater involvement of the cooperator and the legal regulation of abortion which was discussed in Chapter 4.

CATHOLIC HOSPITALS

What about the case of Catholic hospitals today? Recent discussions of this question have concentrated on the legal perspective. Court cases have been brought against Catholic hospitals to make them perform operations which they believe are illicit, but as of early 1974 there has been no final decision ordering a Catholic hospital to perform a sterilization.[23] In the case of abortion the Supreme Court in the Georgia case upheld the constitutionality of a conscience clause permitting exemptions both for personnel and hospitals from performing abortions if it was against their conscientious beliefs.[24]

23. Schulte, *Hospital Progress,* LV (February 1974), pp. 52–56.
24. Stephen M. Blaes, "Litigation: Preparation and Response," *Hospital Progress,* LIV (August 1973), 70–72.

From tne legal perspective one can argue that the situation of the Catholic hospital is now changed because often it is a hospital serving the total community and because it receives much money from government sources in terms of Hill-Burton funds, exemptions from personal income and property taxes, and tax dollars in Medicare and Medicaid. Therefore the state has the right to make sure all citizens can be served in these hospitals and can have operations which are medically indicated even though against the moral code of the sponsoring agent of the hospital. The opposite side argues that the right to practice religion in the dispensation of health care is a constitutional right protected by the First Amendment. If the corporate by-laws of Catholic hospitals show their adherence to a moral code, these rights to practice in this way must be upheld by society.[25]

The discussion in this article will consider only the moral aspects of the problem although these are quite intertwined with some of the legal aspects. No one can deny the right of the Catholic hospital to exist and to follow its own moral code. Does the fact that Catholic hospitals serve a total community and receive government funds do away with this right? Here again there is a collision of rights—the right of the Catholic hospital to exist and to put into practice its own moral teaching and the right of all citizens to have the medical care and treatment deemed appropriate. There is no doubt that in many situations in large metropolitan centers both rights can be guaranteed without harm to others. Collisions could arise and will arise where the Catholic facility is the only one serving a particular area.

One could make a case for the Catholic hospital's right to live by its moral code even in the midst of our pluralistic society. I would urge a more nuanced approach to the question and distinguish again between the cases of sterilization

25. Regan, *Hospital Progress,* LV (February 1974), 66–68.

and of abortion. The Catholic hospital could maintain its own prescribed teaching on sterilization and still recognize the rights of other people to act in accord with their own personal decision. Since no innocent persons would be hurt by such a procedure and since the society as such would not be hurt, I see no reason why Catholic hospitals could not in good moral conscience make the decision to allow people to have sterilizations in Catholic hospitals. The cooperation of the hospital is less proximate than that of the doctor doing the sterilization. Once again in this case one can argue that the Catholic hospital in no way approves the particular action taken but acknowledges the right of the individual to act in accord with conscience provided that the rights of other innocent persons and of society are not harmed.

There are other considerations which also argue in favor of this position. Above all, one must recognize the fact that within Roman Catholicism today there is much dissent on the question of sterilization. Many Roman Catholic theologians and people believe there is nothing morally wrong with contraceptive sterilization in many circumstances.[26] In theory and in practice one must admit the possibility of dissent in the question of contraceptive sterilization. Is it possible then for the Church to operate Catholic hospitals in which Catholics are not able to exercise their right to dissent? This intra-Catholic disagreement at the present time is an even stronger reason for allowing sterilizations in Catholic hospitals.

Some of the arguments proposed by Catholics to sustain their moral and legal right to operate hospitals according to their ethical code properly point out that other religious groups within society are also striving to maintain their rights

26. For my reasons in favor of contraceptive sterilization, see "Sterilization: Roman Catholic Theory and Practice," *Linacre Quarterly,* XL (1973), 97–108; also, *New Perspectives in Moral Theology,* pp. 194–211.

to act in accordance with their own principles. For example, mention is frequently made of the practice of the Mennonites and Amish with regard to education. I applaud the defense of the religious freedom of these groups, but there are differences. The problem concerns the non-Catholic in Catholic hospitals and the freedom of that person. There is also an important ecclesiological difference between Roman Catholicism and many forms of sectarian Christianity. Roman Catholicism as a Church has opted for a stance of cooperation with the world even though it recognizes at times it should and must disagree with what is happening in the world. On the other hand the sectarian groups in Christianity have generally based their beliefs on a withdrawal from the world and the recognition of an inherent incompatibility between the world and the gospel message. Thus, from an ecclesiological viewpoint one cannot make a perfect identity between the sects who wish to follow their own teaching and the Catholic Church which by definition has always been much more open to cooperation with the world.

What about abortion? Just as in the case of the individual doctor so too in the case of the hospital there is an important new element in this case. Present official Catholic teaching believes that one must act as if human life is present from the very beginning of conception; therefore direct abortion is looked upon as the killing of innocent human life. One could argue very strongly in this case that the Catholic hospitals should never cooperate with direct abortion because to do so would bring harm to the innocent human being who Catholic ethical teaching believes to be present. Here it is not just a question of providing another person with the opportunity to act in accord with the personal decision that has been reached, but there is the added factor of the innocent human life. Thus I believe a distinction can and should be made between cooperation in cases of sterilization on the part of the Catholic hospital and cooperation in cases of abortion.

The argument can also be made from the ethical perspective that society should always respect the conscience of the individual when it comes to a matter of taking human life. In many ways this argument has been one of the principal reasons proposed by those, including the American bishops, who have argued in the United States for the existence of selective conscientious objection to participation in war.[27] It is admitted that in a pluralistic society there are bound to be conflicts of beliefs and of rights but society also recognizes that the most important value we have is the value of human life. To uphold the belief of those who do not want to participate in what they believe to be the wrong killing of human life is one very important way in which society can promote the sanctity and dignity of human life. In this regard it seems that the action of the Supreme Court in the Georgia case asserting the right of conscientious exemption in the matter of abortion is in accord with the best ethical understanding of society and the role of government in society.

One must also raise here the fact that even on the matter of abortion there can be dissent within the Roman Catholic Church. As a matter of fact, there is some dissent on abortion but much less than in the matter of sterilization.[28] However, because of the nature of what is involved I believe even those who dissent should be willing to uphold the right of the majority of Roman Catholics at the present time to give this communal witness in our society.

This study has attempted to revise the theoretical understanding of cooperation in a pluralistic society in the light of the teaching proposed in the Declaration on Religious Free-

27. "Declaration on Conscientious Objection and Selective Conscientious Objection," available from the Publications Office of the United States Catholic Conference.

28. For the most publicized example of dissent, see Bruno Ribes, "Les chretiens face à l'avortement," *Etudes,* CCCXXXIX (1973), 405–423; 571–583.

dom.[29] By accepting both a qualified right of the individual to act in accord with the dictates of conscience and the limitations which can be placed on that right, a different concept of cooperation has been proposed and applied specifically to the cooperation of doctors and Catholic hospitals in the questions of sterilization and of abortion.

29. For approaches to cooperation which seem to imply the reasoning developed in this article, see "Report of the CTSA Commission," *Proceedings of the Catholic Theological Society of America,* XXVII (1972), 263–265; Edward J. Ryle, "Pregnancy Counseling and the Request for Abortion: Tentative Suggestions for Catholic Charities Agencies," *The Catholic Charities Review,* LVII (June 1973), 8–15.

8

Paul Ramsey and Traditional

Roman Catholic Natural Law Theory

The ecumenical dimension of Christian ethics and moral theology has come to the fore only in the last few years. Present day literature shows that Roman Catholic ethicians read and are influenced by Protestant authors and vice versa. A Protestant or a Roman Catholic ethician today must be in constant ecumenical dialogue. Such, however, was not the case even a few years ago.

The greater openness within Roman Catholicism generally associated with the thought and the spirit of Vatican II has greatly influenced contemporary Roman Catholic moral theology. Before that time even in the United States there was no real dialogue with the Protestant ethical tradition. Important figures in the Catholic tradition such as John A. Ryan and Paul Hanly Furfey indicate in their writings little or no contact with Protestant thought. Likewise, on the part of Protestant ethicians, there was little or no dialogue with the contemporary Catholic thought either in this country or abroad. Walter Rauschenbusch expressed no positive appreciation of the Catholic tradition. In fact, Robert Cross has commented that Rauschenbusch's discussion of the development of asceticism, sacramentalism, hierarchy, and dogma reads today like a parody of the extreme evangelical Protestant critique of Roman Catholicism.[1] Reinhold Niebuhr, according to Stone, had some understanding and appreciation of the Catholic tradition, resisted one-sided and anti-Catholic approaches, and praised some of the changes sanctioned by Vatican Council II; but he had been upset with the reactionary position of the Roman Catholic Church in some of its political alignments in the 1930's and always criticized Catholic pretensions to absolute truth and authority.[2] Niebuhr recognized some truth in the natural law approach, but his references were usually just to the teaching of Aquinas.[3]

It is safe to say that no Protestant ethician in this century has shown in his writings greater interest in and appreciation of Roman Catholic ethical thought than Paul Ramsey. So strong is this Catholic influence that there seems to be a feeling among some that Ramsey is a crypto-Catholic. Ramsey has called for Protestant ethicians to pay more attention to the legitimate place of natural law in Christian ethics. The Methodist theologian from Princeton has studied and employed such traditional Catholic approaches as the just war theory, the principle of the double effect, and the distinction between ordinary and extraordinary means of preserving human life. In addition, Ramsey has often sided with positions proposed by Roman Catholicism in areas of abortion and medical ethics. He has also been a very forceful advocate of the place of universal, exceptionless norms in moral theology and has staunchly attacked the approaches of situation ethics. In the past few years when even many Roman Catholics have been disagreeing with older Catholic teaching espe-

1. Robert D. Cross, "Introduction to the Torchbook Edition," in Walter Rauschenbusch, *Christianity and the Social Crisis* (New York: Harper and Row Torchbook, 1964), p. xiv.

2. Ronald H. Stone, *Reinhold Niebuhr: Prophet to Politicians* (Nashville and New York: Abingdon Press, 1972), pp. 219–222.

3. *Love and Justice: Selections from the Shorter Writings of Reinhold Niebuhr,* ed. D.B. Robertson (Cleveland and New York: Meridian Books, 1967).

cially as found in the addresses of Pope Pius XII and other popes, Ramsey has often gone out of his way to praise papal teaching and on one occasion refers to Pope Pius XII as at least a minor prophet for raising his voice against a prevalent attempt to have the personal aspect of human reproduction replaced by categories of manufacturing and product making.[4]

Any full appreciation of Paul Ramsey's Christian ethics must include a discussion of his relationship with traditional Roman Catholic theology, especially the natural law theory, but there are some problems in attempting such an evaluation. First, there is a difficulty from the viewpoint of traditional Roman Catholic theology. Roman Catholic moral theology has changed greatly in the last few years. One cannot even speak today about Roman Catholic moral theology as a monolithic theory or methodology, although there do continue to be some traditional emphases. Earlier chapters in this book have shown there is now a greater appreciation of the possibility and actuality of dissent within Roman Catholicism from the teaching of the hierarchical magisterium on specific moral questions. Interestingly, Ramsey has expressed his disagreement on occasion with some of these newer developments within Roman Catholic ethics.[5] This essay will use the term traditional Catholic moral theology to refer to that comparatively monolithic discipline which existed before the Second Vatican Council. In a sense, I dislike using the term traditional in this manner, but the meaning is clear if understood in the limited meaning described above.

Difficulties for this study also arise from the way in which Paul Ramsey has done Christian ethics in the course of his

4. Paul Ramsey, "Shall We 'Reproduce'? II. Rejoinders and Future Forecasts", *Journal of the American Medical Association,* CCXX (1972), 1483.
5. Paul Ramsey, *The Patient as Person* (New Haven: Yale University Press, 1970), p. 178.

teaching and writing career. Ramsey has not written a defini-
tive, systematic treatise on Christian ethics. His most systematic work is *Basic Christian Ethics,* which was his first
work published in 1950 and the one which shows least
knowledge of and appreciation for Roman Catholic moral
theology. It is a tribute to Ramsey's great intellectual capacities that his thought has developed and matured over the
years, but again this development causes some difficulty in
any attempt at evaluation. Ramsey also has the tendency in
considering particular questions to find support for his own
contentions in the approaches of others without necessarily
accepting all the methodological presuppositions involved in
what others might hold. His obvious delight in engaging in
controversy and his rhetorical flair also make the task of
accurate interpretation more difficult. In the light of the
nonsystematic, developmental and somewhat polemical aspects of Ramsey's writing, it is necessary to nuance carefully
and accurately Ramsey's attitude toward traditional Roman
Catholic moral theology.

I. RAMSEY'S INTERPRETATION
OF NATURAL LAW IN MARITAIN

In his 1962 publication *Nine Modern Moralists,* Ramsey
develops his own approach to Christian ethics in dialogue
with and criticism of other moralists and specifically calls for
Protestant theologians to accept a concept of natural law or
justice. Ramsey here accepts what he interprets to be a
revisionist theory of natural law proposed by Jacques Maritain and by Edmond Cahn according to which there is some
wisdom in man's natural decisions.[6] Ramsey, however, does
not want to accept some of the characteristics often asso-

6. Paul Ramsey, *Nine Modern Moralists* (Englewood Cliffs, New Jersey:
Prentice-Hall, Inc., 1962), pp. 209–256.

ciated with natural law, such as: natural law conceived as a realm of universal principles; an excessive rationalism which deduces universal norms from prior principles; a realm of clear light unaffected by the distortions of sin; a self-sufficient ethical stance in which Christian love does not enter to re-shape, enlarge, sensitize, and sovereignly direct our apprehensions based on nature alone of the meaning of right and wrong action.[7]

Ramsey also rejects the Catholic republication of the natural law by the authoritative Church teaching which in his judgment makes the natural law approach too inflexible and takes the final decision out of the court of human reason.[8] The heavy emphasis in this book is not on these particular problems he finds in many Catholic presentations of natural law; rather he concentrates on explaining his interpretation of Maritain and urges other Protestant ethicians to accept such an approach.

Both Jacques Maritain and Edmond Cahn, in Ramsey's judgment, affirm a natural law teaching based on the wisdom of the human judgment, made by inclination and not by rational deduction, in the prism of the case. Ramsey interprets Maritain as rejecting the rationalistic, deductive and inflexible concept of natural law often proposed by or at least associated with Roman Catholicism in the past. Nonetheless, there has been a development within Maritain himself as is evident in comparing his earlier book, *The Rights of Man and Natural Law,* with his later exposition in *Man and Society.*[9]

Ramsey interprets the later Maritain in this way. The natural law involves knowing what is right or wrong through inclination or a vital knowledge of connaturality or congeni-

7. *Ibid.,* pp. 4–5.
8. *Ibid.,* pp. 227–230.
9. *Ibid.,* pp. 209–256.

ality and not through a deductive reasoning process. Natural
law in this sense is known only *in medias res,* in social
contexts, or in the prism of actual cases. Natural law is
distinguished from *ius gentium,* which is the area of conceptual reason and deduction. But even in Maritain the domain
of natural law and that of *ius gentium* are not totally distinct.
The French philosopher even suggests that the natural law
has been first manifested not in inclinations but in social
patterns; that is, in *ius gentium. Ius gentium* seems to contain
characteristics which pertain both to natural law as well as
characteristics which go beyond natural law, such as deduction by rational inference. The prohibition of murder can
belong to both natural law and to *ius gentium.* [10]

Ramsey also finds some inconsistencies in Maritain's approach which he attributes to a failure to break cleanly with
a deductive and conceptual approach to natural law which
even Maritain had somewhat accepted in his earlier writings.
While in *Man and Society,* Maritain insists that the natural
law is based on knowledge through inclination and not rational deduction, he still does write that the principles of the
natural law are like conclusions derived from common principles. He also still maintains that the natural law follows
from the first principle—do good and avoid evil—in a necessary way. Ramsey sees it as a contradiction to say that the
natural law follows from the first principle, and especially to
say that it follows in a necessary manner. Also Maritain at
times still uses the word conceptualization to refer to natural
law even though he has reserved this word to describe the *ius
gentium.* [11]

These inconsistencies indicate that, despite the remarkable
departure that Maritain's understanding of natural law as
knowledge through inclination represents from the tradi-

10. *Ibid.,* pp. 217–223.
11. *Ibid.,* pp. 219–220.

tional scheme of rational, deductive natural law, he occasionally lapses into the older expressions. Thus Maritain proposes a flexible, nonrational, nondeductive, contextual understanding of natural law as the moral judgment of inclination in the prism of the case. In the light of Ramsey's later writings, it is interesting to note how often he refers to this understanding of natural law as a contextual judgment made in the prism of the concrete context.

How accurate is Ramsey's interpretation of Maritain? In my judgment Ramsey has somewhat distorted Maritain's position so that it buttresses his own understanding of natural law as being flexible, nonrationalistic, nondeductive, and contextual. At the very minimum, one cannot so totally neglect Maritain's theory on *ius gentium* and act as if it has no place in his total ethical system. Natural law is now understood by Maritain in a restricted way, but it is only a part of his total ethical theory.

Even more importantly, I believe that Maritain's theory is less flexible and contextual than Ramsey believes. Some of Maritain's emphasis on what follows in a necessary way is not merely a carry-over from a position Maritain has now abandoned but rather remains an integral part of his position. Maritain explains that natural law includes two elements—an ontological element and a second, or gnoseological, element.[12] Ramsey does acknowledge in a number of places in his discussion that Maritain's theory is based on an essentialist understanding of the human and that Maritain does insist on the distinction between the being of natural law and our knowledge of it.[13] However, Ramsey merely accepts the fact that there is an essence to human beings and does not accept the detailed ontology proposed by Maritain. The Princeton

12. Jacques Maritain, *Man and the State* (Chicago: Chicago University Press, Phoenix Book, 1956), pp. 84–94.
13. Ramsey, *Nine Modern Moralists*, pp. 223–224.

theologian does not develop this ontological element of the natural law as distinguished from our knowledge of the natural law.

Maritain begins his comparatively brief description of natural law in *Man and the State* by insisting that the human being has a nature or ontological structure which is a locus of intelligible necessities and possesses ends which necessarily correspond to the essential human constitution and are the same for all. Since the human being is endowed with intelligence and determines one's own ends, one must put oneself in tune with the ends necessarily demanded by human nature. "This means that there is, by the very virtue of human nature, an order or a disposition which human reason can discover and according to which the human will must act in order to attune itself to the essential and necessary ends of the human being. The unwritten law, or natural law, is nothing more than that."[14]

The distinguished Catholic philosopher goes on to speak of the human essence with its unchangeable structure and the intelligible necessities it involves. The gnoseological aspect concerns the knowledge of this unwritten law of human nature which Maritain insists is known by human reason (Ramsey does not want to call it rational) through inclination, which is not clear knowledge through concepts and conceptual judgment but obscure, unsystematic, vital knowledge by connaturality or congeniality.[15]

In this light one can then properly understand the closing paragraph in Maritain's discussion of natural law even though there might remain some verbal problem with his use of conceptualization—a point made by Ramsey. Maritain concludes by saying that the natural law is an unwritten law in the deepest sense of that expression because our knowledge

14. Maritain, p. 86.
15. *Ibid.*, pp. 89–92.

of it is no work of free conceptualization, "but results from a conceptualization bound to the essential inclinations of being, of living nature, and of reason, which are at work in man, and because it develops in proportion to the degree of moral experience and self-reflection, and of social experience also, of which man is capable in the various ages of his history."[16]

Ramsey himself does not accept such an ontological foundation based on essential human nature for natural law and develops his own theory in dialogue with only the second or gnoseological aspect of natural law proposed by Maritain. Ramsey's theory, consequently, differs not only from the traditionally formulated natural law teaching in Roman Catholicism but also from the revision proposed by Maritain. In the light of Maritain's exposition of the ontological aspect of natural law and also of his insistence on the *ius gentium*, his theory is not as radical a revision as Ramsey claims.

To clarify and understand properly the meaning of natural law in Christian ethics in general, and particularly in the ethics of Paul Ramsey, it is necessary to distinguish two related but different functions of natural law. The first or theological aspect responds to the question of whether there is a source of ethical wisdom or knowledge for the Christian which exists apart from the explicit revelation of God in Jesus Christ in the scriptures. Does the Christian share some ethical wisdom and knowledge with all human beings because they share the same basic humanity? If one admits such a source of ethical wisdom and knowledge, how is it related to the explicitly Christian? The second aspect of the question is the more specifically philosophical-ethical which asks how the human is to be understood and how specifically it contributes to Christian ethical decision-making either in terms of virtues, goals, norms, or judgments.

16. *Ibid.*, p. 94.

II. THE THEOLOGICAL ASPECT OF THE QUESTION

In the light of this theological aspect of the natural law question, Ramsey in *Nine Modern Moralists* affirms that there is some virtue in man's ordinary moral decisions. The theological foundation for this validity is the fact of creation and the realization that creation and natural justice are not totally destroyed by sin although sin is definitely present and exerting its influence.[17]   In other places Ramsey frequently condemns a natural law optimism which fails to recognize the presence of sin in the world.[18]   Specifically he has criticized at some length the encyclical *Pacem in Terris* of Pope John XXIII precisely because it failed to take into consideration the existence of human sinfulness.[19]

But for the Christian, Ramsey maintains that natural law or natural justice is not enough nor may it be considered totally closed in itself. Christ is transforming, renewing, reshaping and redirecting natural law. Ramsey thus rejects an understanding of nature and grace or justice and love as two layers with the realm of love always above and the realm of justice below holding sway in its own domain without the transforming influence of love or the supernatural. Christ, or *agape,* always remains the primary, distinctive, and controlling aspect of Christian ethics. Ramsey describes his own approach as Christ transforming natural law.[20]

In another context, Ramsey describes this relationship in Barthian terminology according to which creation is the possibility, promise, and external basis of covenant which remains the internal basis, the meaning, and the purpose of creation. Natural justice provides the relationship of human

17. Ramsey, *Nine Modern Moralists,* pp. 4–5.
18. Paul Ramsey, *The Just War: Force and Political Responsibility* (New York: Charles Scribner's Sons, 1968), pp. xiii; 479–488.
19. *Ibid.,* pp. 70–90.
20. Ramsey, *Nine Modern Moralists,* pp. 233–256.

beings *with* fellow human beings which then must be transformed by love understood as the relationship of human
beings *for* fellow human beings.[21] In *Nine Modern Moralists*
Ramsey employs the symbols of Egypt and Exodus to explain the relationship between natural justice and Christian
love. He acknowledges that there was more in Egypt than the
fleshpots, for there was also a security and integration based
on natural justice. But the closed one worldview of morality
based on natural justice must be molded and reshaped into
the form of God's saving action.[22]

H. Richard Niebuhr, in his *Christ and Culture*, describes the
approach of Thomas Aquinas and Catholic moral theology in
general as Christ above culture—a motif which affirms both
Christ and culture. But there is a gulf and separation between
them so that Christ stays above culture and does not truly
penetrate and transform the realm of the natural or of
culture.[23] It is important to note that Ramsey recognizes
that the Christ above culture description of Roman Catholicism is not totally accurate especially in the light of his
dialogue with Jacques Maritain. Catholic political theory does
not propose that revelation or grace are simply added on to
reason or nature which in themselves remain intact and
sufficiently strong and clear to furnish us with ordered structures of a just political life. In Catholic thought grace perfects
nature and revelation illumines and perfects reason. In this
light Catholic thought insists that reason can with confidence
arrive at ethical truth but also that revelation is necessary to
strengthen and fulfill the suggestions of nature. Thus Ramsey
sees in Maritain and some Catholics a concept of transformism even though he indicates elsewhere that grace does

21. Paul Ramsey, *Christian Ethics and the Sit-In* (New York: Association Press,
1961), pp. 22–26.
22. Ramsey, *Nine Modern Moralists,* pp. 231–232.
23. H. Richard Niebuhr, *Christ and Culture* (New York: Harper and Row
Torchbook, 1956), pp. 129–141.

not always transform natural justice in Roman Catholic thought. The traditional Protestant insistence on both sin and grace puts more emphasis on the transforming aspect of love than Catholic thought does, but the difference between Protestant and Catholic thought is one of degree of emphasis on transformism and not a simple affirmation or denial of transformism.[24]

On specific questions Ramsey shows how his methodology operates and also how it differs from some approaches of Catholic moral theology. In his dialogue with Maritain, Ramsey raises the question of why the individual person should be regarded as a bearer of rights. Is this known through natural justice or through the Exodus which sees the individual in terms of God's first loving and choosing that person? The Princeton ethician interprets even Maritain as admitting that reason and nature alone are not sufficient for firmly establishing the rights and dignity of the individual human person in our society, but these basic human rights are also founded on the religious order's appreciation of the human being's relationship to a transcendent God.[25]

Ramsey himself believes that the morality of Exodus into covenant is needed as the explicit theological premise actively at work in the moral life of human beings in every Egypt of the natural order in order to sustain any proper ethics, to comprehend and interpret it adequately or even to restore it in this hour of moral and political disorder.[26] Against Edmond Cahn, Ramsey asserts that it is only the immediate presence of the claims of the righteousness of God between person and person and not any sense of generic injustice which asks an individual on occasion to be unwilling to save one's own life at the unavoidable cost of another's life.[27]

24. Ramsey, *Nine Modern Moralists*, p. 243.
25. *Ibid.*, pp. 238–244.
26. *Ibid.*, p. 244.
27. *Ibid.*, pp. 245–251.

Thus does Ramsey understand the role and function of love transforming justice in this particular matter of basic human rights.

Does Ramsey consistently carry out the theory of Christ transforming natural law or love transforming justice with its acceptance of the place of natural justice but all the while retaining *agape* or love as the controlling or primary aspect in Christian ethics? His early discussion of war published in 1961 does follow such an approach. Ramsey appreciates the just war tradition as it developed in Roman Catholic theology, but he attempts to show that both historically and theoretically *agape* both justifies the right to war and limits that right in the principle of discrimination. *Agape* demands that the Christian go to the aid of the neighbor whose rights are being attacked, but *agape* also demands that the attack be limited only to those who are actually bearers of force. The principle of discrimination which proclaims the immunity of noncombatants from direct attack is based primarily on Christian love and not on justice.[28]

Can love transforming justice adequately describe Ramsey's social ethics? I do not think so. Ramsey developed and articulated this approach in the late 1950's and early 1960's. In a somewhat polemical manner, he was attempting to indicate to his fellow Protestant ethicians that there is some value in the traditional Catholic approach to natural law and natural justice even though he did modify such an approach.

One can notice a change in his thought with an ever stronger emphasis on the need for order and force in the social realm, because of the presence of sin, and less emphasis on love and justice in his writings on social ethics in the 1960's and 1970's. Ramsey laments the fact that the liberal consensus in Protestant, and to some extent in Catholic,

28. Paul Ramsey, *War and the Christian Conscience: How Shall Modern War Be Conducted Justly?* (Durham, North Carolina: Duke University Press, 1961) pp. 3–90.

ethics forgets the presence of sin and decries the need for power and even armed force in politics.[29] *The Just War* begins with a one page fable showing that our present life and existence are heavily influenced by sin and the fall.[30] Thus Ramsey's later writings in the area of political ethics with their somewhat polemical character emphasize the presence of sin in human existence and do not really develop at length the aspect of justice or of love transforming justice.

Nine Modern Moralists, in the chapter considering Emil Brunner, claims that the proper understanding of Christian life in society is based on the threefold divine activity of creation, preservation, and redemption. Interestingly, on the level of the human moral activity corresponding to the three-fold divine activity, Ramsey explicitly speaks only of the twofold work of love and justice although the concept of justice does include a heavy emphasis on order.[31]

Christian Ethics and the Sit-In speaks of the three-fold activity of God as creating, preserving, and redeeming and relates this to the need for order, justice, and love in society. But in practice there seems to be such a heavy influence on order that love and justice do not really exert that much influence on the solution of particular questions, such as voluntary and limited busing of black students out of their neighborhood into more predominantly white schools and the question of integration within the churches themselves. [32] The concept of the state proposed in *War and the Christian Conscience* really downplays the role and function of justice in the state[33] and seems to go against an isolated statement found in *Nine Modern Moralists* according to which Augus-

29. Ramsey, *The Just War*, pp. 5–9.
30. *Ibid.*, p. xxi.
31. Ramsey, *Nine Modern Moralists*, pp. 207–208.
32. Ramsey, *Christian Ethics and the Sit-In*, pp. 40–65.
33. Ramsey, *War and the Christian Conscience*, pp. 15–33.

tine does not pay sufficient attention to justice in his under-standing of the state.[34]

Subsequent writings from 1967 to the present give an even greater emphasis to the negative and preserving aspect of the state in response to human sinfulness. In Ramsey's later discussions of the state he speaks primarily of the function of preservation based on the covenant which God made with Noah never again to destroy the world. The state thus is seen as the means by which God will deep the world from destroy-ing itself with no balancing development of a more positive aspect of the state based on justice.[35] In my judgment as enunciated elsewhere in greater detail the political ethics expounded by Ramsey in his writings from the middle sixties to the present cannot be described as employing the method-ology of Christ transforming natural law or love transforming justice.[36]

There is another question of consistency concerning Ram-sey's theory of Christ transforming natural law with its accep-tance of a place for natural law and justice in his system of Christian ethics. Such an approach was proposed in *Nine Modern Moralists*. Is this position consonant with the posi-tion Ramsey took in *Basic Christian Ethics* which was pub-lished in 1950? The author himself indicates on a number of occasions that there is no contradiction between the two books. The introduction to *Nine Modern Moralists* maintains

34. Ramsey, *Nine Modern Moralists*, p. 181.

35. Paul Ramsey, "Does the Church Have Any Political Wisdom for the 70's?" *The Perkins School of Theology Journal*, XXVI (Fall 1972), 29–40; Ramsey, "Force and Political Responsibility," in *Ethics and World Politics: Four Perspec-tives*, ed. Ernest W. Lefever (Baltimore: The Johns Hopkins University Press, 1972), pp. 43–73; Ramsey, "A Political Ethics Context for Strategic Thinking," in *Strategic Thinking and Its Moral Implications*, ed. Morton A. Kaplan (Chicago: University of Chicago Press, 1973), pp. 101–147.

36. Charles E. Curran, *Politics, Medicine and Christian Ethics: A Dialogue with Paul Ramsey* (Philadelphia: Fortress Press, 1973), pp. 11–26.

that *Basic Christian Ethics* develops the meaning of Christian love which is the primary and distinctive aspect of Christian ethics, but such an approach did not deny that there could be a role and a place for natural law and natural justice in a complete system of Christian ethics. *Nine Modern Moralists* just makes explicit the concept of Christ transforming natural law which could even be found somewhat in *Basic Christian Ethics*.[37]

In *Deeds and Rules in Christian Ethics,* Ramsey again defends himself against the charge of any inconsistency between his exposition in *Basic Christian Ethics* and in *Nine Modern Moralists.* In the first book he was stressing only what was primary and distinctive in Christian ethics, whereas in the second book he developed the proper place and function of natural law or natural justice.[38] In fairness to Ramsey it must be pointed out that even in *Basic Christian Ethics* he does employ the same description of love as primary and distinctive in Christian ethics so that his defense of his consistency is not merely a later rationalization on his part.[39]

In my judgment, nevertheless, there is more discontinuity between *Basic Christian Ethics* and *Nine Modern Moralists* than Ramsey is willing to admit. The problem is not that *Basic Christian Ethics* emphasizes just the primary and specific aspect of Christian ethics and says nothing about natural law; but, rather, aspects of the theory proposed in *Basic Christian Ethics* do not allow a place for natural law and justice.

The theory of Christ transforming natural law or love transforming justice, which Ramsey proposes in *Nine Modern*

37. Ramsey, *Nine Modern Moralists,* pp. 6–7.
38. Paul Ramsey, *Deeds and Rules in Christian Ethics* (New York: Charles Scribner's Sons, 1967), p. 122.
39. Paul Ramsey, *Basic Christian Ethics* (New York: Charles Scribner's Sons, 1950), p. 86.

Moralists, should logically affect some of the theological considerations developed in *Basic Christian Ethics.* As Ramsey points out in *Nine Modern Moralists,* the acceptance of the natural law or natural justice is related to the Christian teaching on creation, but nowhere in *Basic Christian Ethics* does Ramsey give sufficient development to the role of creation in Christian theological ethics. The central emphasis on Christ and on redemption seems not only primary but close to exclusive, despite some remarks to the contrary. Christian ethics looks only to Jesus Christ and is derived not from man but from Jesus Christ according to Ramsey's exposition in *Basic Christian Ethics.* This Christocentrism not only does not positively develop the place of creation, but it seems to exclude a real role for creation in Christian ethics, so that there is nothing for Christ to transform.

The narrow and almost exclusive Christocentrism of *Basic Christian Ethics* also serves as the foundation for Ramsey's concept of Christian love. Ramsey sees love in terms of the covenant love of God for his people and the love of Jesus for men. His approach does not seem to allow enough of human love so that it truly can be transformed by *agape.*[40]

III. THE PHILOSOPHICAL-ETHICAL ASPECT OF NATURAL LAW

The previous section of this chapter has considered what was called the theological aspect of the question of natural law. Once a Christian ethicist accepts the validity of natural law or natural justice, then the question arises as to what is meant by natural law and natural justice and how ethical wisdom is derived from it. A proper evaluation of the use of natural law in Christian ethics must always make this impor-

---

40. Ramsey, *Basic Christian Ethics,* pp. 1–190.

tant distinction between the two understandings of the term. This twofold question is inherent in the term "natural" as employed in traditional Roman Catholic theology. On the one hand, nature is distinguished from supernature and refers to what belongs to human beings as such, apart from the gift of grace. But nature is also understood in a philosophical sense as the principle of operation in every living thing so that actions should follow from nature. The natural law in traditional Roman Catholic ethics includes both meanings of nature.

As already mentioned in the discussion with Maritain, Ramsey does not really accept the ontological and metaphysical concept of nature on which traditional Catholic natural law theory was built. Without any extensive philosophical analysis, Ramsey merely proposes the existence of an innate sense of justice or of injustice by which the person in the context of the prism of the case can discern the right thing to do. The failure to distinguish the two different aspects of natural law in Christian ethics can readily give the impression that Ramsey has accepted the traditional Roman Catholic natural law theory with its ontological grounding in a universal human nature. Ramsey's insistence that he is following Maritain and his own failure to point out explicitly that he does not accept the Catholic ontological basis of natural law give added reason to think that his understanding of natural law is the same or at least very similar to the Catholic understanding.

There is also another important factor that mistakenly can support the contention that Ramsey in accepting a place for natural law in his theory accepted the Catholic concept of natural law. Catholic natural law theory, precisely because of its philosophical-ethical understanding of nature, has insisted on the existence of universal norms which are binding on all occasions and has staunchly opposed any situation ethics. In later years Paul Ramsey has very strongly opposed situation ethics and stands out as the most prominent antisituationist,

Protestant ethician in the United States. But the reasons for the antisituationist approach are quite different in traditional Catholic natural law and in Ramsey.

Paul Ramsey himself astutely points out two factors that contribute to the emphasis on universal norms in Catholic moral teaching and to a certain type of inflexibility which he cannot accept—the republication of natural law by the authoritative teaching of the Catholic Church and the deductive logic by which conclusions are derived from first principles. Ramsey has correctly realized that these two factors do influence the acceptance of universal norms in Catholic thought. A more fundamental factor, in my judgment, is the ontological basis of natural law—the universal human nature which is present in every individual. It is precisely this universal nature together with a poor understanding of it in terms of a physical nature which has been the primary reason for the insistence on universal norms in Catholic moral thought. At least this has been the ultimate philosophical basis for such an insistence. Earlier discussions in this book show my disagreement with the "traditional" Catholic natural law theory and some of its conclusions.

Although Ramsey has admitted a place for natural law in Christian ethics, his insistence on universal, exceptionless norms in moral theology does not come from his concept of natural law. He has accepted a type of natural law which affirms a sense of justice or injustice found in the concrete judgment in the prism of the case. Our author occasionally does employ terminology reminiscent of the Catholic approach; as for example, when he speaks of general rules founded upon an apprehension of the nature of the person, his needs, and fulfillment.[41] However, the nature of the person is not the foundation for Ramsey's insistence on the existence of exceptionless rules in Christian ethics.

41. Ramsey, *Deeds and Rules in Christian Ethics*, p. 7.

Ramsey's own position on the place of norms in Christian ethics and his justification of general rules has evolved in the course of his writings. There is one chapter in *Basic Christian Ethics* which can readily be interpreted as opposed to any universal norms and principles in Christian ethics.[42] Yet later, Ramsey staunchly defends the existence of such norms. In my judgment, there is some but not as much discontinuity in Ramsey's developing teaching on universal, exceptionless norms as might appear on the surface.

Many of the statements appearing in *Basic Christian Ethics* should be interpreted in the light of a Protestant rhetoric against the law and its use in Christian ethics. The first basis for Ramsey's later insistence on exceptionless norms in Christian ethics is the concept of *agape* or Christian love which he first expounded at great length in *Basic Christian Ethics*. Christian love is obedient love of the neighbor and the neighbor's needs in the same way that God has loved us. As God is faithful to his covenant, so must human beings keep theirs; as God shows mercy and forgiveness, so must human beings; as God's love gives all according to need and not merit, so should the Christian. Christian *agape* is disinterested and unclaiming regard for the needs of the neighbor.[43] Later Ramsey describes our love for God and our love for our neighbor under the one univocal term of faithfulness.[44]

Deeds and Rules in Christian Ethics tries to show that the very meaning of *agape*, understood as faithful love, will at times result in universal ways of acting. There are bonds of fidelity existing among persons, and the individual is not free at any given moment to break these bonds. Rules properly

---

42. Ramsey, *Basic Christian Ethics*, pp. 46–91. For such an interpretation, see James Sellers, *Public Ethics: American Morals and Manners* (New York: Harper and Row, 1970), p. 196.

43. Ramsey, *Basic Christian Ethics*, pp. 1–152.

44. Ramsey, *Nine Modern Moralists*, p. 290.

understood are in no sense opposed to *agape,* but rather *agape* itself leads to the existence of universal, exceptionless rules. The Christian in no sense opposes rules to *agape.* [45] Ramsey calls this pure rule-agapism, as distinguished from act-agapism and summary rule-agapism, and it constitutes one of the ways in which *agape* goes into practice.[46] Thus the concept of love which Ramsey first proposed at great length in *Basic Christian Ethics* is the primary reason or at least the reason Ramsey propounded first and in greatest detail to prove that there are exceptionless moral norms in Christian ethics. Ramsey in 1968 further developed this concept of exceptionless rules based on *agape* in terms of canons of loyalty.[47]

The notion of *agape* which Ramsey accepts logically involves an emphasis on exceptionless rules. Ramsey admits that if agapism is not a distinctive type of ethical theory which is neither teleology nor deontology, then it is more truly called a type of deontology. This approach is consonant with Ramsey's theory of eschatology, for right action cannot be derived from any consequences or goods to be obtained in an age which is being fast liquidated. In *Basic Christian Ethics* Ramsey frequently (e.g., p. 85) points out that Christian ethics is cut from God and not from man. Such a deontological understanding of *agape* in Christian ethics is opposed to a situationist's view that would see good consequences and benefits as a justification for breaking norms in certain circumstances.

The American edition of *Deeds and Rules in Christian Ethics* published in 1967 contains three new chapters which

---

45. Ramsey, *Deeds and Rules in Christian Ethics,* pp. 44–45.

46. *Ibid.,* pp. 104–122.

47. Paul Ramsey, "The Case of the Curious Exception," in *Norm and Context in Christian Ethics,* ed. Gene H. Outka and Paul Ramsey (New York: Charles Scribner's Sons, 1968), pp. 120–135.

were not in the original version published in Scotland in 1965. Especially in the first of these new chapters Ramsey develops an additional reason for the existence of exception-less norms in Christian ethics. Relying on the theory of John Rawls, Ramsey now sees the need for rules of practice in Christian ethics. He goes so far as to contend that the very existence of Christian social ethics depends upon whether this second possible justification of general rules has a legitimate place in systematic reflection on the Christian life.[48]

In his insistence on the existence of rules of practice Ramsey also introduces what can properly be described as the third reason for his insistence on the existence of exceptionless rules—the use of analytic philosophy. It is this type of philosophical ethics, rather than Catholic natural law theory, that the later Ramsey uses to bolster his contention about the existence of exceptionless rules. He often appeals to the principle of generalizability or universalizability which is frequently mentioned in contemporary philosophical literature. The influence of analytic thought is readily seen in his 1968 essay, "The Case of the Curious Exception."[49] Ramsey explicitly acknowledges his dependence on such philosophical insights rather than on traditional Catholic natural law theory as the best theoretical explanation of and warrant for general moral norms.[50] Thus Ramsey's insistence on exceptionless moral norms comes from reasons other than the traditional Catholic natural law theory. In fact, Ramsey himself does not accept the philosophical and ontological understanding of nature which in the judgment of many is the ultimate philosophical basis for the traditional Catholic acceptance of absolute norms.

48. Ramsey, *Deeds and Rules in Christian Ethics*, pp. 123–144.
49. *Norm and Context in Christian Ethics*, pp. 67–135.
50. Paul Ramsey, "Abortion: A Review Article," *The Thomist*, XXXVII (1973), 210.

IV. THE PRINCIPLE OF DOUBLE EFFECT

There has been no particular aspect of Catholic natural law theory which Ramsey has emphasized more than the principle of double effect. A study of his use and understanding of this traditional Catholic concept will also be quite revealing and support the contention that Ramsey really does not depend that much upon Catholic natural law theory. In an early (1968) extended discussion of abortion, Ramsey argues that Protestants should adopt as a rule of practice a distinction between direct and indirect abortion which Roman Catholicism unfolds for the charitable protection of human life in case of irreconcilable conflict of equals.[51]

In a 1973 article on abortion, Ramsey claims there are only three possible solutions to conflict situations involving human lives: (1) One can remain an equalitarian and stand aside from cases of lives in conflict. (2) One can abandon equalitarianism and justify taking one life on the basis of comparable value and worth. (3) One can, while not standing aside, remain an equalitarian and be driven to moral reasoning in conformity with the famous principle of the double effect. Ramsey puts himself in the third category but in the process so revises the principle of double effect that in my judgment it is no longer recognizable as such.[52]

Ramsey first utilized the principle of the double effect in his discussion of just war. The same Christian love which justified war to protect the neighbor in need also gave rise to the principle of discrimination affirming the immunity of noncombatants from direct attack because they are not bearers of force or harm. The concept of direct attack is then

---

51. Paul Ramsey, "The Morality of Abortion," in *Life or Death: Ethics and Options,* ed. Daniel H. Labby (Seattle: University of Washington Press, 1968), p. 78.

52. Ramsey, *The Thomist,* XXXVII (1973), pp. 212ff.

explained in great historical and theoretical detail in the light of the Catholic teaching on the principle of the double effect, and Ramsey also points out his differences with the Catholic position.[53] Chapter 6 has explained and criticized Ramsey's discussion.

Ramsey's explanation of the principle of discrimination, not only in his earliest works but consistently throughout his writing on war, has been based on the understanding of direct attack which has been developed in Catholic natural law theory. It is not merely a question of intention but also involves the doing of the deed itself. In *War and the Christian Conscience* and in *Nine Modern Moralists,* Ramsey states just one area in which he disagrees with the Catholic understanding of direct and indirect and its application to conflict situations involving life. In the comparatively rare situation of the birth-room conflict between the life of the mother and the life of the fetus, Catholic moral theology will not allow either life to be directly taken even if the result is that both will die. In Ramsey's judgment this is truly a case where morality must exit from the closed system of natural law and be transformed by love which would allow the direct killing of the fetus to save the life of the mother.[54]

Through the work of Bouscaren,[55] Ramsey is aware of controversies that arose in the last two decades of the nineteenth century within Roman Catholicism about permitting the direct killing of the fetus to save the life of the mother. However, Church authority intervened through decrees of the Holy Office and declared that the fetus could never be directly aborted. Ramsey points to this authoritative inter-

53. *War and the Christian Conscience,* pp. 45–59; 135–153.
54. *War and the Christian Conscience,* pp. 172–183; *Nine Modern Moralists,* pp. 25–256.
55. T. Lincoln Bouscaren, *Ethics of Ectopic Operations* (2nd ed.; Milwaukee: Bruce Publishing Co., 1944), pp. 3–24.

vention to indicate again that the problem of inflexibility in Roman Catholic natural law ethics might not come from the concept of natural law itself but rather its republication or authoritative interpretation by the Church. In his discussions of war Ramsey has continued to rely on the notion of direct effect to explain the principle of discrimination which for him is the primary limiting factor in the question of war. [56]

In his first article devoted exclusively to abortion, which was originally delivered as a paper in 1966, Ramsey continues his criticism of what he understands as the Catholic teaching which allows the unjust aggressor to be directly killed because by personal guilt the attacker has lost the right to life. In Ramsey's perspective of Christian love and righteousness, the determination of right conduct cannot be based on innocence or guilt. It is not formal aggression (guilt or innocence) but material aggression which justifies the taking of life to prevent the aggressive action just as in the case of warfare. In the conflict situation involving the life of the fetus and the life of the mother Ramsey no longer appeals to *agape* to justify the killing. In this conflict situation the act is directed toward the incapacitation of the fetus from doing what it is doing to the life of the mother and is not directed toward the death of the fetus as such. Ramsey suggests that such an approach is truly in keeping with the teaching of Aquinas himself. "The stopping of materially aggressive action is the highest possible warrant for the killing of men by men (if life cannot otherwise be saved), not the aggressor-innocent distinction."[57] In a later version of this article Ramsey recognizes in the light of comments made by Richard McCormick that in accord with the teaching of Aquinas such an action should be called indirect, but he still prefers the term justifi-

56. *War and the Christian Conscience*, pp. 172–183.
57. *Life or Death: Ethics and Options*, p. 86.

able direct abortion because such terminology requires all to accept the fact that there are two personal termini of a single action and that truly the life of the fetus is taken.[58]

There were some comparatively minor clarifications made in his ensuing discussions, but for our purposes it is sufficient to consider his last extended discussion of abortion—a long review article of the books by Daniel Callahan and Germain Grisez which he published in 1973. Here again Ramsey retains his position that the crucial question is whether the target of the deadly deed is the life of the fetus or what it is doing to the mother. The act is done with physical or observable directness but is justifiable if the target is the death dealing function of the fetus. From what Ramsey has written it is fair to describe the act as physically or observably direct because the fetus is directly killed but morally indirect because the act is targeted against the death dealing function of the fetus.[59]

In the light of Ramsey's discussion of double effect, three comments are in order. First, his earlier disagreement with Catholic teaching in the conflict situation of the life of the fetus and the life of the mother appealed to the concept of love transforming justice, but later he employed purely rational arguments against the traditional Catholic teaching. This definitely indicates a change in his thinking and may also show that the concept of love transforming justice is no longer as central in his thinking as it was in an earlier period.

Secondly, as pointed out in Chapter 6, I think Ramsey has consistently misinterpreted, at least to a degree, the Catholic teaching on directly killing an unjust aggressor. Ramsey interprets the majority contemporary Catholic position as holding

58. Paul Ramsey, "The Morality of Abortion," in *Moral Problems: A Collection of Philosophical Essays,* ed. James Rachels (New York: Harper and Row, 1971), pp. 22–23.
59. *The Thomist,* XXXVII (1973), 220–221.

that the aggressor by guilty action has lost the right to life and therefore can be directly killed both in the order of intention and in the order of the material act itself. He indicates that Thomas was still influenced by Christian love in maintaining that one could kill but not directly intend the death of the aggressor. However, the Catholic position was not based on the subjective guilt or innocence of the person, even though there might be some reasons because of which one could arrive at that conclusion. Even a materially unjust aggressor could be directly killed, so that it is not the guilt or innocence which is the determining factor but the very fact of being a bearer of force or an aggressor.

In fairness to Ramsey there are, in my judgment, some ambiguities and even inconsistencies in the majority Catholic opinion that could bring about Ramsey's confusion. Those who allowed the direct killing of the aggressor to save one's own life, then restricted the principle of the double effect to the killing of the innocent on one's own authority.[60] The term "innocent" certainly favors Ramsey's interpretation, but one must recall that this same theory did allow direct killing of a materially unjust aggressor so that the decisive factor is not subjective guilt or innocence but the material fact of aggression or attack.

It is also true that at the time of the decisions of the Holy Office in the late nineteenth and early twentieth century, Catholic theology did not allow the application of the teaching on directly killing an unjust aggressor to be applied to the fetus in the womb. But the reason proposed for not applying such a teaching (at least by all the twentieth century manuals I have read, and supported by Bouscaren) is not that the fetus cannot be guilty but that the fetus in the womb is not

---

60. Marcellinus Zalba, *Theologiae Moralis Summa,* Vol. II: *Theologia Moralis Specialis; Tractatus de Mandatis Dei et Ecclesiae* (Madrid: Biblioteca de Autores Cristianos, 1953), pp. 275–286.

truly involved in aggression but is only trying to live and survive. These authors deny that the action of the fetus constitutes aggression.[61]

In response to remarks of Germain Grisez that he is really talking about materially unjust aggression, Ramsey says that he was in no way thinking of the category of *materially unjust* aggression but only of actual aggression of one innocent human upon another.[62] Despite the inaccurate terminology, I believe that by materially unjust aggression the Catholic tradition meant actual aggression and it did not consider the guilt or innocence of the person. One could directly kill a person who was a bearer of aggression and thus threatening one's life. In my judgment the justification for killing an unjust aggressor in the Catholic tradition was not based on the fact that the aggressor through guilt lost the right to life. Thus it seems that Ramsey and the traditional Catholic teaching were closer than he recognized at this point. This interpretation, together with Ramsey's own later development of not relying on love transforming justice to explain his approach to conflict situations, casts some doubt on his theory that Thomas still felt the influence of *agape* in his treatment of unjust aggression whereas the modern Catholic opinion was based on justice, since the guilty aggressor lost the right to life.

The third and most important observation about Ramsey's continuing application of the principle of double effect is that in his latest statement of it and even earlier he has really not revised the traditional Catholic theory but has rejected it. However, he himself never admits that he has rejected it. The most significant and important condition of the double ef-

---

61. Bouscaren, pp. 3–64.
62. *The Thomist*, XXXVII (1973), 219–220.

fect, according to Catholic discussions, is the condition which holds that the good effect must be equally as immediate as the evil effect in the order of physical causality. The evil effect cannot be the means by which the good effect is produced. Ramsey properly understood this because he described the principle of the double effect as requiring that the good must not only be the formal object of the intention but also the immediate material object of the physical act. [63] Likewise, Ramsey employed this understanding of the concept of direct in describing the principle of discrimination.

In conflict situations, he is now denying that the act is wrong if the abortion is the immediate material object of the physical act. In fact, the physical structure of the act is no longer determinative for Ramsey in this case. Life can be taken with observable and physical directness, but the crucial moral problem is whether the intention of the act is the incapacitation of the fetus from doing what it is doing, the prevention of the aggressive function or the stopping of the deadly deed perpetrated on the mother. Ramsey limits his consideration to the conflict situation involving the life of the fetus and the life of the mother, but even in other conflict situations involving abortion and other values he would have to settle the morality not on the basis of the immediate material object of the act but merely on the basis of proportionality. Ramsey could readily maintain that the only proportionate reason justifying an abortion is the life of the mother, but as I have pointed out elsewhere there is some ambivalence in Ramsey on this point.[64] It is clear, however, that Ramsey, as well as many Catholic authors writing today, does not apply the contemporary understanding of the principle of the double effect to abortion cases.

63. *War and the Christian Conscience,* p. 55.
64. Curran, *Politics, Medicine and Christian Ethics,* pp. 128–130.

CONCLUSION

Paul Ramsey both agrees and disagrees with traditional Catholic natural law theory, but the area of disagreement is much greater than might appear at first sight. From the perspective of the theological aspect of natural law, he accepts a place for natural law or natural justice but rightly insists on its being integrated into the Christian vision including sin and transformation by love. From the philosophical perspective, he does not accept the ontological basis for natural law proposed in the manuals of moral theology, which was a very important, if not the primary, source of the Catholic insistence on universal norms in moral theology. Ramsey's own insistence on exceptionless rules does not follow from his acceptance of natural law. Although Ramsey frequently says that he is following the principle of the double effect, his own teaching on the solution to conflict situations in abortions does not follow that principle. He does, however, follow the concept of direct killing in his exposition of the meaning of the principle of discrimination which protects noncombatants from deliberate direct attack.

Finally, Ramsey's revision of traditional Catholic moral theology can be briefly compared with the revision I have proposed in this book and elsewhere. From the theological perspective, there should be a place for "the natural" and the role of human reason in ethics, but this must be integrated into a more complete perspective which is best described in terms of the fivefold Christian mysteries of creation, sin, incarnation, redemption, and resurrection destiny.[65] From the philosophical perspective, the older essentialist understanding of human nature is being revised in the light of more historical categories. The insistence of absolute norms in

---

65. Charles E. Curran, *New Perspectives in Moral Theology* (Notre Dame, Indiana: Fides Publishers, 1974), pp. 47–86.

Roman Catholic moral theology is being questioned in the light of the changing and more historical understanding of the human and especially in the light of the right of dissent from authoritative noninfallible teaching with the resultant pluralism within Roman Catholic moral theology. Chapter 6 has also agreed with the basic trust implied by Ramsey but never explicitly admitted by him that the principle of the double effect must be revised and cannot rely on defining "direct" only in terms of the physical causality of the act.

9

Ongoing Revision:

Personal and Theological Reflections

This essay intends to look in a reflexive way on how events, ideas and personal experience have influenced my theological development and contribution to the ongoing revision of moral theology. Both personal and intellectual experiences have helped to shape the thinking of every scholar. The theologian is also influenced by experiences within Christianity and within the Church. This chapter will reflect on the personal, intellectual and ecclesial influences which have shaped my own theological reflection in the area of moral theology or Christian ethics.

Reflection shows that my personal experience has been influential in shaping my approach to moral theology even on the most abstract and fundamental questions. One of the basic questions in any ethical theory is the ultimate ethical model. In theory, I have been influenced on this question by the thought of H. Richard Niebuhr and his disciples. Traditionally, ethics has been divided into either teleological or deontological types, although lately a third type of a relationality-responsibility model has been introduced. The teleological model understands ethics in terms of the goal or end and the means to obtain it. One first determines what is the ultimate end and then coordinates and subordinates more proximate ends and means as the way of achieving the ultimate end. Thomistic ethics generally follows such an approach as is evident from the fact that Thomas Aquinas begins his discussion of ethics by considering the ultimate end of man. Deontology sees the ethical life primarily in terms of duties, laws and obligations and is well illustrated in the philosophical approach of Immanuel Kant. In practice the ethics proposed for daily living in the Catholic Church with its heavy emphasis on law and the commandments followed the deontological model, which was probably common for most Christian Churches.

Theoretical reason argues that the teleological model is too purposive and ordered. Likewise, in the midst of both enormous complexity and great historical change the older understanding of eternal laws based either on the scriptural revelation or on the essential nature of human beings does not seem adequate as the primary ethical model. These and other reasons only exclude the deontological or the teleological as the ultimate ethical models even though there must always be some place for norms and for goals and ends in moral theology.

My own life and development as a theologian and as a person did not follow the teleological or the deontological model. I did not sit down and figure out what my goal was and decide on the best means to achieve it. My personal and professional development as a theologian has been something that I did not and could not see in advance. My theological growth depended very much on my response to the new and changing situations with which I came into contact and was not the unfolding of a well conceived plan. There were too many aspects in my own development over which I had no control. I never experienced the luxury of feeling that everything was under my influence and I could plan my own future development in a very detailed way for a long period of time. Obviously some such plan is always necessary for organization and results, but reflection made me realize how often I was called upon to respond to other events that entered my life.

I never planned to write an essay on this subject, but after some hesitation I responded positively to the suggestion. The conscious awareness of the influence of experience on my theological development as mentioned above led me to accept this invitation for further reflection. Perhaps a chronological arrangement will be the most logical way to proceed, although at times other considerations will be introduced.

THEOLOGICAL STUDIES

My theological studies were done in the context of preparation for priestly ministry at the North American College in Rome. I was studying for the Catholic priesthood for the diocese of Rochester, New York, and had received my B.A. from St. Bernard's Seminary in Rochester having followed the usual college-seminary course. I began my theological studies at the Gregorian University in Rome in September of 1955 without any intention or goal of ultimately becoming a teacher or scholar in the area of theology. In fact, I had purposely not chosen a religious community because I had no overwhelming drive at that time to devote my life to either teaching or scholarship.

Theology in Rome in the 1950's was still generally unaffected by the winds of change which would come with the advent of the Second Vatican Council. The teaching methods were of the old school—the professor read his lectures, which would often be available in mimeograph form, to an audience of students which regularly numbered well into the hundreds. (There were many more students on the first day and on the last day of class!) No papers were required, and there was just one final examination (oral in the major subjects) at the end of the year. Lectures and the examinations were all in Latin which was not too great a problem for me. Despite all these very negative aspects of the education itself, I still remain grateful for the experience. It put me into contact with working theologians and even at a distance I was able to appreciate some aspects of what they were trying to do. Later I would change many of the ideas I learned in those years, but I remain grateful for the experience.

I was in no sense a rebel student, but would have accurately been described as a docile student who worked hard and was faithful in class attendance—doing also a moderate amount of outside reading. Now I can recall only two or three issues on which I seriously disagreed with a professor—the question of religious liberty and the fate of unbaptized infants. I did not see how the mercy of God could not find some way to bring these "souls" to the fullness of life. I was ordained in 1958 at the end of my third year of theology, and shortly thereafter the Bishop of Rochester told me that I would be staying on for graduate studies in moral theology because I was going to teach moral theology at St. Bernard's Seminary. I had no burning desire to teach; but after more than three years of theology the prospect of teaching seemed acceptable, although naturally I had no say whatsoever in the matter. At the time I thought it might be more interesting to study and to teach canon law because the practical application and concrete working out of ideas have always been appealing to me.

My two years of graduate study proved most formative. I was told to obtain my doctorate at the Gregorian University. With the exception of a newer vision and approach to moral theology which Fr. Joseph Fuchs was trying to impart, my earlier theological formation at the Gregorian University had been in terms of very traditional moral theology. However, I was very much attracted to my professors such as the German Franz Hürth, who was known as a most influential member of the Holy Office, with whom I occasionally chatted for lengthy periods in Latin about different kinds of moral problems. Since I was familiar with the approach to moral theology of the professors at the Gregorian, I tried to broaden my horizons. I enrolled in courses at the Academia Alfonsiana, which under the direction of the Redemptorists at that time was in the process of initiating a program of studies leading to a doctorate in moral theology. In the end I obtained a doctorate from both institutions.

My experience at the Alfonsiana brought me into contact with a much broader view of moral theology. This institution demanded much more course work on the doctoral level than the Gregorian and opened up vistas in the area of biblical and patristic morality, the historical development of moral theology, and different philosophical approaches. These newer approaches and vistas were epitomized in Fr. Bernard Häring, who almost singlehandedly pointed Catholic moral theology in new directions in the pre-Vatican II Church. Häring's insistence on overcoming the dichotomy between moral theology and spiritual theology not only countered the legalism and minimalism of the manuals of theology but also gave moral theology a scriptural and liturgical dimension which it had previously lacked. Häring's insistence on the biblical call to perfection also brought with it an emphasis on growth, change and development in the Christian life which paved the way for my own future appreciation of historicity. Likewise, his dependence on Max Scheler's philosophy also opened up new philosophical horizons for me. In the light of Häring's insistence on the primacy of the Spirit and the virtue of *epikeia* (equity), positive laws and exceptions to such laws were more properly understood. Häring in those days created quite a stir by maintaining that the obligation to pray the breviary was such that at times one should not use Latin if the language becomes an obstacle to the primary purpose of prayer.

A practical and compassionate side of Häring's moral theology was also underscored in the law of growth which would not insist on imposing more than an individual was able to do at a given time. What appealed so profoundly to me was the wholeness of his approach which was mirrored in his own life and personality. There was an authenticity about his teaching and his life which spoke volumes. Ours was not a particularly close relationship at the time, but my enthusiasm for his moral theology was demonstrated by the number of fellow graduate students from the North American College whom I invited to attend some of his lectures.

Our personal relationship grew with the years. I was instrumental in setting up Häring's first theology week in this country in Buffalo in 1962, although the primary invitation had already been extended to him by the Benedictine Fathers at Conception Abbey for a six week summer course. Very significant for me personally was the backing Häring gave me in the midst of two public struggles I later had. In 1972 I was happy to be able to express publicly my gratitude to Bernard Häring by dedicating my new book to him on the occasion of his sixtieth birthday.

As the 1960's moved on and the postconciliar period of the Church opened, I was somewhat disappointed to realize that Häring's publications were no longer breaking new ground in a systematic way. We had a discussion about this while he was a visiting professor at Yale Divinity School in the 1966–1967 school year. Häring pointed out that he was devoting much of his time and energy to bringing the idea of renewal in the Church to an ever wider public, for he felt this was the most important need for the Church at the present time. I respected that decision and could understand it very well. One can say without fear of contradiction that no one has spoken to more people in more countries about contemporary Christian moral life than Bernard Häring. In the process it has been impossible for him to publish on a high, scholarly level, and thus he has not been able to continue charting the future course of moral theology. However, even now his insights are often valuable and fruitful for the discipline of moral theology. The moral theologian who is a committed Christian and churchman will always experience the tension between the scholarly understanding of Christian ethics and the practical proclamation of the gospel as it affects the lives of people.

Graduate study in moral theology thus gave me a new vision of the subject and made me very discontent with the older approaches. Here the seeds were already sown for many of my own future developments, but my doctoral research did not wholly mirror these new attitudes. My doctoral dissertation at the Gregorian University under the direction of Fr. Francis Furlong was of a very traditional variety—*The Prevention of Conception After Rape*. At the Alfonsiana I wrote a dissertation of a more historical nature on *Invincible Ignorance of the Natural Law in Saint Alphonsus*. My director, Fr. Domenico Capone, also helped me by insisting on the need for a systematic approach to put together all the other aspects of moral theology.

One incident just before returning from Rome in the summer of 1961 stands out in memory. Francis X. Murphy taught patristic theology at the Alfonsiana, and we had lunch together just before I left Rome. (Some of our conversation that day, plus the fact I knew his mother's maiden name was Rynne, helped me partially solve the riddle of the author of what later appeared as the famous letters from Rome about the Vatican Council in *The New Yorker* magazine.) We discussed what would happen upon my return to the States to teach moral theology. Murphy encouraged me to write and continue my scholarly pursuits, but also cautioned me to go slow and not make too many waves, because he was aware of my dissatisfaction with the older approach to moral theology. He suggested that I begin by teaching my classes in Latin (this had been somewhat of a tradition in the past at St. Bernard's Seminary in Rochester) so that first attention would not focus on the newer approaches I was teaching. The strategy worked quite well—for a while. I was known as the one who taught in Latin for the first three weeks before going into English at the request of the students.

THE FIRST YEARS

Teaching a new approach to moral theology in a pre-Vatican II seminary environment was an exhilarating experience—especially since my approach was different from that of all the other theological professors. Newer approaches to theology challenged many students and created a real interest in theological study. The faculty was expected to follow a textbook, but my "introductions" became notorious. One year the introduction finished in March, and only then did I bring the textbook into class. A number of faculty colleagues were also quite supportive in many different ways even though they might not have fully appreciated what I was trying to do.

My first venture in writing was in response to a request for a pamphlet on Christian morality for a Doctrinal Pamphlet Series to be published by Paulist Press. This pamphlet was written in the spring of 1962 and published early that summer. (Two years ago my final take-home examination for students in the introductory course in moral theology was to criticize this particular pamphlet. They were quite negative—and rightly so!) Also, there were a few other comparatively small and insignificant articles. Probably because there was no other Catholic theologian who had shown in print any sympathy for the newer developments in moral theology, I was invited to give a paper on conscience at the Roman Catholic-Protestant Colloquium sponsored by Harvard University in March of 1963. I was fearful about accepting, but finally agreed and enjoyed the entire experience. After that time I tried to deepen my contact with Protestant ethical thought and often taught seminars on the subject here at Catholic University, which gave me the opportunity to read and discuss with my graduate students the outstanding figures in the Protestant ethical tradition. Previously, as was typical of most pre-Vatican II Roman Catholic theologians, I had little or no contact with Protestant ethical thought.

During the early 1960's I began to give talks not only in the Rochester area but also in various places around the country on topics of renewal in Catholic moral theology including an address to the convention of the Canon Law Society of America in 1964, arguing against the continued need for the promises to be taken by both parties to a mixed marriage to raise all the children in the Catholic faith. I was also warned on a number of occasions by officials of the Diocese of Rochester that my teaching was at times too progressive and I should be more careful.

The major issue at the time was artificial contraception. Only at the end of 1963, did some Catholic theologians begin openly to question the teaching of the Church on artificial contraception. I followed the debates and reported on them sympathetically in an article published in the summer of 1964 in *Jubilee*. Shortly thereafter I became convinced of the need to change the teaching of the Roman Catholic Church on birth control and before the year was out wrote an article to explain my change and gave addresses on this topic.

As a moral theologian teaching in a diocesan seminary and as a priest helping out weekends in a parish, I came into contact with a large number of young married couples. Often I was asked in those years to give talks to parish groups on questions of marriage. Likewise, many couples were sent to me by others to talk about their problems. I was jarred by the discrepancy between theory and practice. These couples who were practicing artificial contraception did not seem to be sinning. At first I had justified their position by saying that objectively what they did was sinful, but subjectively there was no sin. They were showing all the signs of a good Christian life. What was wrong with what they were doing? I was also troubled by the fact that many other couples who were trying to follow the teaching of the Church seemed to be under such difficult pressures and tensions in their lives.

This somewhat jarring personal experience caused me to reconsider the reasons which had been proposed in favor of the teaching against artificial contraception. Looking back at that article which was written in 1964, I see that it really set the parameters for much of my work in the next few years— although I obviously did not recognize it or understand it at the time. Any thoughtful discussion of the question of artificial contraception must face the question of natural law and the teaching authority of the Church. These were the two areas I discussed in that article. The teaching against artificial contraception seemed to be based on only one aspect of the human—the biological; but the moral judgment can never be absolutely identified with the biological. Research for my thesis helped me to show that the Catholic teaching was proposed at a time when all thought the seed was the only active element of human reproduction, so that every single act of sexual intercourse was open to procreation. Today we know that this is not true. In the section on the teaching authority of the Church I pointed out the possibility of change in the light of the change in other Church teachings and also based on the changing understanding of human sexuality and reproduction.

In retrospect, so much of my scholarly interests for the last decade were set by that discussion. In September of 1973 I published an article in *Theological Studies* on the present state of Roman Catholic moral theology arguing for a pluralism in moral methodology and a pluralism with respect to specific moral teachings in the Catholic Church. This article had originally been given as the presidential address to the American Society of Christian Ethics. Two of the three major divisions of that article were natural law and authoritarianism in Church teaching. In the ensuing years I had investigated in greater detail the question of natural law, since it was generally accepted that Roman Catholic moral teaching was based on natural law. An interest in history and an appreciation of historical-mindedness (which I learned explicitly from my former professor, Bernard Lonergan) helped me to show that for the most part Roman Catholic moral teachings were not based on *the* natural law, understood as a monolithic, philosophical system with an agreed upon body of ethical content in existence throughout the centuries. Although many thinkers had employed the term "natural law" in the course of history, they did not mean the same thing by it. In addition, it seemed that the individual teachings came into existence first and only later was the theory introduced as a way to explain the already existing teachings. However, in the nineteenth century the authoritative, hierarchical teaching office of the Church imposed thomistic philosophy and theology as *the* Roman Catholic approach. In ethics, emphasis was placed on the natural law as the Catholic approach. Most contemporaries grew up in the context created by the nineteenth century and thus did not realize that Catholic moral teaching for the most part had not been based on *the* natural law.

The very ambiguities in the concept of natural law occasioned problems. Ulpian, a Roman lawyer in the third century, had defined the natural law as that which is common to man and to all the animals, such as the procreation and education of offspring. He distinguished natural law from the *ius gentium* which was proper to man because of human reason. Thomas Aquinas later defined the natural law as right reason, but at times he did accept Ulpian's understanding of natural law as that which is common to man and all the animals. Consequently, the natural easily becomes identified with the physical and the biological, and human reason cannot interfere in these natural processes. This seemed to me what happened in the Church teaching on contraception and in the famous teaching on the primary end of marriage. But it also explained other problems in moral theology. In fact, the debate about situation ethics in the late 1960's, in my judgment, ultimately centered on those areas where the human was identified with the physical and the biological— questions of medical ethics such as contraception and sterilization; the question of when human life begins; the solution of conflict situations by the principle of double effect which defined the direct effect in terms of the physical structure of the act; sexuality in which the sexual act as described in physical terms is always wrong outside marriage; and there are also traces of this problem in the treatment of the problem of divorce. I do not at times deny that the moral and the physical can be identified, but this insight helped to explain, understand and situate much of the debate about situation ethics.

The early treatment of the teaching office of the Church in moral matters, as found in that article written in 1964, centered on the possibility of change in such teaching. Later reading and investigations showed other instances of such changes, and again the recognition of the importance of historical consciousness gave a theoretical basis for such change. Even before the Encyclical *Humanae Vitae* in 1968, I insisted on the accepted Catholic teaching about the right to dissent from authoritative, noninfallible Church teaching. This aspect has developed at much greater length in the controversy following the organized theological dissent against the papal condemnation of artificial contraception in 1968. Naturally, too, the possibility of dissent was seen as extending to all other specific moral questions because in the midst of such complexities one cannot achieve a level of certitude on specific moral questions which can exclude the possibility of error. Thus, my first articles set the tone and the parameters of much of my theological writings for the next ten years. But we are getting too far ahead of the chronology.

Back in 1964 and early 1965 a call for change in the teaching of the Catholic Church on contraception was bound to cause some ripples. There were pressures put upon officials in the Diocese of Rochester from outside the diocese, but there was also discontent within the diocese itself—although there existed for sometime a reluctance to touch me. There were some warnings, and I knew the situation was tense. I tried to strengthen my own position by sending to the diocesan officials various offers I had to teach at Catholic universities in the United States, but in all cases they told me that I could not be spared from St. Bernard's. In late July of 1965, the axe fell. I was called in and told that I would no longer be teaching at St. Bernard's, but I was free to accept the offer from Catholic University or any other offer I had received. My reaction was not very strong, for I was realistic enough to know that sooner or later this was bound to happen. I can truthfully say that neither then nor since have I really experienced any great bitterness over it, but I have always been grateful for those who supported me and spoke up in my defense at that time.

CATHOLIC UNIVERSITY AND CONTROVERSIES

After a few weeks of negotiations, mostly by telephone, I accepted the invitation of Dean Walter Schmitz and the faculty of the School of Theology of Catholic University of America to join them. I had previously taught in the summer sessions of the Department of Religious Education of that university under the chairpersonship of Gerard Sloyan who had also wanted me to join his faculty full time, but Fr. Schmitz had originally contacted me more than three years previously. Early in September after I had just arrived at the university, I was called in by the Vice-Rector on the basis of a letter that had been sent to all clerical members of the faculty questioning my orthodoxy because of the various positions I had taken.

I enjoyed the new surroundings and was made to feel at home by my colleagues, some of whom had been in graduate studies with me. I continued my work which in the light of the circumstances included continued writing and speaking on the question of artificial contraception. In the fall of 1965 I arranged with Fides Publishers of Notre Dame to publish a collection of essays under the title *Christian Morality Today*. The book was published in September of 1966 and contained essays on many facets of the Christian moral life emphasizing newer developments in terms of scripture, the liturgy, and the gospel call to perfection as well as discussions of natural law, authentic Church teaching, contraception, servile work and the promises in mixed marriages. There were also further meetings in which University authorities expressed misgivings about my teachings. In October of 1966, my faculty unanimously expressed confidence in my teaching and orthodoxy and objected to the harassment of me and the unspecified charges made against me.

In June of 1966, I was scheduled to give a paper on masturbation at the annual meeting of the Catholic Theological Society of America and spent the second semester working on the subject. Again, the approach followed the same format as in the case of contraception. Catholic teaching maintained that in the objective order masturbation was always a grave sin, although in the subjective order grave fault might not always be present. The actual practice and experience of people seemed to contradict that statement. In the light of a better understanding of the meaning of sin, in the

light of a more personal and less biological view of masturbatory activity, I argued that even in the objective order masturbation should not always be considered grave matter.
Historical investigation pointed up the poor biological understanding which may have influenced the teaching attaching
such great importance to human semen. To my knowledge,
this was the first article by a Catholic theologian attacking
the accepted position that masturbation always involves grave
matter.

It seemed expedient at that time to show that the call for
new methodological approaches in Catholic moral theology
and for a change in some of the past teachings on specific
questions was coming from more than just a few theologians
on the fringe. I conceived the idea of a book on the question
of absolute norms in moral theology concerning many of the
disputed topics, with articles written by various professors
teaching in Catholic universities and seminaries. In Feburary
of 1967 a contract was signed with Corpus Books, and I
contacted seven other Catholic theologians, working out specific articles with them. With the help of my colleague and
friend, Daniel Maguire, the edited book finally was published
in the spring of 1968. But the spring of 1967 was to bring its
own surprises.

On April 17th I was called by the Rector (president) and
finally asked to come to his room. He was flanked by all the
executive officers of the University and informed me and
Dean Schmitz, who at great personal sacrifice has courageously supported me ever since my coming to Catholic University, that at the Spring meeting the Board of Trustees
voted not to renew my contract. The Rector insisted that he
was not speaking in his own name but as an agent for the
Board of Trustees. The Board of Trustees had met in Chicago
on April 10th. Later newspaper reports indicated that about
twenty cardinals, archbishops, and bishops participated in the
voting while the six laymen on the Board of Trustees ab-

stained. (At that time the Board of Trustees of Catholic University consisted of every archbishop in the United States as an *ex officio* member plus some other members including laymen.) These same later reports indicated that a committee composed of Cardinal Krol, Archbishop Hannan, and Rector McDonald had been constituted to undertake a study of my writings and make a report. It seems they looked at the book from Fides and also at the paper on masturbation published in the *Proceedings of the Catholic Theological Society of America*. Newspaper reports at the time also indicated the hand of the Apostolic Delegate, Archbishop Vagnozzi, in the matter. A few years later Roy Meachem, a journalist who covered the whole affair, wrote in the *Washingtonian* that Archbishop Vagnozzi, the Apostolic Delegate to the United States, told Meachem in an interview that he was responsible for my firing because Rome wanted to make an example out of a liberal American priest, and I was chosen.

Since there had been previous meetings with officials of the University, I was quite suspicious when I was called to the Rector's rooms. My reaction to the Rector's news was to protest that I had been given no hearing. I pointed out that the action was all the more incongruous because earlier in the academic year the faculty of the School of Theology and the Academic Senate of the University voted unanimously that I be given a new contract in September and promoted to the rank of Associate Professor. After realizing the decision was final, I mentioned that the only recourse available to me was to bring the whole affair to public attention, but I agreed to keep it quiet for twenty-four hours. I left the Rector's rooms and went to teach my 11:00 a.m. class as if nothing had happened.

That afternoon (Monday, April 17) I told a few friends and colleagues. From there things quickly spread. The theology faculty met on Tuesday at noon. A public rally was scheduled for Tuesday night, and the crowd overflowed the 400 seat meeting hall. The rally had all been arranged by a very efficient and hastily put together faculty-student group covering all the various schools of the university. Here for the first time the facts were made public. The steering committee of students had sent out flyers advertising the meeting, and my faculty colleagues, Robert Hunt, Daniel Maguire and Sean Quinlan spoke eloquently and moved the crowd. Petitions were signed demanding the trustees rescind their action. The momentum was obviously building. The Wednesday morning *Washington Post* headlined the story on the front page, and at ten o'clock that morning a rally of over 2,000 persons was held in front of the Rector's quarters. At Wednesday noon the theology faculty voted unanimously that, "We cannot and will not function unless and until Fr. Curran is reinstated. We invite our colleagues in other schools of the university to join with us in our protest."

As the front pages of Thursday's newspapers continued to tell about the story, students quickly joined in the cessation of classroom activities. Faculties of other schools met and with one exception joined in the strike. On Thursday afternoon the entire faculty assembled and voted to endorse the strike, but even on Thursday morning classrooms were empty. The strike was on. Demonstrations and rallies continued. My room was turned into "strike headquarters," but the whole operation was truly collegial with many people working together who had never even known one another before. The media continued to give immense coverage to the strike both in daily papers and on evening television news programs.

The pressure was building. There were some cracks among the hierarchy as Cardinals Cushing and Sheehan as well as some other bishops spoke out against either the firing itself or the way in which it was done. Negotiations began, with Dean Schmitz steadfastly standing up for his faculty's decision. Finally after a long Monday afternoon meeting between the Chancellor of the University, Archbishop O'Boyle, the Rector and the theology faculty, it was announced publicly at 6:00 p.m. that evening (April 24th) by Archbishop O'Boyle and the Rector to a crowd assembled in front of the library that the action of the trustees was rescinded and I would be given a new contract with a promotion to associate professor as of September 1, 1967.

Throughout the strike we purposely made every effort to keep the basic issue as narrow as possible—proper academic procedure was violated because the trustees fired me without giving reasons or a hearing despite the unanimous decision of my peers that I be promoted. This was the formal reason, but everyone knew the real reason was my teaching, especially in the areas of artificial contraception and also masturbation. In the final victory our tone was also purposely restrained—we have now been given not an ultimate victory but an opportunity and a mandate to continue our efforts on behalf of Catholic University, scholarship, and Catholic theological investigation.

This successful strike of an entire university community in 1967 was unique. One campus historian claimed that it had not occurred since the Middle Ages! But I am also sure that it could never happen again. The fortuitous confluence of many circumstances allowed it to happen. I was a comparatively unknown figure on the campus outside my faculty, having been here for only two years. I taught no undergraduate students. However, there had been long smoldering resentments against the administration of Rector McDonald. Academic freedom and theology had been involved in many earlier issues, especially the banning of four prominent, liberal theologians from speaking on campus and the "firing" of a scripture scholar, Fr. Siegman. There were also many other dissatisfactions about arbitrary decisions and the bypassing of the Academic Senate. The time was ripe. My incident just ignited the immense mound of tinder that had

been accumulating over the years. The timing was fortunate—
who wants to picket in the middle of winter? Or who wants
to go on strike the week before final examinations are to
begin? In my judgment, all those factors would never again
come together to make possible a strike by the entire university community. For one thing, after ten years on the same
campus and having been scarred in many battles, I am sure
that I could never get the type of unanimous support which I
obtained at that time! Such are the contingencies of history.

Little did I realize that this event set the stage for a future
development. The 1967—68 school year proceeded with the
usual ups and downs. I prepared another collection of essays
for publication (*A New Look at Christian Morality,* published
by Fides) which touched on a wide range of subjects beginning with a discussion of the radical ethical teaching of Jesus
and including a long chapter on conversion as the fundamental moral message for the Christian. There was no explicit
chapter on contraception, but the essay on masturbation was
included. I obviously did not want to see my function only in
terms of speaking out on the one issue of artificial contraception. But that question did not die.

I had hoped that ultimately the problem of birth control
would be handled in such a way that artificial contraception
in practice would not constitute a moral question or problem
for Roman Catholics. As 1968 dawned there were signs that
perhaps Pope Paul would not take the recommendations of
the majority of his special commission studying the question
of birth control who called for a change in the teaching of
the Church. That summer I had agreed to give six lectures at
St. Bonaventure's University in Olean, New York, and would
spend the rest of my summer there reading and writing. In
July rumors began to fly that an encyclical condemning
artificial contraception was imminent. I was in frequent contact with colleagues at Catholic University and throughout
the country. The strike at Catholic University the year before

had the effect of catapulting me into a very prominent leadership role on this question of artificial contraception and the Roman Catholic Church.

We tried in vain to raise enough publicity to prevent the issuance of any encyclical. In my judgment an encyclical at that time reaffirming the older teaching would be catastrophic. Many people would think that they could no longer be loyal Roman Catholics because of their decision to practice artificial contraception. Priests would be searching for guidance and would also be thrown into great crises of conscience. I was convinced that most Catholics and priests did not even know about the right to dissent from authoritative, noninfallible, hierarchical teaching. Plans then began to take shape to formulate a response to the encyclical which was rumored to be imminent.

On Sunday evening, July 28, it was reliably reported on radio and television that an encyclical would be issued on Monday, July 29th. The encyclical was released in Rome on that Monday morning (at 4:30 a.m., New York time). I already had contingency reservations to fly back to Washington about noon on Monday. After numerous phone calls Sunday evening and Monday morning, a meeting was set for Caldwell Hall (my residence) at Catholic University that afternoon for a group of theologians to assemble and discuss a response to the encyclical. Copies of the encyclical were promised to us at that time. Other calls were made to theologians around the country telling them that a statement would be forthcoming and asking them to be prepared for a phone call later that evening asking them to sign the statement.

A group of about ten theologians met in Caldwell Hall, read the encyclical, and discussed a response. I insisted that the statement could not hedge, but would have to meet head-on the question of dissent. After a fruitful discussion I typed out the final draft with help from Dan Maguire, but the whole enterprise had been the fruit of the contributions of those present at the meeting. It was agreed to hold a press conference Tuesday morning to announce the statement, and in the meantime we telephoned the other theologians around the country to obtain their signatures for the statement. At the press conference I was the spokesman for the group and issued the statement in the name of eighty-seven American theologians. The number later swelled to over six hundred signatures of people qualified in the sacred sciences as a result of a mailing to members of various professional organizations. Naturally this response received headline news throughout the United States and in all the television media. In fact we were able to hold subsequent press conferences in the next few days in an attempt to obtain as much coverage as possible.

Our quick, forceful response supported by so many theologians accomplished its purpose. The day after the encyclical was promulgated American Catholics could read in their morning papers about their right to dissent and the fact that Catholics could in theory and practice disagree with the papal teaching and still be loyal Roman Catholics. Other theologians around the world joined in and also even individual bishops and later some conferences of bishops. But our response as a quick, well-organized, collegial effort was unique. This, I hope, solved some problems for many Catholics, although I am sure that it also created problems for many other Catholics, who could not understand this type of dissent.

The statement that a small group put together within hours after the encyclical was published has in my prejudiced judgment stood the test of time remarkably well. It was short and respectful, pointing out the good aspects of the encyclical, but also clearly showing its flaws both from the viewpoint of moral theology and ecclesiology. It ended with a short reminder about the existence of the right to dissent in the Roman Catholic Church from such authoritative, noninfallible, papal teaching, and clearly applied that right to dissent both in theory and in practice to the use of artificial contraception. In the ensuing furor, two false charges tended to ruffle me more than usual. Some claimed that we never read the encyclical. (It is true that our response was published before even many bishops had received the encyclical.) Such a charge is not only false, but anyone who read our short critique had to be convinced that it was a direct response to the reasoning of the encyclical itself. Others claim that our action was precipitous. My answer to that is: What is the virtue in delay? Our statement has stood the test of time much better than many that were written weeks or even months later. No, it was imperative to act both with speed and theological accuracy to accomplish our purpose. There was absolutely no virtue in delay.

As was to be expected, this organized dissent caused quite a stir in the Roman Catholic Church in the United States. Catholic University was the center of focus in the academic discussion because the core group had many members associated with the University, and I was recognized as the principal animator of the group. There were a number of meetings and discussions which have been described elsewhere between dissenting theologians and bishops. A special meeting of the Board of Trustees at Catholic University was called to discuss the matter. Cardinal McIntyre of Los Angeles introduced a long resolution stating that the utterances of Fr. Curran, his followers and associates with regard to the encyclical *Humanae Vitae* constitute a breach of contract which admits of no other consideration than termination. Such an approach did not prevail, perhaps because of the experience occasioned by the strike the year before. The Board of Trustees finally called for an inquiry in accord with academic norms and due process to determine if the theologians had violated their manifold responsibilities.

The academic process was a full scale hearing before a faculty committee at which we were given [wrongly] the burden of defending our actions. Thanks to the inestimable generosity of the law firm of Cravath, Swaine and Moore of New York City, and to the professional skill and extraordinary personal concern of John F. Hunt, a member of the firm, and his associate Terrence R. Connelly, our case was presented in a most cogent and professional manner, both in terms of written submissions and of oral argument. The hearing dragged on for almost the entire academic year, and it was only at the beginning of April that the unanimous decision of the faculty hearing committee acknowledged that we had in no way violated our responsibilities. All "the subject professors" worked together on our defense; but my friend and colleague, Bob Hunt, and I organized and directed the effort. The written submissions were modified somewhat and published by Sheed and Ward as two books—one written primarily by the theologians considering the theological aspect of the question and the other written primarily by the lawyers discussing the academic freedom aspects of the case.

Although my colleagues and I were vindicated, I was not totally exultant. In many ways the entire situation was an unnecessary tragedy. Unfortunately, there were others who followed our lead but suffered because they lacked the academic protections we enjoyed. I am thinking particularly of the priests of Washington, D.C. and of other theologians such as some faculty members at the seminary in Buffalo spearheaded by my friend Tom Dailey, who lost their teaching jobs because of signing our statement.

The longer, more detailed study of dissent on this occasion opened up the further door in my thinking that such dissent was going to be more and more frequent on specific moral issues in the Roman Catholic Church because on such issues one could never attain the type of certitude that excludes the possibility of error. Thus, in the future the dispute over contraception would be paradigmatic of a growing pluralism in the Roman Catholic Church on such issues as abortion, divorce, medical ethics, and some questions of sexuality. In all probability, as discussion on these issues becomes more public there will be further tensions within the Roman Catholic Church. The Church must learn that its unity is not to be found in terms of absolute agreement on such specific moral teachings.

The reaction to the papal encyclical was obviously a very significant event in terms of the life of the Church, of Catholic theology, and of my own development. My participation in it also increased my own desire to continue my theological investigations as best I could in the field of Roman Catholic theology. Over the years, despite the problems involved in this and other disputes, I had also experienced support and encouragement from many different people. In my view this only made it more incumbent upon me to continue my theological research.

OTHER INFLUENCES

One of the fortuitous and influential developments affecting my thinking was contact with the ethical thought of other Christian communities. This gave me another vantage point in the attempts to criticize my own tradition. But my critique of the Catholic tradition was also heavily based on a critique from within, considering especially scriptural, historical, and contemporary insights. Despite these criticisms by myself and others which have called for significant changes both in methodology and in the teaching on specific questions, I believe my own theological ethic stands firmly within the tradition of Roman Catholic theology. I wholeheartedly accept the fundamental premise of that theology which insists that God often and usually acts mediately with human

beings—through the medium of creation and not just through
Jesus Christ, through the medium of the ongoing tradition
and not just through the revelation in scripture, through the
"koinonia" of the Christian Church with its hierarchical
teaching office and not just through an immediate I-Thou
relationship between God and the individual.

My more concentrated study of Protestant ethicians has
reminded me that my theological approach is basically within
the Roman Catholic tradition. I spent a sabbatical year in
1972 at the Kennedy Center for Bioethics at Georgetown
doing research on the Christian ethics of Paul Ramsey. Ramsey often comes to conclusions quite congenial with more
traditional Roman Catholic conclusions and is thought by
many to be a crypto-Catholic in his ethics. On the other
hand, some in the Catholic Church claim that I follow a
Protestant ethic. Late one night in one of many sessions
discussing with Ramsey, I told him that I could correctly
summarize my research by saying that the differences between us are that Ramsey is more Protestant than most
people think and I am more Catholic than most people think!
Chapter 8 has attempted to prove this thesis.

In theological ethics the Roman Catholic approach asserts
the ability of human beings through reason to arrive at
ethical wisdom and truth. The Catholic moral methodology
based on natural law tries to incarnate this basic reality, but
in my judgment certain aspects of this approach have to be
changed. Protestant and some contemporary Catholic approaches have helped me in developing a criticism of what I
believe is a fundamentally sound assumption. The natural is
not an order in itself, totally cut off from the "supernatural."
There is only one historical existence for all of us. By
concentrating only on the natural and human reason, Roman
Catholic moral theology tended either to forget and ignore all
that belongs to the "supernatural" order or at most saw the
"supernatural" as something added on to the "natural."

Many recent emphases in Catholic moral theology have followed from a better understanding of the question of the natural and the supernatural—the call of all Christians to perfection; the need for continuing change of heart; the fact that the kingdom of God calls us now to cooperate in trying to build a new heaven and a new earth; a call to strive constantly to change the structures of society in the light of the fullness of the kingdom; an emphasis on the Spirit and a corresponding growth in the moral life; the role of the scriptures in moral theology; the importance of the liturgy in the Christian moral life; an attempt in theory and in practice to overcome the dichotomy between faith and the daily life of Christians; a corresponding realization that one could no longer accept such a dichotomy between Church and world.

The recognition that we live in only one historical order also influenced my understanding of the relationship between Christian and non-Christian morality. The question of the self-identity of Roman Catholic ethical teaching first came to the light in terms of its relationship to Protestant ethics and prompted my investigations into pluralism in Catholic moral theology, including a pluralism on specific moral teachings. In the light of personal experience and historical evidence, buttressed especially by the reaization that all human beings live in one and the same order, I have come to the conclusion that non-Christians can and at times do arrive at the same attitudes, goals, dispositions and concrete acts as Christians. Thus, Christians cannot claim self-sacrificing love as belonging only to Christians. The level of difference is on the transcendental level and not the categorical. Our Christian understanding affects the motives and the reasoning processes employed in ethical thinking. The methodologies on a more reflexive level will be different, but Christians cannot claim for themselves a monopoly on such attitudes as love, care for others, or willingness to give oneself for others. Chapter 1 developed this position in great detail.

Also the Roman Catholic insistence on reason and the goodness of the natural tended to forget about the effect of sin. Protestant thought exemplified in Reinhold Niebuhr and also in contemporary writings by Paul Ramsey reminded me of this important aspect missing in Roman Catholic thought, although I would insist that many Protestants of the classic Lutheran tradition as well as Niebuhr and Ramsey have overemphasized the notion of sin. The presence of sin in the world influenced my thinking on a number of significant questions—opposition to utopian views of man's possibility for human progress; acceptance of the need for greater conflict in human affairs, at times even the use of violence in the service of justice; a willingness to accept a somewhat negative judgment about human social and political structures at any given time in history, and the need for change with the realization that all human structures will always be imperfect; a theory of compromise applied, for example, in the question of homosexuality in which the presence of sin in the world (not personal sin) sometimes forces people to be content with less than what would be required if sin were not present and in this sense justifies homosexuality for the individual.

With this background, I was also prepared to realize a danger which emerged in theology in general, and in Catholic theology in particular in the 1960's. In rightfully realizing the importance of overcoming the dichotomy between the natural and the supernatural, some theologians tended to forget the limitations and sinfulness of the present and especially the fact that the fullness of the eschaton is not yet here. Too often a naively optimistic theology arose from a too easy identification of the future of the kingdom with the here and now. The fullness of the kingdom lies beyond history, and we will always live with the tensions of eschatology which is part of our theology.

These various considerations led me to develop what I call a stance, perspective, or horizon of moral theology, which is logically the first step in any systematic development. This perspective is formed by the fivefold Christian mysteries of creation, sin, incarnation, redemption, and resurrection destiny. Any approach to Christian ethics which forgets one of these elements or overemphasizes one element is in my judgment inadequate. What traditional Catholic moral theology said about the ability of human reason is basically correct, but it must be integrated into a more complete picture or perspective.

This perspective also reinforced a fundamental attitude which I came to verbalize and explicitly recognize as governing much of my thought in the last few years. Reality in moral matters is more complex than most people realize. Error more often than not comes not from positive error, but rather from failure to give importance to all the elements which must be considered. This emphasis on complexity and the need for a wholistic approach is appealing to me because I tend to be realistic and practical in my personality rather than idealistic and utopian. In theory it has been developed especially by H. Richard Niebuhr and is often at work in the contemporary writings of James Gustafson. I have been particularly impressed how Gustafson, in his writings as well as in his own person, shows a balanced and sensitive approach—a basic Christian and scriptural vision of reality with a critical openess to philosophical and empirical understandings of the human.

The same insistence on the need for a more wholistic approach which would see all the aspects of the question and not absolutize any one element was behind my critique of the traditional Catholic understanding of the human as incorporated in the Catholic philosophy of natural law. Roman Catholic theology in a few cases absolutized the physical and made the moral and human identical with only the physical aspect, although others have failed to give enough importance to the physical element as exemplified by our contemporary problems of ecology and pollution. Catholic natural law theory overstressed the objective aspect of reality at the expense of more subjective considerations. The emphasis on continuity and the unchanging forgot about discontinuity and change. More relational and personalistic emphases will also change some of the older emphases in the Catholic understanding of the human.

There is no doubt that such an insistence on complexity and on a more wholistic approach with the corresponding danger of polemical exclusion has exerted a great influence on me. I cannot reduce all morality to any one content virtue, even love, nor can I see moral norms based only on consequences unless these are interpreted in the broadest possible sense. My Christian perspective recognizes that the cultural, political, social, and economic structures of society will contain both positive and negative elements. Christian life in the paschal mystery will experience both the suffering of the cross and the joy of the resurrection. Social reform requires both a change of heart on the part of individuals and a change of the cultural and economic structures of society. I am also cognizant of the danger that such an approach, striving to hold in tension all the aspects of our human existence, will at times fail to speak the prophetic voice and be tempted merely to adopt a middle position, but I hope that by constantly asking this question I can avoid some of the pitfalls connected with it.

CRITICAL RETROSPECTION

In retrospect, one should also be critical of the development in one's own thinking. Especially in the light of my basic insistence on complexity and the danger of forgetting or slighting certain aspects of the question, such a critical appraisal of my own development is necessary. I think there have been underemphases in two very important areas of concern for the moral theologian which have been somewhat influenced by the biographical aspects considered in this essay. The Catholic moral theologian is both an academic and a committed Christian member of the Church, and these two aspects will always exist in the person of the theologian and create some tensions. There are the academic concerns of the discipline in attempting more satisfying explanations and synthesis. But there is also the fact that the Catholic moral theologian is intensely interested in the way in which Christians should live out the gospel in daily life and influence the world in which we live.

In terms of the more theoretical aspects of the discipline, the events of the last few years have concentrated attention on some specific teachings accepted in Catholic life and have also witnessed the breakdown of the monolithic Catholic natural law methodology so that today on all levels there is a growing pluralism within the Church as illustrated in Chapter 2.

The next step must be to attempt a more positive synthesis of moral theology—a step which is just beginning. Here I feel the need for deeper philosophical and empirical understandings which will be necessary to develop more systematic approaches for bringing together all the different aspects contributing to moral meaning in the midst of our complex time and culture. My own philosophical approach up to now has tended to be eclectic bringing in elements from personalistic, phenomenological, transcendental and value philosophies. Despite the gigantic task involved, moral theologians like myself must strive for a more synthetic approach bringing together all the scriptural, theological, philosophical and empirical data. In the future, in the light of my past interests, I must emphasize the philosophical and empirical considerations of the human.

The moral theologian is also intimately involved with the

life of the Church and the living out of the gospel message in the world. The developments of the last few years have focused attention on calling for a change in some of the areas which might be called personal morality. However, I have also tried to stress the call of the Christian to perfection and the need for a more faithful response to the gospel in social life. Social morality and its problems have been discussed, but not enough, because so much attention has been given to particular questions of personal morality. There is need now and in the future to develop at greater depth the Christian recognition of the responsibilities to change society.

In my writings on social morality I have attempted to apply the general fivefold stance so that one can avoid both the danger of utopianism with the resulting fact that after a few years of small or meager success people will just give up the struggle for social change and the opposite danger of merely accepting the status quo. With this and other friendly amendments I accept the basic thrust of contemporary liberation theology, but must also point out that liberation theology has tended to be more theological than ethical—in other words, it has not really analyzed with systematical ethical reflection the concrete problems of social and economic structures.

It seems the most pressing problem facing the Church and the members of the Church concerns the fundamental problem of a better and more equitable distribution of the goods of this world. The Church must raise its own consciousness and the consciousness of its members to this particular problem which is especially apparent in our consumer American society. The Catholic Church in the United States to its great credit has an historical tradition of social liberalism and social justice gained from its attempts to prevent laissez-faire capitalism from overriding the just claims of workers to a share of the goods of this earth. But, in the past this social teaching very often was not present at the level of the pulpit and the daily lives of Christians.

Today the problems are more complex and difficult, but there is even greater need for raising consciousness and attempting some solutions. The problem was somewhat easier when the victims of injustice were "our own"—that is, Catholic workers. Today the problem is more complex because we realize it is worldwide in scope. It is not just a question of a more equal distribution of the goods of creation or of justice for workers in the United States, but our horizons now must be worldwide with all the resulting complexities and difficulties of finding solutions. In addition, even here in the United States, the question is of more equitable distribution of the goods of creation for those people who have been outside the establishment to which Roman Catholics now belong. This is a gigantic task facing the Church, and I believe that moral theologians like myself must strive to make our contribution to it. I am also aware that our efforts in this area will not be as dramatic and as attention-catching as our criticisms of particular past teachings of the Church, but they are even more important than those earlier efforts. It seems we are facing the need for more radical changes in the political and economic sphere.

PERSONAL INFLUENCES

Up to this point my theological development has been considered in terms of events and the thoughts of others that have influenced me. Before closing a few things should be said about me—my personality and how I see this affecting my theology. Obviously, in this area, the possibilities of self-deception are even greater.

I am a committed Christian believer belonging to the Ro-

man Catholic Church. Like many, I have had my ups and
downs, but Christianity and Roman Catholicism are very
significant and important to me. The recognition of complexity and tension together with the understanding of sin
and its effects, even within the Church (in my first years
teaching moral theology in Rochester I caused some conster-
nation by insisting that there were five marks of the true
Church of Jesus Christ—one, holy, catholic, apostolic,—and
sinful!), have helped me to cope with some of the problems
of life in the Church. Although I am constantly impatient
with the rate of change in the Church, the recognition of my
own sinfulness and of how slow I am to change has made me
more patient (perhaps too patient at times) with regard to
progress and change in the Church.

Such a view of the Church has helped me to cope with the
inevitable tensions and oppositions that I have experienced in
the Church. Because of the stands I have taken on a number
of issues, and the wide publicity given to them, as well as the
fact of my professorship at the Catholic University of American, which is supported by the American Catholic bishops
and people, I am a persona non grata for many people in the
Church, especially some bishops and priests. There is still a
long list of dioceses in which I am even now forbidden to
speak. I have been looked upon with suspicion and have
never been appointed to any official Church committes or
theological dialogue groups for my own Roman Catholic
Church. In 1972 the Catholic Theological Society of America
bestowed on me its annual reward for outstanding contribution to Roman Catholic theology, but the prelate who sponsored the award did not agree with that judgment. I am
grateful to the courage of my colleagues who changed the
name of the award and named me the first recipient of the
John Courtney Murray Award! (I shall always treasure the
citation for that award which was written by Richard McCormick, a perceptive critic of all moral theologians but also a

source of personal support and encouragement to me.) However, there have also been other bishops who both publicly
and privately have supported me.

There have been many people whom I have never really
met or known who have in one way or another encouraged
my continued efforts, in addition to the encouragement I
have received from a large number of friends and acquaint-
ances. I realistically expect controversy and do not mind it
(maybe the predominantly Irish genes in my genetic make-up
dispose me to like a fight!). The somewhat vitriolic attacks in
the conservative Catholic press and hate mail are things I can
readily shrug off. By temperament I am not a brooder, so
none of these things really ever gets me down. I can relate
them with very little emotional response on my own part.
Most of these problems never cause me any pain or anger, but
rather I just keep on doing what I feel is right.

The public stands against some Church teachings have attracted attention, and in the eyes of some I am a rebel and a
radical. I do not think that I am, and at times I really wish I
were more of a rebel and more of a radical—something which
might be hard for some people to believe! Although I have
critically called for a change in some teachings of the Church,
I am deeply committed to the Church on a very profound
level. There is no doubt that I am inclined to speak out and
call a spade a spade. Perhaps again this is a part of my
character that wants to see things work out in practice and is
unable to easily accept discrepencies between the theoretical
order and the practical living out of reality. I cannot deny,
however, that there is a stubbornness in me which also
contributes to my willingness to take such stands. Nonetheless, I think that I am today in some way the same type of
person who obeyed the seminary rule because I was convinced that was the right thing to do in practice.

In reviewing one of my books in late 1974, a Catholic
moral theologian identified somewhat with an older approach

described my moral theology as radical even though his tone was sympathetic and open. As for being a radical, no one who stresses complexity can really be a radical. In life and in theory I am not a radical, but there are times when the simplicity of the radical does appeal to me. This is probably why I say that at times I wish I were more radical, but "common sense," or is it "common nonsense," and a sense of practical reality usually win out. My fear is that an acceptance of sin and complexity will at times make my theology too middle-of-the-road.

I am sure that there are many other factors contributing to my own theological development of which I am not even conscious, but I believe that the characteristics and traits mentioned in the last few paragraphs have had some bearing and influence on my own theological development. In fact, my own experience in writing these reflections has made me even more conscious of the influence that personality, events, personal history, and the thoughts of others have had in the ongoing revision of my moral theology.

Index